CUSTOM CURRIC...

What About Sex, Drugs, and . . .?

Hormone Helper

Les Christie and Stan Campbell

The Drug Free Challenge

Jim Marian, Stephen Arterburn, and other youth experts

The Whole Story

Duffy Robbins and Randy Petersen

NEXGEN®

Building the New Generation of Believers

An Imprint of Cook Communications Ministries
Colorado Springs, Colorado

What About Sex, Drugs, and ... ?

© 2003 Cook Communications Ministries

Published by Cook Communications Ministries
4050 Lee Vance View
Colorado Springs, CO 80918
www.cookministries.com

Editorial Manager: Doug Schmidt
Product Developer: Karen Pickering
Series Creator: John Duckworth
Series Editor: Randy Southern
Cover Design: Granite Design
Interior Design: Becky Hawley Design, Inc.

Unit 1: Hormone Helper
© 2003 Cook Communications Ministries
Editor: Randy Southern
Writers: Les Christie and Stan Campbell
Option Writers: John Duckworth, Nelson E. Copeland, Jr., and Ellen Larson
Inside Illustrator: Al Hering

Unit 2: The Drug Free Challenge
© 2003 Cook Communications Ministries
Editor: Rick Wesselhoff
Writers: Stephen Arterburn and Marv Penner
Option Writers: Rick Bundschuh, Rev. Nelson E. Copeland, Jr., Kara Eckmann Powell, Christian Hill, Joel Lusz, Jim Marian, Ginny Olson, Marv Penner, Glenn Procopio, and Joel Walker
Inside Illustrator: Jim Starr

Unit 3: The Whole Story
© 2003 Cook Communications Ministries
Editor: Randy Southern
Writers: Duffy Robbins and Randy Petersen
Option Writers: John Duckworth, Nelson E. Copeland, Jr., and Ellen Larson
Inside Illustrator: Al Hering

Printed in the U.S.A.

Contents

Unit Three: The Whole Story

How to Customize Your Curriculum

We know your time is valuable. That's why we've made **Custom Curriculum** as easy as possible. Follow the three steps outlined below to create custom lessons that will meet the needs of *your* group. Let's get started!

Read the basic lesson plan.

Every **Custom Curriculum** session in this book has four or five steps designed to meet five goals. It's important to understand these five goals as you choose the options for your group.

Getting Together

The goal for Getting Together is to break the ice. It may involve a fun way to introduce the lesson.

Getting Thirsty

The goal for Getting Thirsty is to earn students' interest before you dive into the Bible. Why should students care about your topic? Why should they care what the Bible has to say about it? This will motivate your students to dig deeper.

Getting the Word

The goal for Getting the Word is to find out what God has to say about the topic they care about. By exploring and discussing carefully-selected passages, you'll help students find out how God's Word applies to their lives.

Getting the Point

The goal for Getting the Point is to make the leap from ideals and principles to real-world situations students are likely to face. It may involve practicing biblical principles with case studies or roleplays.

Getting Personal

The goal for Getting Personal is to help each group member respond to the lesson with a specific action. What should group members do as a result of this session? This step will help each person find a specific "next step" response that works for him or her.

Consider your options.

Every **Custom Curriculum** session gives you 14 different types of options. How do you choose? First, take a look at the list of option categories below. Then spend some time thinking and praying about your group. How do your students learn best? What kind of goals have you set for your group? Put a check mark by the options that you're most interested in.

 Extra Action—for groups that like physical challenges and learn better when they're moving, interacting, and experiencing the lesson.

 Media—to spice up your meeting with video, music, or other popular media.

 Heard It All Before—for fresh approaches that get past the defenses of students who are jaded by years in church.

 Little Bible Background—to use when most of your students are strangers to the Bible or haven't yet made a Christian commitment.

 Extra Fun—for longer, more "festive" youth meetings where additional emphasis is put on having fun.

 Fellowship and Worship—for building deeper relationships or enabling students to praise God together.

 Mostly Girls—to address girls' concerns and to substitute activities girls might prefer.

 Mostly Guys—to address guys' concerns and to substitute activities guys might prefer.

 Small Group—for adapting activities that might be tough with groups of fewer than eight students.

 Large Group—to alter steps for groups of more than 20 students.

 Urban—for fitting sessions to urban facilities and multiethnic (especially African-American) concerns.

 Short Meeting Time—tips for condensing the meeting. The standard meeting is designed to last 45 to 60 minutes. These include options to cut, replace, or trim time off the standard steps.

 Combined Junior High/High School—to use when you're mixing age levels but an activity or case study would be too "young" or "old" for part of the group.

 Sixth Grade—appearing only in junior high/middle school volumes, this option helps you change steps that sixth graders might find hard to understand or relate to.

 Extra Challenge—appearing only in high school volumes, this option lets you crank up the voltage for students who are ready for more Scripture or more demanding personal application.

Customize your curriculum!

Here's a simple three-step plan to customize each session for your group:

1. Choose your options.

As you read the basic session plan, you'll see icons in the margin. Each icon represents a different type of option. When you see an icon, it means that type of option is offered for that step. The five pages of options are found after the Repro Resource student pages for each session. Turn to the option page noted by the icon and you'll see that option explained.

Let's say you have a small group, mostly guys who get bored if they don't keep moving. You'll want to keep an eye out for three kinds of options: Small Group, Mostly Guys, and Extra Action. As you read the basic session, you might spot icons that tell you there are Small Group options for Step 1 and Step 3—maybe a different way to play a game so that you don't need big teams, and a way to cover several Bible passages when just a few kids are looking them up. Then you see icons telling you that there are Mostly Guys options for Step 2 and Step 4—perhaps a substitute activity that doesn't require too much self-disclosure, and a case study guys will relate to. Finally you see icons indicating Extra Action options for Step 2 and Step 3—maybe an active way to get kids' opinions instead of handing out a survey, and a way to act out some verses instead of just looking them up.

2. Use the checklist.

Once you've picked your options, keep track of them with the simple checklist at the end of the option section (just before the start of the next session plan). This little form gives you a place to write down the materials you'll need too—since they depend on the options you've chosen.

3. Get your stuff together.

Gather your materials; photocopy any Repro Resources (reproducible student sheets) you've decided to use. And…you're ready!

Unit One: Hormone Helper

Talking to Kids about Sex

by Les Christie

I speak to thousands of young people each year about sex and I'm still shocked by the statistics:
- Twelve million teens are sexually active.
- Eight out of 10 males and 7 out of 10 females report having had intercourse while in their teens.
- If present trends continue, 40 percent of today's 14-year-old girls will be pregnant at least once before the age of 20.
- Fifty percent of all sexually active 19-year-old males had their first sexual experience between the ages of 11 and 13.
- By senior year of high school, one in four high school students have had at least four sex partners.

Unfortunately, many young people receive their sex education from the media. The average high school student had the opportunity to watch 14,000 acts of intercourse or innuendo to intercourse on prime time TV in 1991. He or she will watch an average of 10 hours a week of MTV.

However, more unfortunate than the media's influence is the fact that only about 10 percent of young people today receive good, positive, healthy Christian sex education. It is unfortunate that parents and the church have remained more or less silent when it comes to sex education. Sexuality isn't an easy subject to discuss with our kids, but our silence is hurting this generation of young people who desire to hear the truth.

By discussing sexuality with your young people, you may prevent some very negative experiences. You will also be giving the gift of a healthy attitude and godly stewardship of one of God's most special gifts to us, our sexuality.

Tips on Getting Started

As you work through these sessions in *Hormone Helper*, get in touch with the feelings you had about sexuality when you were in high school. How did you feel and what were you thinking about on your first date, your first kiss, the first time you had to say "no," or a time you said "yes" and regretted it?

Also you'll need to keep parents informed. If the parents of your group members aren't kept up-to-date on your plans, your efforts will be wasted. Let parents know what material you will be covering. Send them portions of the material or extra material so they can follow up in their homes. Design questions for parents to discuss with their kids after the *Hormone Helper* series. Most parents feel the weight of responsibility for the sex education of their kids, but do not feel adequate for the task. They are usually grateful when any kind of program is offered in a Christian context.

Over the years, I've faced three areas of objections to having a series on love, sex, and dating. The first objection is that kids are faced with too much sexual information already, and don't need to hear more of it in a church or youth group setting. However, that's the *reason* for this study. Young people need sound, biblical information, not locker-room talk. The second objection is that there are too many controversial issues involved in sex education. This is a valid point; however, there are some absolutes in Scripture. Even the questionable areas—masturbation, premarital petting, contraception—need to be discussed. The third objection goes something like this: "We didn't have a course on sex, and we turned out all right—so our kids can too." The problem with this argument is that not everyone was a "survivor." Many people did not "turn out all right." For many people, a lack of sex education did irreparable damage to their lives. Besides, it's unfair to compare the teens of today with the teens of previous generations. Teens today face *much* more sexual pressure and confusion than even the teens of only one generation ago. Teens of today desperately need help, encouragement, and positive support.

I hope you will feel confident in working through the material in this book. However, at some points in the series, you may want to call in a specialist—a Christian doctor, psychologist, nurse, or teacher—someone who has integrity and wisdom, and can put the kids at ease.

I would caution you about self-disclosure. You may have had difficulty with areas of your own sexuality in the past. Be sensitive about what you share concerning your own experiences. If not handled correctly, your group members may turn you off, look down on you, or convince themselves that because you did something, *they* have a right to do the same thing.

The Big Picture

Our desire for sex is God's idea. He thought it up. He did the plumbing. I used to think God made everything and then went on a coffee break, while Satan snuck in and gave us our sex organs. Sex is not evil or dirty—but it is powerful. Sex is like water or fire. On a hot day a cup of cold water can be refreshing. But water out of control, when a dam breaks, can destroy a town. On a cold night, a warm fire can feel very good. But fire out of control can destroy a home. Sex is wonderful within the framework it was intended. God created sex to be used and enjoyed. But, He created it to be used *within marriage* as an expression of total commitment and unity. Out of control, it can destroy a reputation and a life.

There are stronger desires than sex. For example, the desires for air and food are stronger. If you don't eat for 71 days, you won't be thinking about sex. You won't be thinking about anything. You'll be dead.

We have put sex on a pedestal in our society. Sex by itself will not bring happiness. If intercourse were the ultimate expression of love, then the happiest people on earth would be prostitutes. Instead those sad people find it almost impossible to love or be loved. Love is the warmth and acceptance communicated and demonstrated in hugs, glances, and the quiet moments of just holding each other.

"Going all the way" isn't 15 minutes of ecstasy in the back seat of a car or a bedroom. It's two old people who have been married for 41 years walking hand in hand around the park talking quietly to each other. Two friends and lovers. Any love that lasts that long is "going all the way."

Hugh Hefner, who bragged about going to bed with hundreds of women, got married a couple of years ago. When surprised reporters asked him why, he responded, "Because I'm lonely."

The Bible clearly states in 1 Thessalonians 4:3, "You should avoid sexual immorality." First Corinthians 6:18 instructs, "Flee from sexual immorality." I've heard kids say, "My body is my business." If you're a Christian, your body is the Lord's. The sad fact is that some kids' hearts are not broken by breaking the heart of God. God gives us His loving counsel on sex to make us *more* sexual, not less. God wants to teach us how to really love.

Consider Joseph, who was tempted by Potiphar's wife. He fled from her wearing only his jockey shorts. He didn't say "no" because he might get caught. He didn't say "no" because she might get pregnant. He didn't say "no" because he might get a sexually transmitted disease. He said "no" because it was a sin against God. "How then could I do such a wicked thing and sin against God?" he asked (Gen. 39:9). Imagine if your group members assumed a similar attitude.

May God bless and guide you as you embark on the journey of educating your group members concerning one of His most mysterious and precious gifts—sexuality.

Les Christie is a 26-year veteran of youth ministry. He has been at the same church for 21 years. Les is a sought-after, popular national convention speaker to both youth and adults. He has authored dozens of articles and books, including Unsung Heroes *(Youth Specialties). He is married, has two children, and lives in Placentia, California.*

The images on these two pages are designed to help you promote this course within your church and community. Feel free to photocopy anything here and adapt it to fit your publicity needs. The stuff on this page could be used as a flier that you send or hand out to kids— or as a bulletin insert. The stuff on the next page could be used to add visual interest to newsletters, calendars, bulletin boards, or other promotions. Be creative and have fun!

Ever Had Thoughts about Sex?

If not, you can stay home.
But if you have, join us as we start a new course called *Hormone Helper*.

Who:

When:

Where:

Questions? Call:

Unit One: Hormone Helper

The "S" word.

(Write your own message
in the thought balloon)

"Two thumbs up!!"

Questions about sex?

(Write your own message on the tag, like:
"Do not open until marriage"
or "To: [name of your group] From: God")

The Keys and the Car, but No License to Drive

YOUR GOALS FOR THIS SESSION:
Choose one or more

☐ To help kids become comfortable with the fact that they might be experiencing sexual feelings.

☐ To help kids understand that while sex is a wonderful gift from God, it is incomplete (and inappropriate) outside the bond of marriage.

☐ To help kids determine which physical aspects of sex are appropriate for this stage of their lives and commit to remain within those limitations.

☐ Other:_____
_____

Your Bible Base:

Genesis 38
Ephesians 5:1-14
1 Thessalonians 4:1-12

Sexual Scavenger Hunt

(Needed: Recent popular magazines, TV Guides, newspapers)

Form three or four teams, and give each team an equal number of magazines and newspapers. If possible, include a *TV Guide* for each team. Set a time limit (five to ten minutes), and announce that teams will be competing in a sexual scavenger hunt. Their goal will be to list the most references to sex (either overt or suggestive) from these sources:

- The newspapers you have provided (editorials, articles, comics, and so forth)
- Magazines you have provided (ads, articles, opinion columns, etc.)
- Listings in the *TV Guides*
- Any examples from recent TV programs that team members can recall
- Any examples from films or videos that team members have seen
- Any examples from song lyrics that team members can quote.

At the end of your predetermined time limit, have teams read their lists. The lists should be somewhat lengthy because any single source might provide numerous sexual references. The purpose of this exercise is to demonstrate the amount of sexual material that your young people are exposed to on a regular basis. As each list is read, the response from others is likely to be, "Oh, I didn't even think of that one."

Acknowledge the team that came up with the longest list. Then have group members quickly go back through their lists and identify any examples that they feel are pure or biblical examples of sexuality as opposed to those that contradict biblical standards. Have them figure a percentage of *positive* references based on the total.

Ask: **To what extent are you affected by the sexual messages you receive through the media?** If the tendency is to say, "Not at all," or "Very little," point out how many anti-Christian messages they were able to list at a moment's notice. Repetition is the key to any system of brainwashing, and the repeated references to more and better sex are certainly influential on young people. Your group members may be successfully repelling the messages—so far—yet it must certainly be a struggle for some of them to do so.

In what specific ways are you affected by all of these sexual messages? (Do sexy models in ads influence purchases of cologne, clothing, etc.? When the discussion turns to sex, do any of your group members feel inferior or left out? Does anyone act as if he or she is more experienced than he or she truly is, just to fit in?)

Why do you think so many people are uncomfortable talking about sex, even to the point of referring to it as "the birds and the bees," "doing the wild thing," and other such phrases? (Lack of adequate knowledge about the subject; embarrassment; to make it seem more commonplace and less special.)

Where do you get information that you trust about sex?

Is That in the Bible?

(Needed: Copies of Repro Resource 1, pens)

It is hoped that group members have a good understanding of what the Bible has to say about sexual purity. But some may be living under the assumption that the Bible is a bit behind the times when it comes to "current" issues such as romance and sexual activity. Hand out copies of "Is *That* in the Bible?" (Repro Resource 1). Have group members complete the quiz. When they're finished, discuss their answers. The correct responses are:

(1) B [Prov. 30:18-19, New International Version]
(2) B [Prov. 11:22, Living Bible]
(3) L [D. H. Lawrence]
(4) F
(5) B [Eccl. 4:11, Living Bible]
(6) B [S. of S. 1:2, Living Bible]
(7) B [S. of S. 3:1, New International Version]
(8) L [Francis Edward Smedley]
(9) B [S. of S. 7:1-3, Living Bible]
(10) B [I Cor. 7:3-5, Living Bible]
(11) L [Emily Dickinson]
(12) B [S. of S. 7:7-9, Living Bible]
(13) L [James Thurber]
(14) B [I Cor. 7:9, Living Bible]
(15) F [Though the first sentence is quoted from Gen. 2:25, Living Bible]

[Note: No quotations were taken from Dr. Ruth. Were any of your group members fooled?]

Point out that God created sex to be one of the most pleasurable experiences people can ever have. Sex is intended to be a wonderful gift. But like any gift of God, it can be misused and corrupted. Sex outside the bond of marriage causes a number of problems. And while these sessions will focus on several of those problems, we should never forget that sex was created as a unique, thrilling gift to bring two married people as close together as they can possibly be.

STEP
3

Caught after the Act

(Needed: Bibles, pens, paper)

OPTIONS

Say: **You may discover that the Bible has a lot to say about sex that you don't know about. One story you probably never heard as a kid is found in Genesis 38. It's a bit complicated, but then so are most relationships where sexual activity is involved. It begins with Judah, who was one of the 12 sons of Jacob** (Israel). **He had three sons of his own—Er, Onan, and Shelah. When Er got old enough, Judah arranged for him to marry a girl named Tamar. But Er was not a good person, and God allowed him to die. According to the custom of the time, it then became the responsibility of the husband's brother to provide for the wife. And one of the means of "providing" was to marry her so she could bear children who would look after her** (Deut. 25:5-6). Direct group members to Genesis 38. Have them read the chapter independently (or in small groups if they would be comfortable doing so). As they do, ask them to compile a list of "current" sexual issues they find—things that many young people are dealing with. Their discoveries should include

- using a partner for sexual fulfillment with no true commitment (vss. 9-10)
- use of sex as a technique to manipulate someone else
- double standards (Judah was just as guilty as Tamar, but he was ready to kill *her.*)
- multiple sexual partners
- seduction (vs. 14)
- incest (vs. 16)
- potential scandal (vs. 24)
- birth control (vs. 9)
- prostitution

- rumor and accusation (vs. 24)
- blackmail (vs. 25)

Explain that in this case, the problems were resolved. Judah was caught after the act—red faced, no doubt—and took responsibility for his actions. Tamar got the child(ren) she wanted, even though her method was by no means honorable. And one of the babies born from the sexual liaison between Judah and Tamar was Perez, an ancestor of King David (Ruth 4:18-22), and subsequently, of Jesus. So God can create good things, even from the mistakes we make.

Summarize: **The Bible contains many similar stories of the unfortunate and often tragic consequences of sexual misconduct: homosexual acts, incest, abuse, rape, and so forth. However, it also tells us how we can avoid the potential pitfalls of getting involved in a relationship built entirely on sexual drive rather than genuine love.**

STEP 4

Sex: Now and Then

(Needed: Note paper, pens, fake microphone)

Spend a little time explaining how our society's thinking has evolved in regard to marriage (and consequently, "permissible" sex). Explain that in Bible times, marriages took place much sooner after puberty. As soon as someone was able to *become* a parent, he or she had the *opportunity* to do so as well. The person simply got married and started a family. But our current society has come up with the concept of *adolescence,* a period during which time teenagers have the sexual capacities of an adult, but are expected to wait for several years until they are "mature" enough to get married.

See if you can find one or two volunteers who will speak out in favor of marriage (and "legitimate" sex) at this point in their lives, and a couple of others willing to cope with not acting on their hormonal urges for several more years until they do get married. (Explain that these are the only two biblically acceptable options for young people wishing to become sexually active.) Call these volunteers to the front as you play the role of a talk show host. Wander through the group with a fake microphone, letting members ask questions or make comments, and try to generate a good discussion. Keep the conversation

OPTIONS

SMALL GROUP

HEARD IT ALL BEFORE

LITTLE BIBLE BACKGROUND

MOSTLY GUYS

MEDIA

URBAN

balanced, alternating between the pros and cons of either side. Questions to consider might include:

- **Do you think it's fair to be expected to wait several years before acting on sexual urges you may already feel? Why or why not?**
- **If you could get married as soon as you began to get sexual urges, how do you think it would affect your lifestyle? Your behavior? Your other relationships (parents, friends, etc.)?**
- **What would you think about having your parents arrange a marriage for you, as parents frequently did in ancient cultures?**
- **Would you rather be treated as an adult right now—with all the responsibilities of finding a job, providing for a family, etc.—or would you prefer having a few more years of "carefree" adolescence, even though you may still be treated as a child by parents, teachers, and so forth?**

After the discussion, summarize: **Regardless of your opinion, the fact is that in our society most of you are expected to wait for a number of years before you get married. In the meantime, you are likely to have some strong sexual urges.**

What reasons do young people give to justify having sex before they get married? (They love each other; everyone else is doing it; they plan to marry the other person eventually; sex is no big deal anymore; sex is a "rite of passage" into adulthood; etc.)

What do you say in response to your friends who have these opinions? Let group members comment, but let them know that you will be providing them with some good answers in this and subsequent sessions.

Group members may fully believe that God has condemned premarital sex, but not know exactly where to find proof. The seventh commandment, "You shall not commit adultery" (Exod. 20:14), doesn't say anything about *premarital* sex.

Divide into groups. Have each group read one of the two following passages and create a list of things people need to keep in mind as they deal with sex on a physical basis—guidelines, warnings, challenges, etc. (Suggested responses are provided.) One person from each group should report his or her group's answers to the whole group.

Ephesians 5:1-14
- We should imitate God (in purity, holiness, etc.).
- Our actions should not even *hint* of sexual immorality.
- Dirty jokes and obscene language should be avoided.
- We shouldn't be fooled by people who try to deceive us into believing lies.
- What people do in secret will be exposed.

I Thessalonians 4:1-12
- We should live to please God (rather than ourselves).
- God's people are to be "sanctified" (distinctive as compared to the rest of the sinful world).
- We should learn to control our bodies and avoid sexual immorality.
- Sex should not be considered an option, because it takes advantage of someone else.
- God will punish sexual immorality.
- We should be more concerned with earning others' respect than keeping up with them sexually.

A Hands-Off Approach

(Needed: Copies of Repro Resource 2, pens)

Astute group members may have noted by this time that not *all* physical aspects of sex are necessarily wrong. If not, challenge the assumption that being "sexual" means having intercourse.

Ask: **Are there appropriate ways for someone your age to express physical attraction toward someone of the opposite sex? If so, what are they?** List responses. In some cases, there may be disagreement as to the appropriateness of certain actions. If so, save discussion for later. You're simply making a list of responses right now.

Hand out copies of "Let's Get Physical" (Repro Resource 2), which lists several types of physical expression. Let group members add anything they came up with that isn't already listed. Then have them place each activity at the point on the scale where they feel it belongs. (As they do, be sure to have them consult the lists of biblical guidelines they compiled earlier.) For example, one person might be a "hugger" who in all innocence enjoys the warm and fuzzy feeling a hug brings. To someone else, however, it might invoke lustful thoughts and lead to temptation. So while the first person would find hugging "Perfectly Acceptable," the other person might need to list as "Potentially Dangerous."

When group members finish, let willing volunteers compare their sheets and see if there are any significant differences. As members discover what behaviors others feel are appropriate, they may become more comfortable as they relate to each other.

O P T I O N S

LARGE GROUP

MOSTLY GIRLS

JR. HIGH
HIGH SCHOOL
COMBINED

Challenge each person to learn to enjoy the sexual physical sensations that are appropriate for him or her at this time, and to avoid going farther and getting more involved than he or she intends to.

Summarize: **It may seem to you that the sexual feelings you have are something like being given a brand new Porsche, having the keys in your hand, and knowing everything you think you need to know about driving— yet being several years away from being able to get a driver's license. As tempting as it might be to go ahead and take all the risks involved with breaking the law, if you do, you're almost certain to face severe consequences somewhere down the line.**

Worth the Wait? (Part 1)

(Needed: Paper, pens)

OPTIONS

Each of these sessions will conclude with three specific reasons why it is worth saving sexual intercourse for marriage. Group members should be encouraged to add other reasons of their own. Essentially, the only reasons young people give for having premarital sex are: (1) to "prove" love; (2) because they just couldn't stop when they got involved; or (3) because it's "no big deal." All of these "justifications" will be refuted. But in the meantime, the list of reasons to save sex for marriage should be significantly longer and should make a lot of sense. (And if group members come up with the reasons themselves, they might be more willing to follow their own advice.)

Begin by thinking only of the *physical* reasons to save sex for marriage. A few of the things your young people should come up with are listed below.

When you save sex for marriage:

- All risk of premarital pregnancy (and its many complications) is eliminated.
- The risk of contracting the sexually transmitted HIV (AIDS) virus is greatly reduced.
- The risk of contracting other sexually transmitted diseases (syphilis, gonorrhea, etc.) disappears.

If these were the only three reasons to put off having sex, they should be plenty, but there are many more to come. Birth control pills, condoms, and other paraphernalia may reduce such risks, but can never entirely prevent them. Faithfulness within a monogamous marriage relationship is the only genuine "safe" sex.

Keep in mind that many times the sex drive is strong enough to overrule logic. As you close in prayer, ask God to provide your group members with the physical willpower and emotional integrity they need to remain sexually pure in an age of promiscuous activity. And if you plan to go on with this series, tell them that the emotional aspects of sex may be even more significant than the physical ones—as they'll find out next time.

Is That in the
BIBLE?

Read each of the following quotations. If you think it comes from the Bible, place a "B" beside the quote. If you think it comes from a famous literary writer, mark it with an "L." If you think it comes from Dr. Ruth, use a "D." And if you think we just made it up, give it an "F" (for "fictional"). Be warned, however, that we used the Living Bible for some of the biblical quotes so you wouldn't get any clues from the "thees" and "thous."

_____ 1. "There are three things that are too amazing for me, four that I do not understand: the way of an eagle in the sky, the way of a snake on a rock, the way of a ship on the high seas, and the way of a man with a maiden."

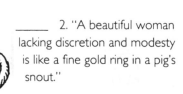

_____ 2. "A beautiful woman lacking discretion and modesty is like a fine gold ring in a pig's snout."

_____ 3. "Sex and beauty are inseparable, like life and consciousness. And the intelligence which goes with sex and beauty, and arises out of sex and beauty, is intuition."

_____ 4. "God has a specific person selected for you, and when the time is right, you will know His will in the matter."

_____ 5. "On a cold night, two under the same blanket gain warmth from each other, but how can one be warm alone?"

_____ 6. "Kiss me again and again, for your love is sweeter than wine."

_____ 7. "All night long on my bed I looked for the one my heart loves; I looked for him but did not find him."

_____ 8. "All's fair in love and war."

_____ 9. "How beautiful your tripping feet, O queenly maiden. Your rounded thighs are like jewels....Your navel is lovely as a goblet filled with wine. Your waist is like a heap of wheat set about with lilies. Your two breasts are like two fawns, yes, lovely twins."

_____ 10. "The man should give his wife all that is her right as a married woman, and the wife should do the same for her husband: for a girl who marries no longer has full right to her own body, for her husband then has his rights to it, too; and in the same way the husband no longer has full right to his own body, for it belongs also to his wife. So do not refuse these rights to each other."

_____ 11. "That Love is all there is, is all we know of Love."

_____ 12. "You are tall and slim like a palm tree, and your breasts are like its clusters of dates. I said, I will climb up into the palm tree and take hold of its branches. Now may your breasts be like grape clusters, and the scent of your breath like apples, and your kisses as exciting as the best of wine, smooth and sweet, causing the lips of those who are asleep to speak."

_____ 13. "I love the idea of there being two sexes, don't you?"

_____ 14. "It is better to marry than to burn with lust."

_____ 15. "Now although the man and his wife were both naked, neither of them was embarrassed or ashamed. And God said, 'You two try to control yourselves, OK?'"

Let's Get Physical

Sex has a lot of different physical aspects. One is intercourse, which you are told is wrong before marriage. Another is holding hands, which even your parents will admit is "Oh, how cute!" And in between the two is a whole range of other possibilities. Some of these may be things that seem acceptable for other people, yet which make you uncomfortable. So this scale is for you. Go through the list of physical sensations and place the number of each one in the box where you feel it belongs.

1. Holding hands on a moonlit night

2. Slow dancing

3. "Full contact" dancing

4. Going "all the way"

5. A goodnight peck on the cheek

6. Hugging

7. Giving a back rub

8. Getting a back rub

9. A heavy "back seat" make-out session

10. Mutual fondling to the point of arousal

11. Oral sex

12. Playing "Post Office," "Spin the Bottle," etc.

13. Calling "900" numbers for sexual conversations

14. Full body massage

15. Passionate kissing

CLEARLY WRONG

POTENTIALLY DANGEROUS

PERFECTLY ACCEPTABLE

STEP 1

If cutting up magazines wouldn't be active enough for your group, try this variation. Before the session, cut at least a dozen photos of "beautiful people" (plus a few ordinary ones) from magazines. To start your meeting, give each person one or more pictures. When you give the signal, kids have to arrange the faces in a line on the floor in order of "sexiness" from left to right, least to most. When there's a disagreement over the place a picture should have, majority rules. Then discuss the fact that sexiness is in the eye of the beholder. Ask: **Why do we think some people are sexy and others aren't? If sex is a personal, private thing, why do many people try so hard to look sexy? How do you think God feels about the question of what's sexy and what isn't?**

STEP 3

Instead of studying Genesis 38, read Genesis 1:26-28; 2:18-25 aloud. Have kids run up to the board and draw the "male" symbol (a circle connected to an arrow) whenever a male is mentioned, and a "female" sign (a circle connected to a cross) whenever a female is mentioned—and a heart shape whenever something is mentioned involving the two of them. Ask: **What can we learn from these verses about sex and God's attitude toward it?** (Possible answers: God created the sexes; He declared them [including their bodies] good; the male and female needed each other; God expected them to have sex [as part of multiplying and in order to be one flesh]; the man and woman were meant to have no shame about their bodies or their sexuality.)

STEP 1

When discussing a sensitive subject like sexuality, there can be safety in numbers; kids who are embarrassed can hope that someone else will answer your questions. But if you're one of just two or three kids, there's nowhere to hide. Unless your kids are especially comfortable with each other, don't expect them to warm up easily to discussion. Arrange seating as informally as you can, with seats at a 45-degree angle to each other rather than making kids face each other head-on. Ask potentially embarrassing questions in the third person instead of first person. Give kids time to think about questions that they don't feel comfortable answering aloud. In Step 1, if your group is too small to make the scavenger hunt a team effort, let kids compete individually.

STEP 4

If you have fewer than eight group members, it may be tough to make the talk-show format work. Try substituting a radio call-in format so that panelists won't be needed. Bring a disconnected phone receiver. Act as the host, throwing out questions for "callers" to answer. Give the phone to a group member; then ask the first question. He or she answers, then gives the phone to someone else. If you like, announce that you'll ask a question of "the fifteenth caller," and have kids pass the phone around that many times before asking the next question.

STEP 3

If your group is large enough, provide added incentive for reading Genesis 38 by dividing the group into five teams: lawyers for Tamar, lawyers for Judah, prosecutors who have charged Tamar with prostitution and blackmail, prosecutors who have charged Judah with buying the services of a prostitute, and members of the Society for More Decent Bibles, who believe all references to sex should be removed from Scripture. After giving teams time to read the chapter, the lawyers and prosecutors should make their cases to the rest of the group. Then have the members of the Society for More Decent Bibles tell how they'd like to censor the chapter—allowing you to lead into a discussion of how Scripture frankly treats the subject of sex.

STEP 5

Sharing and comparing kids' responses to Repro Resource 2 may be difficult to do thoroughly in a large group. To expedite the process, divide your meeting place into three zones: Clearly Wrong, Potentially Dangerous, and Perfectly Acceptable. As you read the items on the list, give kids time to arrange themselves in the three zones to show how they responded. Let volunteers explain their answers before moving from one item to the next.

STEP 4

Kids who have spent much time in church won't be surprised to hear that the Bible opposes sexual immorality. They may question the relevance of such an old book to the urgent drives they feel. So ease into discussion of biblical morality with the following simulation. Say: **The year is 2418. You have just been appointed commander of a space station orbiting the planet Gamma IV in the Andromeda galaxy. You have inherited all kinds of problems from the last commander. Sexually transmitted diseases are running rampant throughout the station, killing several key personnel each year; 25 percent of your unmarried teenage girls are having babies, placing an added burden on your life support system; several rapes are reported each week. Yet none of these problems exist on Gamma IV, where an alien civilization lives by a strict rule: no sexual relations outside of marriage. Your space station has no rules governing sexual behavior, but offers free condoms, free abortions, and free meetings with android prostitutes. What do you do about your problems, and why?**

STEP 6

Jaded kids might rattle off the right "why wait" answers, knowing what's expected. But the answers may have no connection to their behavior. Instead of asking such kids to list physical reasons why *they* should abstain from premarital sex, ask what they would tell younger brothers or sisters to do. Then ask whether the same advice should apply to themselves, and why.

STEP 3

Given the complexity of Genesis 38, you may be better off reading Genesis 1:26-28; 2:18-25 (see "Extra Action" option). If you want to use Genesis 38, you'll need to explain three things:

• Some of ancient Israel's customs (such as taking the wife of a deceased brother) differed from those we should follow today. In some cases God gave commands that fit Israel's situation and not ours, and in some cases Moses allowed less-than-perfect practices because people resisted following God's way (as with divorce; see Matt. 19:7-9).

• People in Bible times felt a stronger need to have large families than many people in our culture feel today. Children were needed as helpers in an agricultural society, and the death rate for babies was high. This helps to explain, though not excuse, Tamar's behavior.

• The Bible reports all kinds of behavior, good and bad. It doesn't always go into detail about the wrongness of all the sins it reports. We shouldn't assume that just because something's mentioned here that it's okay.

STEP 4

Before asking kids to analyze the Ephesians and 1 Thessalonians passages, you may want to explain that the Greek word translated "sexual immorality" here is *porneia*. It refers to a wide range of sexual activities condemned by God—such as adultery, intercourse before and outside of marriage, prostitution, incest, and other perversions or distortions of the way God meant sex to be. Kids may think these verses fail to specifically prohibit premarital sex, but the fact is that they condemn premarital sex and much more.

STEP 1

Kids may feel nervous and a little embarrassed when they hear sexuality is the subject of this session. Acknowledge those feelings while helping kids get to know each other with the following activity. Form pairs, mixing guys and girls as much as possible. Give each pair a small amount of "blusher" makeup and a brush, sponge, or cotton ball with which to apply it. (If some girls in your group have makeup in their purses, let them use it.) One person in each pair should brush a little blusher on his or her partner's cheeks while the one receiving the blush describes an "embarrassing moment" he or she has experienced. Then have the partners switch roles. When everyone is "blushing," note that it sometimes feels embarrassing to talk about sex—but that you won't be putting anybody on the spot in this meeting. Be sure to provide plenty of makeup remover for kids to use as you move into the rest of the session.

STEP 6

To conclude, ask kids to close their eyes and to imagine that they've traveled back in time to the creation of the world. They're watching God at work in the Garden of Eden. Read or have a volunteer read Genesis 1:26-28, 31 and Psalm 139:13-16. Then, with kids' eyes still closed, say something like this: **God invented sex. He also invented you, every bit of you, including your sexuality. You may not always feel like a great invention, but you are. Take a minute now to tell God how you feel about being a guy or a girl and to thank Him for inventing sex and inventing you.** Then close in prayer yourself, thanking God for the kids in your group and the way He's created them.

STEP 1

After discussing sexual messages and influences, distribute paper and pencils and ask the girls to write the names of the adults in their immediate world (parents, teachers, church leaders). Have them mark the ones they think are appropriate models of biblical standards for human sexuality. Then ask the girls to use one corner of their paper to write their responses to the following questions. **Do you think you know everything you need to know about how your body functions? About a guy's body? Who are the people on your list you can talk to for more information?**

STEP 5

After discussing Repro Resource 2, have the girls talk about the items on the sheet that may be acceptable but could become potentially dangerous. Form teams of three or four girls and give each team a different item. Ask each team to suggest a few things that might be done if an acceptable situation begins to change. For example, what if a back rub isn't limited to your back, or a friendly hug becomes more. Ask: **What can you do or say? What if the guy is someone you admire and whose friendship you don't want to lose?**

STEP 4

If your group is mainly male, or if you're splitting the group along gender lines for these sessions, you may want to focus on issues many guys face. Have one team read the Ephesians verses and discuss: **Does a hint of sexual immorality** (vs. 3) **make a guy more attractive to girls? Does it make him feel better about himself? Does a hint of sexual immorality make a girl more or less attractive? Why? Do you agree that dirty jokes** (vs. 4) **are always out of place? Why or why not? Which do you think is more attractive to most guys: dirty jokes or giving thanks? How does one tend to prevent the other?** Have another team read the I Thessalonians passage and discuss: **How could a guy tell that he hadn't learned to control his own body** (vs. 4)**? What are some places you might avoid if you were trying to learn to control your sexual appetite? How might a Christian guy wrong another Christian sexually** (vs. 6)**? How could brotherly (or sisterly) love** (vs. 9) **prevent that?**

STEP 6

For many adolescent males, the sex drive is so strong that abstinence sounds like a guarantee of physical suffering. They lose sight of the fact that sex is not a life-or-death physical need like breathing, eating, and drinking. Give them a visual reminder of this fact by taping on the wall the following pictures you've drawn or photocopied and labeled beforehand: a human skull labeled "Three hours without breathing"; a human skull labeled "Three months without food"; a human skull labeled "Three months without water"; and a smiling, healthy guy labeled "Three years without sex."

STEP 1

Stage a two-team relay race. Kids from one team (The Pleasure Seekers) try to make it across the room to pick up cookies one at a time and bring them back. Kids from the other team (The Pleasure Police) try to keep the Pleasure Seekers from accomplishing their goal. If a police officer tags a cookie smuggler, the latter has to put the cookie back. The Pleasure Seekers have three minutes (or another time limit that fits the size of your group) to get all the cookies. If they succeed, they keep the cookies. If not, the cookies go to the Pleasure Police. After the contest, lead into the question of whether God is like the Pleasure Police—trying to keep people from enjoying their natural sexuality.

STEP 6

After the meeting, set up a refreshment table. At first put "Hands Off!" and "Do Not Touch!" signs on everything kids might like. Then take those signs off and put up signs that limit the amount each person can take, plus some that indicate in what order kids can eat the items. Point out that God's approach is to give us limits for our own good, not to deny us what is good.

STEP 1

During the week before the meeting, use a VCR to tape a TV program like *Entertainment Tonight* or a music video show. Include the commercials. To start your meeting, play the program for your group—but in the fast-forward or "search" mode, so that kids can see the show in fast motion. (Note: so that images don't flash by too quickly to see, tape the program on your VCR's "SP" speed.) Encourage kids to mentally keep track of the number of images they see that seem to be using sex or sexiness to get attention. After watching for about five minutes, see who came up with the most and least images and why. Then pick up the basic session's Step 1 with the question: **To what extent are you affected by the sexual messages you receive through the media?**

STEP 4

Rather than using the talk-show format, play a song for the group: the Beach Boys' "Wouldn't It Be Nice." This oldie sounds downright quaint today, expressing a boy's yearning for the intimacy he'd have with his girlfriend if they were only older and married. If you have time, play a current song that takes for granted a sexual relationship without any reference to commitment. Contrast the two songs. Whether playing one song or both, ask: **What percentage of dating teenagers today do you think have the attitude of the singer in "Wouldn't It Be Nice"? Why does this song sound old-fashioned today?** Then use the talk-show questions in the basic session's Step 4.

STEP 1

Combine Steps 1 and 2 into a single opener. Before the meeting, cut a variety of ads, especially movie and clothing ads, from magazines; cut the quotes from Repro Resource 1, separating each quote from the rest. Put all of these items in a pile in the middle of your meeting place. As your session begins, designate one wall "Goes Along with the Bible" and another "Doesn't Go Along with the Bible." Kids should line up at the pile, each taking one ad or quote and taping it on one wall or the other without comment. Then let the whole group look at the two walls and discuss whether they agree or disagree with the way the quotes and ads were categorized.

STEP 3

Skip the study of Genesis 38 and return to the nine biblical quotes on Repro Resource 1. Have kids cross out the six that aren't from the Bible, and discuss the way love and sex are viewed in these quotes. Note that sex and love are tied together; that sex is seen in a mostly positive light, and that sexuality is treated frankly. Are group members surprised by this? What has been their impression of the Bible's view of sex until now? Then read Step 4's Ephesians or I Thessalonians passage. After pulling out the main points, move back to the middle of Step 4 and ask the whole group just one or two of the "talk-show" questions. If time is very limited, skip Steps 5 and 6. In their place, pass out photocopies of a portion of Les Christie's article, "Talking to Kids about Sex," from the beginning of this unit. The portion you should photocopy begins with the subhead, "The Big Picture," and finishes three paragraphs from the end of the article, with the sentence, "God wants to teach us how to really love." Let kids take this home to read.

STEP 1

Instead of using magazines, do this activity with music CDs or albums. The objective is to write down as many sexual inferences as can be found in the albums before the time is up. Have your teens bring CDs or albums of their favorite R & B and rap artists. The activity will work best if you have a wide range of contemporary artists (Public Enemy, 2 Live Crew, Shabba Ranks, MC Hammer, Whitney Houston, BBD, Mariah Carey, etc.). Display the CDs or albums exhibition style on tables around the room. Then give your group members a time limit for the activity. When you say go, they will move around the room, writing down the sexual inferences they find on the CDs or albums.

STEP 4

The talk-show format can have a further impact by including teenagers (male and female) who already have children. To a number of urban churches and youth groups this is an accessible reality. Interestingly, these young people tend to preach a "gospel of sexual responsibility" after having a child. They want to share with their peers the lessons they did not heed concerning sexual responsibility. They will probably share in direct and straightforward language that marriage and/or sexual responsibility ought to be considered. This type of peer counseling will cause good and frank discussion among teens, and will get them beyond the intimidation of asking the youth worker sexual questions in a public format.

STEP 1

If possible, separate junior high and high school students while leading these sessions. If you can't, remember that some junior highers are in the confusion of mid-puberty, while older kids may be battling (or succumbing to) temptation. Assume that all the kids are curious about sex and that some may be experienced, but don't assume that all kids are dating or that all understand the biological basics. Keep discussion in the third person as much as possible to avoid putting younger kids on the spot (Example: Instead of asking, **Where do you get information about sex?** ask, **Where do the kids you know get information about sex?**) Give kids from both age groups a nonthreatening way to ask specific questions by using a question box (a shoebox with a slot in the top), into which kids can drop written queries for you to answer. For Step 3, use the "Extra Action" option (reading Gen. 1:26-28; 2:18-25 instead of Gen. 38). In Step 4, don't expect younger kids to have answers to the questions asked by the "talk-show host"; you may want to address these to older kids. In the same step, use either the Ephesians or the I Thessalonians passage, not both, and try to include a mix of ages in each small group so that older kids can help younger ones.

STEP 5

Kids who have struggled with the "How far can I go?" question may find Repro Resource 2 helpful. But some younger students may find it confusing and a little scary—and their parents may fear that explicit discussion of petting will "put ideas in" kids' minds. If you think the latter is the case in your group, delete the sheet and discuss ways in which kids have seen people on TV and in movies express affection. Which would they be comfortable with? Which ways do they think are OK? Which aren't?

STEP 1

If cutting up magazines would seem too much like a grade-school craft project to your young people, open with a slightly more cerebral activity. Pass out paper and pens. Each person must write a one-hundred-word description of a typical day in his or her life—without using the letters S, E, or X. Allow up to five minutes for kids to meet this challenge; if you like, give a prize to anyone who is successful. After noting the difficulty of the assignment, tie it into the challenge of life without SEX—living without being sexually active, even though one has the physical ability to have sex.

STEP 6

At the end of the session, form pairs. Offer a prize to any pairs who take on one of the following assignments this week: (1) Write a "book report" on the section of your school health textbook that deals with sexuality, and read it to the group next week; (2) prepare to debate each other for five minutes on the subject of whether school-based clinics should be allowed to distribute condoms; or (3) prepare (and perform next week) a skit in which characters from a show like *Melrose Place* or *Beverly Hills 90210* discover that they won't die if they don't have sex.

DATE USED:

Approx. Time

STEP 1: *Sexual Scavenger Hunt* _____
- ❏ Extra Action
- ❏ Small Group
- ❏ Fellowship & Worship
- ❏ Mostly Girls
- ❏ Extra Fun
- ❏ Media
- ❏ Short Meeting Time
- ❏ Urban
- ❏ Combined Junior High/High School
- ❏ Extra Challenge
Things needed:

STEP 2: *Is That in the Bible?* _____
Things needed:

STEP 3: *Caught after the Act* _____
- ❏ Extra Action
- ❏ Large Group
- ❏ Little Bible Background
- ❏ Short Meeting Time
Things needed:

STEP 4: *Sex: Then and Now* _____
- ❏ Small Group
- ❏ Heard It All Before
- ❏ Little Bible Background
- ❏ Mostly Guys
- ❏ Media
- ❏ Urban
Things needed:

STEP 5: *A Hands-Off Approach* _____
- ❏ Large Group
- ❏ Mostly Girls
- ❏ Combined Junior High/High School
Things needed:

STEP 6: *Worth the Wait? (Part 1)* _____
- ❏ Heard It All Before
- ❏ Fellowship & Worship
- ❏ Mostly Guys
- ❏ Extra Fun
- ❏ Extra Challenge
Things needed:

R-E-S-P-E-C-T: That's What Sex Should Mean to Thee

YOUR GOALS FOR THIS SESSION:

Choose one or more

☐ To help kids realize that sex is not the most natural or logical result of genuine love during a relationship prior to marriage.

☐ To help kids identify and deal with the many emotions that accompany sexual desire and/or activity.

☐ To help kids begin to associate the importance of respect with any type of sexual desire and/or opportunity.

☐ Other:_____

_____

Your Bible Base:

Genesis 34
Galatians 5:22-23

STEP 1

Picture This Emotion

(Needed: Written-out sets of emotions, drawing paper, pens, "Love Indicator" circles)

O P T I O N S

SMALL GROUP

FELLOWSHIP & WORSHIP

EXTRA FUN

SHORT MEETING TIME

EXTRA CHALLENGE

Form teams and provide each team with a pen and plenty of paper. Have teams assemble in the corners of the room, as far from each other as possible. In the center of the room, provide for each team a set of folded slips of paper which contain a variety of emotions, behaviors, and feelings (joy, hatred, lust, hunger, grief, despair, disappointment, peace, kindness, loneliness, greed, and so forth). Each slip of paper should contain one emotion. An identical set of folded slips should be provided for each team. At your signal, one person from each team should run to his or her stack, draw one slip of paper, run back to his or her team members, and attempt to draw the word using *Pictionary* rules (no talking, no use of letters or numbers, etc.). After the word is guessed, the next person in the group should repeat the process. Team members should alternate until all the slips are gone or until you call time. The first team to draw and guess all the words successfully, or that completes the most within your time limit, is the winner.

Explain that as young people begin to have sexual feelings and try to work through what they are experiencing, they go through a wide range of emotions. The emotions can vary from day to day. To find out what your group members are feeling *now*, convert your room into a "Love Indicator" machine—like one you might find at a carnival or arcade (the kind where the person puts in a quarter and a light bulb comes on to indicate how "sexy" he or she is). Put down circles or squares of paper across the room, with escalating levels such as "Ice Queen/King," "Cold Fish," "Cool and Clammy," "Meek and Mild," "Middle of the Road," "On the Spicy Side," "Hot Tamale," and "Volcano."

Let group members choose where they think they belong and stand on that spot. After all group members have taken a position, see if they agree with each other's self-assessments. Discuss: **How does it make you feel to be perceived as less romantic than you really are? How do you feel to be thought of as "sexier" than you think you are?**

A Skit and It Shall Be Done for You

Ask for volunteers to perform some skits. Volunteers should act out one or more of the following scenes and focus on the *feelings* of the person(s) involved. Read each scenario and give volunteers a few minutes to put something together.

(1) Andrew has never had a date, though most of his friends have been dating for a number of years. But out of the blue, Angie asks him to a turnabout event at school. They have a wonderful time, and Andrew suddenly realizes the thrill of dating. Volunteers should put together a before-and-after skit to contrast Andrew's emotional state prior to the party with how he acts the day after.

(2) Jane has begun to date Ted. Jane has never dated much, but Ted has had several relationships—some of them involving considerable sexual activity. The guys in the locker room like to hear Ted talk about his dates and the things he has done. Jane and Ted haven't gotten involved more than an occasional good-night kiss. None of Ted's other girlfriends really meant that much to him, but he really likes Jane. The problem is that his friends press him for "the juicy details" in the locker room every Monday. Volunteers should enact the locker room as the guys try to get Ted to talk. Will he tell them the truth, or what they want to hear?

(3) Jeannie and Jason are the "perfect couple" at school. Both are smart and athletic, and have big plans for the future. They have dated for about three years, and are planning to attend the same college. However, on this particular day, Jeannie pulls Jason aside (some of their friends might be hanging around) to tell him that she is pregnant. Jason and Jeannie should express what they are feeling toward each other, and begin to explore their options.

(4) The biblical Mary confronts the biblical Joseph to tell him she is pregnant—and why. Mary and Joseph should express their feelings and explore their options as Jason and Jeannie did in the previous example.

Summarize: **Sex is certainly a physical act, and can have physical consequences—pregnancy, sexually transmitted diseases, etc. Yet perhaps even more powerful are the emotions that accompany a sexual relationship. The emotions we feel during the early stages of love, or romance, at least, can be so incredibly thrilling that we never want them to end. We want more and more. But if we allow emotions to lead us to sexual activity, we suddenly find ourselves facing a whole load of other emotions. The physical thrill of sex is short-lived. The emotions are ongoing—almost continual. That's why God designed sex to take place only within the context of marriage. When two people are wholly and eternally committed to each other, sex brings them together and makes them feel wonderful. But outside of marriage, sex ignites the wrong emotions: fear, shame, jealousy, guilt, and more.**

STEP 3

Hitting below the Belt

(Needed: Bibles, pens, paper)

Explain that many times the strong emotions that accompany premarital sex aren't limited to the two people who become sexually active. Many others may be involved as well—parents, friends, children who might result from such a union, etc.

For a case in point, divide into groups, hand out paper and pens, and have group members read Genesis 34. This chapter provides the account of Shechem's rape of Dinah (the daughter of Jacob). As group members read through the chapter, have them list all the emotions they discover, either stated or implied. Also ask them to put themselves into the roles of the characters in the account and list the emotions they think they would be feeling. They should put together a long list, including:

- Betrayal (vs. 1—Dinah had been to visit the women of the land, strangers to her)
- Lust (vs. 2)
- "Love" (vs. 3)
- Passion/desire (vs. 4)
- "Grief and fury" (vs. 7)
- Disgrace/shame (vs. 7)
- Deceit (vss. 13-17)

O P T I O N S

EXTRA ACTION

HEARD IT ALL BEFORE

LITTLE BIBLE BACKGROUND

SHORT MEETING TIME

URBAN

JR. HIGH HIGH SCHOOL COMBINED

- Delight (vs. 19)
- Greed (vss. 20-23)
- Revenge (vss. 25-26)
- Retribution (vss. 27-29)
- Fear (vs. 30)
- Honor (vs. 31)

Ask: **How did Dinah feel about what had happened?**
(We don't know. Of all the emotions listed in this chapter, we are
unable to determine how *she* felt. Was she glad that her brothers had
wiped out the family of Shechem? Or would she have liked to have
married him, in spite of what he had done to her? Though she was
the victim in this story, we know less of what *she* felt than of what
all the others were feeling.)

**Put yourself in Dinah's place. You can see, to some extent,
the depth of emotions that resulted from one sexual
encounter. Some of the people around you are excited.
Others are violently angry. And most of them are confused
and acting in irrational ways. The same thing happens every
time someone chooses to have sex prior to marriage.
The person's life can never be the same, nor can the lives
of his or her family members.**

Name That Feeling

(Needed: Pens, paper, copies of Repro Resources 3 and 4)

Hand out pens and paper as you explain that you are going to read
a number of statements kids might hear at school. After each statement,
group members should immediately write the emotion(s) they would
feel upon hearing that statement. When they're finished (give them just a
few seconds), have group members simultaneously hold up what they
have written. This should both encourage group members to be honest
and allow them to see how often other people may feel the same way
they do. It will also allow you to get some insight into how they truly feel
as they deal with sexual issues at school. The following are some sample
statements, but feel free to add others that you know would be specifically applicable to your group.

- **A person you really like, but you don't think likes you, walks up and says, "I have two tickets to a concert this weekend. Would you like to go?"**
- **A person you barely know, but find very annoying, walks up and says, "I have two tickets to a concert this weekend. Would you like to go?"**
- **Your best friend pulls you aside and tells you, "Chris and I went 'all the way' last night!"**
- **Your friend Gina has a boyfriend named Scott that you've never liked at all. Gina tells you, "Scott forced me to have sex with him last night. I kept saying no, but he just wouldn't stop."**
- **One of your biggest adversaries walks up to you in front of a crowd of people and says, quite loudly, "Is it true what I hear? Are you a virgin?!"**
- **A casual friend says, "You and a date are invited to a party at Bill's tonight. It's couples only, and his parents won't be home—if you know what I mean."**

In some cases, it may be difficult for group members to identify exactly what they would be feeling. Summarize: **As you can see, sexual activity can arouse a lot of strong emotions—even if you aren't the one involved in the sexual activity. The emotions range from sheer joy to horrifying terror. That's why it's so important to do everything in your power to avoid those strong, negative emotions.**

Distribute copies of "The Gift." Repro Resources 3 and 4 are designed to look alike, but there are subtle and significant differences. Half of your group members should get one version and the other half should get the other version. But all group members should assume they're getting the same assignment.

After group members read the parable, ask: **What do you think the "gift" represents?** (Sexual intercourse.)

Who do you think the giver is? (Though we may tend to think we give sex to someone we love, it is first and foremost a gift to each of us from God.)

Do you identify at all with the anticipation Joe felt?
Do you think Joe did the right thing?
Is Joe's model one that you would like to follow?
How do you think Joe felt at the end of the story?

Try to start with some questions that everyone will agree with, but eventually let group members discover that two versions of the story have been circulated. Explain that it's the same way in life—we all have pretty much the same opportunities, and it's how we respond to those opportunities that shapes our attitudes toward the people we date, the sexual act itself, and pretty much our whole state of mind.

The Logical Results

(Needed: Bibles)

It is likely that group members will agree with much of what you have said so far. Many of them probably have friends who have been hurt by getting too involved with sex too quickly. Yet most young people struggle with the "big" question, so let them deal with it now: **What if you really love the other person? Isn't sex a logical, natural, and justifiable way of deepening that love?** (A related question is "What if you have every intention to marry the other person? What's the big deal about getting started a little early with the sexual activity?")

Let group members discuss their opinions. Perhaps some of them have thought through the issue and have good answers. But for others, it might still be a struggle. When the discussion begins to wane a bit, have someone read aloud Galatians 5:22-23. Then ask: **If we're living as the Christians God has created us to be, what will be the logical results of love?**

Let group members discover the characteristics associated with love in regard to the fruit of the Spirit. Ask: **Do you think these qualities really apply to romantic and sexual relationships?** (Yes. In the context of the chapter, they are contrasted with such things as "sexual immorality," "debauchery," and "orgies" [Gal. 5:19-22].)

One at a time, read the qualities associated with love in this passage (joy, peace, patience, kindness, goodness, faithfulness, gentleness, and self-control). In each case, determine whether the characteristic would be evident in most relationships where sexual activity is taking place. Then determine in what ways it might be apparent in relationships where both people have committed to refrain from sex. (For instance, patience would certainly be evident in a relationship in which two people are waiting until they're married to have sex.)

When you finish, summarize: **What all this boils down to is that sexual activity demonstrates a lack of respect for the other person. Genuine love promotes patience, self-control, and gentleness. Premarital sexual involvement is usually based on selfish needs, manipulation, and worse. It is also important to have a sense of respect for one's self. If self-image levels are low—if we feel unworthy of love from others, if we are so hungry for love that we are willing to take it from anyone who offers—then we become susceptible to giving in to the sexual**

O P T I O N S

LARGE GROUP

HEARD IT ALL BEFORE

LITTLE BIBLE BACKGROUND

MOSTLY GUYS

MEDIA

urges we feel. Offer to talk with or recommend counseling to anyone who feels this way.

Your emotional state of mind can influence every decision you make. By committing right now to save sex for marriage, you can avoid a lot of needless emotional suffering in the meantime. I guarantee you'll be glad if you do.

STEP
6

Worth the Wait? (Part 2)

(Needed: The list you started in Session 1)

O P T I O N S

Explain that if sex were purely a physical act, it would be easier to cope with. But the emotions that accompany sexual activity are incredibly powerful. Have group members add to their list of reasons to save sex for marriage, this time focusing entirely on the emotional concerns that are involved. Among other things, they should come up with the following:

- You never have to worry about "getting caught." You can experience peace of mind rather than guilt, shame, and other horrible feelings.
- When you *do* get married, you will have a completely clear conscience and can give complete loyalty to your spouse.
- Your current relationships will be stronger (and probably longer).

Ask group members to recall any recent negative emotions they may have felt in regard to dating relationships. Close in prayer, asking God to remove the strong temptation to have sex, to heal any emotions that are painful, and to provide the strength for group members to make good decisions concerning their future sex lives.

The Gift

The gift sat in a distant corner with the tag in clear sight: "Do not open until Christmas." But Christmas seemed like such a long time away to Joe. The gift was from his favorite relative—the one who always gave the best presents on birthdays and holidays. Most relatives just gave cards, socks, or underwear, but this one gave wonderful, excellent, thrilling gifts. (And the relative had promised that this one would be the best yet.)

The gold foil wrapping and brightly colored bow made it quite a temptation to Joe. The gift looked mysterious and exciting from across the room, and the closer he got to it, the more exotic it appeared. Of course, he got all those warnings from his parents: "Be sure to leave the gift alone until it's the right time to open it." But time was *crawling*. Each hour seemed like a day, and each day seemed like a month.

One day Joe was at home alone while his parents were out shopping. No matter what he tried to do—homework, TV, or whatever—he seemed to end up in the same room with the gift. He wanted to know more about it. He just couldn't help it. He finally wandered closer and picked it up. It even *felt* exciting. He gave it a little shake and the sound from within was *so* tantalizing.

Joe happened to notice that it would be pretty easy to gently slip the bow off of the wrapping, carefully undo the tape at one end, slide the box out of the wrapping, and see exactly what the gift was. He struggled with the temptation, but finally resisted. He put the gift back down and returned to his homework. The thought of the gift kept crossing his mind, but he knew that was only natural. Anything so special was certain to command a lot of thought and attention.

Each time his parents were gone, he again felt the temptation to open the gift and see exactly what it was. But after he had made up his mind not to open the gift, it became a little bit easier to wait as he experienced each recurring temptation. His eagerness and anticipation increased, but he knew he could wait until Christmas came.

When Christmas *finally* arrived, Joe was handed the gift. The giver sat back and watched as Joe opened it. The moment was special for both of them. And, wow, Joe couldn't believe what a great gift it was! If he could have listed every single thing he wanted for Christmas, the whole list wouldn't have been half as good as this single gift.

The gift was something special that Joe treasured throughout his lifetime. He frequently thought back to that very special Christmas. Every time he did, the memory thrilled him. Very few other experiences in life would ever compare to what he felt that day. He was overjoyed that he had managed to wait until the time was right. And Joe—as well as the giver of the gift—lived happily ever after.

The Gift

The gift sat in a distant corner with the tag in clear sight: "Do not open until Christmas." But Christmas seemed like such a long time away to Joe. The gift was from his favorite relative—the one who always gave the best presents on birthdays and holidays. Most relatives just gave cards, socks, or underwear, but this one gave wonderful, excellent, thrilling gifts. (And the relative had promised that this one would be the best yet.)

The gold foil wrapping and brightly colored bow made it quite a temptation to Joe. The gift looked mysterious and exciting from across the room, and the closer he got to it, the more exotic it appeared. Of course, he got all those warnings from his parents: "Be sure to leave the gift alone until it's the right time to open it." But time was *crawling*. Each hour seemed like a day, and each day seemed like a month.

One day Joe was at home alone while his parents were out shopping. No matter what he tried to do—homework, TV, or whatever—he seemed to end up in the same room with the gift. He wanted to know more about it. He just couldn't help it. He finally wandered closer and picked it up. It even *felt* exciting. He gave it a little shake and the sound from within was *so* tantalizing.

Joe happened to notice that it would be pretty easy to gently slip the bow off of the wrapping, carefully undo the tape at one end, slide the box out of the wrapping, and see exactly what the gift was. He struggled with the temptation, and finally gave in. He gingerly opened the gift, and it was great! He quickly had it out of the box and was just starting to enjoy it when he thought he heard his parents. He rapidly bundled it back up, replaced the tape and the bow, and tried to act as if nothing had happened.

Each time his parents were gone, he again felt the temptation to open the gift and enjoy it. And since he had already done so, it became a little bit easier to give in to each recurring temptation. Funny thing, though—every time he opened the gift it seemed a little less exciting and a lot less special. He even began to lose his enthusiasm for Christmas to get here. What else was there to look forward to?

When Christmas *finally* arrived, Joe was handed the gift. The giver watched as he opened it. Joe suspected it was obvious to everyone else that the previously shiny foil had lost its luster and that the bow had become rather shabby looking. He tried to act surprised, but could not seem to show much enthusiasm. His disappointment seemed to rub off on the others, and this Christmas just didn't seem very special.

The gift was something that Joe kept throughout his lifetime. But it never seemed special to him. He frequently thought back and wondered how things would have been different if he hadn't ruined the surprise. He was disappointed—too late—that he hadn't waited until the time was right. And Joe and the giver of the gift were never quite as close after that Christmas.

NOTES

EXTRA ACTION

STEP 3

Form teams. Give each team a supply of poster board and markers. Read Genesis 34 aloud in sections of two or three paragraphs at a time. At the end of each section, call out a number between 3 and 6. Each team must create a newspaper headline summarizing what happened in the section you just read, and the headline must have the number of words that you called out. The first team to complete its headline and carry it up to you wins that round.

STEP 4

If reading the story on the Repro Resources would be too sedate or too difficult for your group, try another way to make a similar point. Before the session, put a fragile (but inexpensive) glass or ceramic figurine in a box. Don't try to protect the figurine with Styrofoam or other packing material. Wrap the box in wedding-gift paper. At this point in the session, play a lively game of floor hockey using the box as the puck. If you don't have hockey sticks or brooms, let kids use their feet. After playing for several minutes, stop the game. Carefully unwrap the figurine and give it as a "wedding present" to the group. Chances are it will be broken; even if it isn't, the box will be in bad shape. Use this as an illustration of the disappointing results of not keeping one's virginity intact as a wedding present for a spouse.

SMALL GROUP

STEP 1

If you don't have enough group members to manage the picture charades, here's another idea. Have kids stand next to each other in a line and hold hands. Anyone who lets go of anyone else's hand is out. Now have kids perform a variety of tasks, using only the hands that are clasped: eating popcorn; signing their names; drinking water from a paper cup; and defending themselves against a barrage of Ping-Pong balls or pillows that you throw. Then talk about how it felt to have such an "intimate" relationship (awkward, frustrating, interesting, etc.). Use this as an illustration of the fact that even physical relationships have an emotional side.

STEP 2

If your pool of willing volunteers isn't large enough to act out one or more of the skits, try this. After describing only the second, third, and fourth situations, have kids write "love notes" from one character to the other, expressing feelings. For example, someone might write a note from Ted to Jane, apologizing for stretching the truth to the guys in the locker room. Someone else might write a note from Jeannie to Jason, expressing her fear of losing him. After sharing and discussing these notes, move to the summary at the end of the step, beginning with, **Sex is certainly a physical act. . . .**

LARGE GROUP

STEP 2

If your group is quite large, improvising skits can present two problems. First, if you have only a few kids putting on skits for the rest, the rest have nothing to do while the actors are preparing. Second, if you have everyone preparing skits, it takes too long to perform all of them (and kids are usually just waiting their turn to act, not paying attention to the other groups). Either way, you can lose the attention of those not performing. To remedy that, call the actors you need up to the front and have them pantomime as you read the situations one at a time (use just #2–#4). When you get to the end of a description, let the whole group suggest what the actors should say and do next. Rather than trying for smooth-running skits, let the actors try out different suggestions and let group members refine the results. Allow up to four minutes for each situation to be played out; then have actors summarize the emotions their characters experienced.

STEP 5

To give as many kids as possible a chance to participate in discussion, form small groups at the start of this step. After asking each of the questions, let the small groups talk things over for a couple of minutes. When you get to the qualities associated with love in the Galatians passage, ask eight kids—each representing one of the qualities—to come to the front. Ask each to tell whether his or her quality would be more evident in a premarital sexual relationship, or in a relationship in which the couple is postponing sex until marriage—and why. Let other group members help out as needed.

STEP 3

Cynical kids may laugh at the implication that premarital sex today always leads to violent revenge by family members as it did in Genesis 34. So instead of concluding the step with the summary statement in the basic session, ask kids to come up with a contemporary soap opera plot that includes all of the emotions (not the events) they listed from Genesis 34. The main characters should be a teenage guy and girl who have recently had sex. This activity should help ease the transition from the ancient example to today's application—that sex outside of marriage often leads to strong, negative emotions for those involved and those who care about them.

STEP 5

Some kids may reject the claim that premarital sex is selfish and manipulative. If they know "nice" sexually active kids who've been going together for a long time, they may think it's possible to have a gentle, self-controlled, respectful, premarital sexual relationship. Arguing the point will prove fruitless, so approach the subject from a slightly different angle. After discussing whether sex is a good way to deepen love, turn the "why-wait-if-you're-in-love" question around: **What if you really love the other person? Why not wait in order to deepen your love?** Have half the group brainstorm ways in which having sex before marriage might deepen love; have the other half list ways in which waiting might deepen love. Share results. Then, rather than looking at the Galatians passage, read 1 Corinthians 13:4-8, concentrating on the last two verses. Point out that biblical love is an "always" thing. It involves a commitment to staying together no matter what. Waiting deepens that kind of love; *not* waiting shows that you're unwilling to make a binding commitment, which calls into question the claim that you're really in love.

STEP 3

Kids with little Bible background may be confused by the customs and violence of Genesis 34. If you anticipate such a response from your group, look at Psalm 51 instead. David wrote this confession after being confronted about his adultery with Bathsheba (2 Sam. 11:1—12:25). Ask kids to list emotions found in this Psalm (guilt, regret, sorrow, hope for forgiveness and restoration) and to suggest the kind of music that would best fit it. Also point out the other results of David's adultery—the murder of Bathsheba's husband as David tried to cover his tracks, and the death of David's infant son.

STEP 5

If you use the Galatians passage, you may need to explain the "fruit of the Spirit" concept. Kids may assume that Galatians 5:22-23 is simply a list of good qualities and that 5:19-21 is a list of bad ones. Point out that "fruit of the Spirit" is what God's Spirit grows in us when we belong to Christ and let Him change us. The fruit is the "produce" or product of the Spirit, the evidence that He's there. If these qualities are nowhere to be found in our lives, we need to ask whether God's Spirit is in us at all. If these qualities aren't showing in our dating relationships, we need to ask whether we're trying to keep God away from that part of our lives.

STEP 1

To start the session with a relational activity, group kids according to the color of their shoes (or another arbitrary criterion such as birth month). Make sure each small group has at least two kids in it. Present each small group with the following problem, which its members must solve by consensus: **All the members of your small group want to go to college. But there's only enough money for one of you to go. If you share the money equally, none of you will get to go more than a semester. And if you don't go this year, it will be at least four years before you can try again. Who gets to go?** After a couple of minutes, ask kids what they decided. Chances are that no consensus was reached—or the decision was made and the left-out ones aren't happy. Point out that men and women who spend their lives together have to make tough decisions like this and live with the results. Having a superficial trait—shoe color, birth month, sexual attraction—in common isn't enough to form the kind of relationship that lasts through tough choices and hard times.

STEP 6

Bring a guitar or other accompaniment. Point out that as the inventor of sex and emotions, God understands how the two work together. He reserves sexual activity for those who are married, not because He wants us to feel frustrated, but in part because He knows what premarital sex can do to people emotionally. Spend some time thanking God that He understands and values our feelings, sexual and otherwise. Then ask kids to suggest a few songs—anything from hymns to Top 40—that engage their emotions. Sing as many of the well-known ones as you have time for, reminding kids that God is Lord of our emotions in and out of church.

MOSTLY **GIRLS**

MOSTLY **GUYS**

EXTRA **FUN**

STEP 2

You'll need to make some changes in the skits at the beginning of Step 2. For Skit #1, change the scenario so that Angie is the one who has never dated—and never even cared that much about dating. Her feelings about dating change, however, when she accepts Andrew's invitation to go to a football game with him. In the skit, Angie should be explaining her new feelings about dating to her friend Joan, who has never had a date. For Skit #2, change the scenario so that Jane is the one with several previous relationships. In the skit Jane should be trying to explain her real feelings about Ted to her friends, who only want to hear the "juicy" details of her dates. For Skit #3, ask a girl to play the role of Jason, and present the skit as it is written.

STEP 4

After the discussion of Repro Resources 3 and 4, focus on the idea of sex being a gift. Ask for several volunteers to debate this question: **Are we the giver or the receiver of the gift of our own sexuality?** Have them consider the question particularly as it relates to the female perspective and responsibility in a dating relationship. After the debate has gone on for a few minutes, ask the following clarifying question: **Is sex ours to give away as we please—or have we received this gift from God and are accountable to use it as the Giver has requested, saving it for marriage?** Discuss how a person's answer to the question would affect her behavior.

STEP 2

If you have a hard time coming up with actors for guy-girl skits, try this instead. Set out an assortment of "used" refreshments: chewed gum, half-eaten cookies, apples with bites taken out of them, etc. When kids are reluctant to partake, ask them why. Discuss how some kids have no problem with using each other sexually, but don't want "used" people when they're looking for a lasting relationship. **How might each of these "used" people feel: (a) a guy who is pressured by his friends to lose his virginity, only to get a girl pregnant when he does so; (b) a girl who "proves" her love by having sex, only to be dumped by the guy; (c) a guy who believed he was "safe" as long as he had "protection," only to get AIDS anyway; (d) a girl who hears her date from last night telling other guys that she was "really hot"?** Then move to the post-skit summary at the end of the step.

STEP 5

Guys may ask the "what-if-you-love-each-other" question only in the interest of justifying what they really want: sex. Point this out by having them run an obstacle course in which the obstacles represent loving (but nonsexual) acts a guy could do for his girlfriend. Examples: running through a row of tires could stand for fixing a flat in the rain; walking several yards with a box over your head could stand for ignoring the charms of other girls; crawling on your knees could stand for praying together. After the race, discuss: **What percentage of guys do you think see the "finish line" of this race as getting to have sex? Do you think most guys would be willing to go through all this stuff without the "reward" of sex? On a list of the top ten truly loving things you could do for a girlfriend, where would sex be? Why?**

STEP 1

Before the session, play any team game your kids like—softball, charades, Frisbee football, etc. Use conventional teams for the first five minutes. Then change the rules, allowing half the kids on each team to play without being committed to either side. These kids can switch loyalties anytime, moving from team to team depending on who's winning, where the sun is, etc. After playing this way for another five minutes, stop the game. Ask: **How did the committed players feel about the uncommitted ones? How much interest could the uncommitted players have in who won the game?** Use this later in the session to illustrate the emotional strain placed on a relationship where partners are "playing around" but not "playing for keeps."

STEP 6

If you have time for another game, try this. You'll need a lock and at least a dozen keys that look like they might fit the lock. Before the meeting, hide the keys around your meeting place so that they're tough to find. Hide the correct key in the toughest place of all. At this point in the session, turn kids loose to look for the right key. The first one to open the lock (if anyone does) will be the winner. Award a prize if you like. After the contest, discuss how frustrating it felt to search for the keys, only to be disappointed when they weren't the right ones. Make a parallel to the much greater emotional upheaval that accompanies going from one sexual relationship to another, looking in vain for true love.

STEP 2

Before your meeting, enlist the help of a few group members to record the following lines of dialogue on audio tape. The lines should be read with as much feeling as possible.

- *(miserable)* "My life is over."
- *(joyful)* "This is great! I can hardly wait to see what's going to happen!"
- *(angry)* "How could you do such a thing? This is all your fault."
- *(fearful)* "I don't know what to do now. I'm scared."
- *(smug)* "Yeah, I'm pretty proud of myself."
- *(amazed)* "You did *what?*"

Instead of acting out the Step 2 situations in your meeting, read the description of each situation. After each, play all the taped lines of dialogue. Ask: **Which of these lines might be spoken in this situation? By whom? What feelings are being expressed?** Then move to the summary at the end of the step.

STEP 5

Before the session, ask several group members to bring a tape of a favorite song that contains the word love. At this point in the session, after raising the question of whether being in love justifies having sex, play as many songs as you have time for. As kids listen, they should write down what they think each song means when it mentions the word love. Then share definitions and ask: **If love has so many different meanings, how can you know when you're "in love enough" to justify having sex?**

STEP 1

Replace Steps 1 and 2 with the following. You (or a kid who has strong self-esteem) will be a human pinball. The pinball wears an inner tube around his or her middle. The rest of the group gets to push him or her around for one minute, using only hands and touching only the inner tube. Kids also get to push the pinball around verbally, hurling insults (warn kids not to use vulgarity or racial slurs). Then make the point: The pinball was physically protected by the inner tube, but couldn't be protected emotionally from the insults. In the same way, "safe sex" precautions may seem to protect people physically, but can't protect against the emotional problems that often accompany premarital sex. As an example of such a problem, read just situation #3 from Step 2 and ask kids to name the emotions the characters might feel. Then move to the summary statement at the end of Step 2.

STEP 3

Genesis 34 requires a lot of reading; use two shorter passages instead. Read Proverbs 6:32-35, which mentions some emotional results of illicit sex. Then read Song of Songs 1:1-4, which displays emotions from the right kind of sexual relationship. Contrast the two passages: **How does someone who has sex outside of marriage end up feeling?** (Destroyed, disgraced, shamed.) **Does sex outside marriage always lead to these feelings?** (Some may feel disgraced right away, others years later. Some people may not feel ashamed until they stand before God to be judged.) **How might family members feel?** (Jealous, furious, vengeful.) **What feelings accompany a healthy, married sexual relationship?** (Joy, excitement, passion, admiration, delight, etc.) To save more time, skip the reactions to the statements at the start of Step 4; go straight to using the story on the Repro Resources.

STEP 2

Use the following two skit options:

(1) Brahim is HIV positive from a sexual relationship he had at 14. Since then, he's had intercourse with many girls. He lived by the philosophy, "If I have to go, I'm taking other people with me." At age 16 he joined the church and has not been sexually active since. However, Brahim and Shaniqua, the pastor's daughter, have fallen in love. Although Brahim and Shaniqua have promised not to have sex with each other, should Brahim tell her (and his past girlfriends) his secret?

(2) Ray and Dontae are good buddies in the youth group. They both seem like nice Christian boys, and are liked by all the girls. One day, Albert, another guy in the youth group, discovered that Ray and Dontae are gay. Albert is not sure what to do. On one hand, he wants to tell the other members of the group; on the other hand, he doesn't want to gossip. What should Albert do?

STEP 3

A controversial topic that will expand the discussion of Dinah's rape is that of sexual abuse. This is an undiscussed reality in a number of urban churches that affects one in three girls and one in seven boys before the age of 18. Ask group members' opinions on incest, harassment, battery, sexual assault, and stalkers. If you think it's appropriate, have each group member write on a piece of paper "yes" or "no" if he or she has been sexually abused. Instruct group members that if they want help with their situations they should write their initials on their papers. Explain that you will contact (privately and discreetly) those who write their initials. Do this *only* if you are willing to genuinely help.

STEP 2

Junior highers often find it hard to improvise skits. And since most of the situations listed involve dating, younger kids may not relate to them. So here's an alternative. Pass out paper bags, one to each group member. You'll be describing some situations; kids are to show with their paper bags how the characters might feel. Kids can show embarrassment by putting the bags over their heads; they can show anger by blowing up and popping the bags; they can show happiness or sadness by using the bags as hand puppets and laughing or crying; they can show nausea or a mixture of intense emotions by pretending to use the sacks as "barf bags." **Situation #1: Ken discovers that the girl he has a crush on is already sexually involved with a much bigger, stronger guy. Situation #2: Maria's boyfriend keeps telling her that everybody else is having sex and they haven't yet, and he wants to know why. Situation #3: Nathan, who has borrowed a *Playboy* magazine from a guy at school, is looking at it in his room when his father walks in. Situation #4: Cathy "fooled around" with a guy for the first time a few weeks ago, and now she thinks she might be pregnant—but isn't sure.** After discussing kids' reactions if they're willing, point out that talking about sex means talking about strong emotions, too.

STEP 3

Condense the Genesis 34 Bible study by reading only verses 1-7 and 25-31. Rather than using small groups (which may flounder unless you have an adult leader guiding each group), read the verses aloud and ask kids to call out the emotions displayed in the passage as you read. Write these feelings on the board; ask kids to rate how strong each feeling was on a scale of 1 to 10, with 10 being the strongest.

STEP 1

If picture charades and the "Love Indicator" seem too unsophisticated for your group, try this instead. Write the following list of emotions on the board: regret, joy, disappointment, fear, contentment, confusion, love, hate, sadness, happiness, anger, obsession, boredom, cynicism. Then display several notebooks and say: **These are the "love diaries" of some famous people. As I hold each one up, tell me which of the emotions on this list you would expect to show up most often in that diary.** Here are some celebrities whose names you might use in addition to those currently "hot" with your group: Magic Johnson, Madonna, Roy Rogers and Dale Evans, Adam and Eve. Ask kids to explain their answers. Use this activity to lead into a discussion of the unbreakable tie between sex and emotions.

STEP 6

Rather than just listing some of the negative emotions that can result from premarital sex, help kids think through those feelings by using the following simulation. Form small groups. Say: **Your group is starting a new greeting card company. In the next five minutes, your job is to come up with a card that people could send to one of the following: (a) an unmarried teenage girl who's just discovered that she's pregnant; (b) a guy whose plans for college have just fallen through because he has to marry his pregnant girlfriend; (c) a girl who's just been dumped by her boyfriend after "proving" her love by having sex with him; (d) a guy who's just found out that he has AIDS; or (e) the parents of any of these kids.** Then have kids share their cards and discuss the emotions they identified. Ask: **On a scale of 1 to 10, with 10 being the toughest, how hard was it to be encouraging in these situations?**

DATE USED:

Approx. Time

STEP 1: *Picture This Emotion* _____
- ❑ Small Group
- ❑ Fellowship & Worship
- ❑ Extra Fun
- ❑ Short Meeting Time
- ❑ Extra Challenge
- Things needed:

STEP 2: *A Skit and It Shall Be...* _____
- ❑ Small Group
- ❑ Large Group
- ❑ Mostly Girls
- ❑ Mostly Guys
- ❑ Media
- ❑ Urban
- ❑ Combined Junior High/High School
- Things needed:

STEP 3: *Hitting below the Belt* _____
- ❑ Extra Action
- ❑ Heard It All Before
- ❑ Little Bible Background
- ❑ Short Meeting Time
- ❑ Urban
- ❑ Combined Junior High/High School
- Things needed:

STEP 4: *Name That Emotion* _____
- ❑ Extra Action
- ❑ Mostly Girls
- Things needed:

STEP 5: *The Logical Results* _____
- ❑ Large Group
- ❑ Heard It All Before
- ❑ Little Bible Background
- ❑ Mostly Guys
- ❑ Media
- Things needed:

STEP 6: *Worth the Wait (Part 2)* _____
- ❑ Fellowship & Worship
- ❑ Extra Fun
- ❑ Extra Challenge
- Things needed:

Sex on the Mind

YOUR GOALS FOR THIS SESSION:
Choose one or more

☐ To help kids realize that much of their focus on sex initiates in their minds.

☐ To help kids understand how their thoughts tend to influence their actions.

☐ To help kids replace sinful sexual thoughts with more positive and productive ones.

☐ Other:_____

_____

Your Bible Base:

2 Samuel 13:1-29
Philippians 4:8-9

STEP 1

How Come?

As soon as group members arrive, present them with a "How Come?" riddle. For example: **A man looks at the menu in a restaurant and sees that the special is porpoise. He has never ordered it before, so he decides to try it. When it arrives, he takes one bite, screams hysterically, and runs out of the restaurant. How come?**

Let kids ask yes-or-no questions until they arrive at the answer. (The man had been on a ship that wrecked on a remote island. Several people died. Food supplies were short. The ship's cook had served "porpoise" quite frequently until the survivors were eventually rescued. Yet with one taste in the restaurant, the man realized that what he had eaten on the island tasted nothing like the porpoise on his plate. ...)

Here's a less-extreme example (for more squeamish groups): **A man walks into a bar and asks for a glass of water. The bartender pulls out a gun and points it at the man. The man says "Thanks" and walks out. How come?** (He had hiccups and the bartender had successfully scared them out of him.)

[More of these "How Come" puzzles can be found in *Games* magazine, August 1992.]

Explain that most people enjoy mysteries and problem solving. Yet when the topic is sex, sometimes the mystery seems too much to understand. We have a natural curiosity about things we don't understand—especially sex. When we first discover how our physiology works, we tend to ask, "How come?" And it is normal to spend much of our teenage years thinking about sexual things.

Dear Abby

(Needed: Collection of advice column questions, pens, paper)

Try to deal with some of the specific "mysteries" of sex by reading a number of queries submitted to advice columnists. Teen magazines will probably provide some of the best examples. Select one of the questions, read it aloud, and let each group member write a short response. Collect the responses (which can remain anonymous) and read some of them aloud. Then compare their responses to the actual response from the columnist. In many cases your group members may discover that they know more than they thought. In fact their Christian perspective on many issues may actually provide better advice than a secular columnist.

After you let group members respond to a few questions from other young people, let *them* ask the questions. Again, keep it anonymous. Have them write down any questions they have about sex. Then collect the papers and read the questions at random, with no names attached. Be open and honest as you deal with the things they wish to know about sexual issues and/or relationships.

It's What's Inside That Counts

(Needed: Copies of Repro Resource 5, pens)

Explain that while some people tend to get caught up in "external" anatomy as they begin to think about sex, more concern should be given to two *internal* sex organs—the brain and the heart. Many young people spend endless hours trying to appear sexy on the outside. Millions of dollars are spent each year on acne creams, industrial strength deodorant, colognes and perfumes, hair products, makeup, clothes and accessories, and so forth—anything that might help make someone more attractive to the opposite gender. Yet if we focus more on outward appearance than inner character, we do ourselves (and other people) a grave injustice.

Hand out copies of "Scrambled Wisdom" (Repro Resource 5), folded into thirds so each scrambled passage is on a separate third of the paper. Ask group members not to look at the first passage until you give the signal, and to not go on to the next one until you say so. Then let them work as individuals or in small groups to unscramble the passages one at a time. Don't let them look in their Bibles unless they absolutely can't figure out the passages. After each scrambled passage is solved, discuss what it means. The unscrambled passages are as follows:

- "I the Lord search the heart and examine the mind, to reward a man according to his conduct, according to what his deeds deserve" (Jer. 17:10). (God is aware of the things that go through our hearts and minds—both good and bad.)
- "Since, then, you have been raised with Christ, set your hearts on things above, where Christ is seated at the right hand of God. Set your minds on things above, not on earthly things" (Col. 3:1-2). (We choose the things we think about, and are capable of "setting our minds" on things that are godly rather than harmful for us.)
- "Do not conform any longer to the pattern of this world, but be transformed by the renewing of your mind. Then you will be able to test and approve what God's will is—his good, pleasing and perfect will" (Rom. 12:2). (When we choose not to conform to the "regular" [worldly] way of thinking, God is able to transform and renew our thoughts.)

STEP 4

OPTIONS

Horrible Thoughts, Horrible Actions

(Needed: Bibles)

To show how impure thoughts, when left unchecked, can lead to tragic results, have group members read the story of Amnon and Tamar in 2 Samuel 13:1-22. (If you have already done Session 1 as a group, explain that this is not the same Tamar as in the Genesis 38 account.) Depending on the maturity level of your group, you can either have volunteers read aloud, section by section, or have everyone read silently and then discuss the content.

2 Samuel 13:1-6

Do you understand how the people in this story are related, and what the problem was between them? (Absalom and Tamar were children of King David. Amnon was also David's son [his oldest], but by a different mother. Jonadab was a cousin of the three children. Amnon was in "love" with Tamar, his half-sister, but marriage between them was forbidden under their law [Lev. 20:17].)

Why do you think Amnon was "frustrated to the point of illness" (vs. 2)**?** (Perhaps because he continued to dwell on his misplaced "love" until it became an obsession. Rather than yield to God's law, he kept his mind focused on improper possibilities.)

What made Amnon's problem even worse? (He listened to an untrustworthy source of information. He found someone who told him what he wanted to hear, and acted on bad advice.)

Can you think of a recent time when you had a problem and kept asking around until you found someone who told you what you wanted to hear? What were the results?

2 Samuel 13:7-14

Do you know people who remind you of Amnon in the way they think? (Some people seem to be consumed with thinking about sex [and potential encounters] all the time. They plot and plan and hope for any opportunity, without much thought about the potential consequences of their actions.)

What kind of person do you think Tamar was? Why? (She vehemently tried to protect her purity. *Her* mind seems to have been filled with logic, intelligence, and common sense.)

What appeals did Tamar make in attempting to convince Amnon to leave her alone? (She brought up her own purity, Amnon's reputation, and the legal aspects of his intended action; she even came up with a possible solution to the situation that wouldn't have involved sin or violence.)

Tamar made a lot of sense. Why do you think Amnon didn't listen to her? (He had one selfish goal, and he didn't care what he had to do to accomplish it. Perhaps his mental fantasies were so powerful that he refused to miss this opportunity.)

2 Samuel 13:15-22

Do you think Amnon's "love" for Tamar was genuine? Why? (His feelings for her proved to be merely lust, or he wouldn't have "hated her more than he had loved her" [vs. 15] after he forced her to have sex.)

How did Tamar's response differ from Amnon's? (Her remorse was genuine. Amnon should have married her after raping her, even though his reputation would have been affected [Deut. 22:28-29]. *Her* reputation was destroyed. Not only did she have to suffer through

Amnon's rape, but his refusal to marry her meant she wasn't likely to *ever* find a husband due to the cultural stigma of the time.)

King David was "furious" when he heard what had happened, but why do you think he didn't punish Amnon for his actions? (Perhaps David recalled his own recent affair with Bathsheba [2 Sam. 11], which had resulted in adultery, deceit, and the eventual murder of Bathsheba's husband. It would have been difficult for him to chastise his son for doing something so similar to what he himself had done.)

Explain that Amnon didn't go unpunished for long, however. Tamar's full brother, Absalom, waited two years for the right opportunity, and had Amnon killed. As a result, David not only lost Amnon as a son, but Absalom ran away and eventually became a major adversary to David (2 Sam. 13:23-39).

When fantasies go unchecked, the results are not always what we think. It was certainly true for Amnon. It took only one actual sexual encounter to destroy his "love," the girl's reputation, the stability of his family, and even his life. We should learn from his experience the importance of not allowing ourselves to be consumed by mental fantasies.

STEP 5

Lust Busters

(Needed: Bibles, copies of Repro Resource 6)

Where do fantasies come from? (Most people have a natural curiosity about sex when they get to a certain age. But as they begin to try to satisfy that curiosity, many people let it become an obsession. At this point, some look for answers in pornographic publications.)

Is it wrong to think a lot about sex? (It depends. There is certainly nothing wrong with getting the facts and gathering enough information to make wise decisions. But dwelling on the topic can possibly lead to lust, disrespect for the other gender as a whole, and an inability to think clearly and rationally. And for those involved with pornography, it is very difficult to remove or ignore the mental images that have been formed. Thinking about sex isn't necessarily wrong, but *lust* is.)

Why do you think teenagers think about sex so much? (Their bodies are changing, which initiates normal questions; it's a

OPTIONS

EXTRA ACTION

LARGE GROUP

HEARD IT ALL BEFORE

MOSTLY GIRLS

MOSTLY GUYS

MEDIA

popular topic of discussion; they are exposed to vast amounts of sexual material in ads, TV shows, and movies; etc.)

Hand out copies of "It's All in Your Head" (Repro Resource 6). Let group members determine which of the items listed they would classify as "things of beauty," which would be "objects of lust," and which would be somewhere in between. When they finish, discuss their responses.

Then discuss: **Suppose you're standing on the beach and see two people pass you going in opposite directions. One is a girl in a thong bathing suit, or guy in Speedo trunks. The other looks very much the same, but is dressed more modestly. Which one would your eyes follow down the beach? Why?** It is hoped that group members wouldn't be trying to pick up *any* stranger off the beach; yet many might confess to paying more attention to the skimpily clothed person. They may even have some good reasons to try to justify their actions.

Would you consider your attitude "lustful"? Why?

What if you were the modestly clothed person and were rejected simply because someone else was more naked than you were? How would you like to be evaluated purely on how little you wear or how good your body looked?

Do you think it's OK to pay more attention to people who "turn you on," or do you think it's wrong to do so? (It's a form of judging others on appearance. And while it's a natural reaction, Christians should have the "supernatural" goal of not showing favoritism for any reason—race, gender, age, or cut of a bathing suit.)

Summarize: **Lust is one of the hardest emotions to cope with. We want to think that other people like us and find us attractive. But if we keep going and begin to dwell on what kind of wonderful lovers we would be, we've gone too far. And if we don't do something to control those thoughts, we may one day find ourselves with the opportunity to do something, and without the resistance to stop.**

So in conclusion, let us repeat the Lustbusters Code. Repeat after me. (Stop at marked intervals and let group members echo your words.) **Whatever is true/ whatever is noble/ whatever is right/ whatever is pure/ whatever is lovely/ whatever is admirable/ if anything is excellent or praiseworthy/ think about such things/ And the God of peace will be with you/ Philippians 4:8-9.**

In a world filled with 976 numbers for sexual fantasy and sensual pleasure, challenge group members to memorize the 489 number (Phil. 4:8-9). As they replace lustful thoughts with pure ones on a regular basis, they will see inevitable changes in their attitudes and behaviors as well. Have them memorize the verses at this point in the session if time permits.

Worth the Wait? (Part 3)

(Needed: The list you worked on in Sessions 1 and 2)

Conclude by having group members think of additional reasons to save sex for marriage, this time based on the intellectual/mental aspects of sex. This will probably be a bit harder to do than the physical or emotional aspects were, but group members should be able to come up with a few good reasons. Alert them that sexual activity tends to consume one's thoughts, as well as his or her emotional energy. Consequently, by committing to postpone sex until marriage:

- you find more efficient uses for your mental time and energy;
- you are able to focus better on schoolwork, jobs, etc;
- you find that abstinence is a source of creative power. Rather than dwelling on the lust involved in sexual desire, you can develop other ways to express your powerful feelings (songs, poems, plays, etc.).

Explain that as pleasant as romance and sexual things can be to think about, sex can have a powerful way of consuming our mental energy if we don't watch out. If bad habits have already been formed in this area, it may be hard to break them. But it is a freeing experience to take control of our thoughts and learn once more how to think about a variety of worthwhile and productive things.

NOTES

SCRAMBLeD
WISDOM

The words of the following verses have been taken out of order and alphabetized. It's up to you to restore them to their proper places—without using your Bibles. When you think you have the solution, have your leader check it. Don't go on to the next verse until you are told to do so.

PASSAGE #1 (One sentence)

a / according / according / and / conduct, / deeds / deserve" / examine / heart / his / his / "I / Lord / man / mind, / reward / search / the / the / the / to / to / to / what / (Jeremiah 17:10).

PASSAGE #2 (Two sentences)

above / above, / at / been / Christ, / Christ / earthly / God. / hand / have / hearts / is / minds / not / of / on / on / on / raised / right / seated / Set / set / "Since, / the / then, / things / things / things" / where / with / you / your / your / (Colossians 3:1, 2).

PASSAGE #3 (Two sentences)

able / and / and / any / approve / be / be / but / by / conform / "Do / God's / good, / his / is— / longer / mind. / not / of / of / pattern / perfect / pleasing / renewing / test / the / the / Then / this / to / to / transformed / what / will / will / will" / world, / you / your / (Romans 12:2).

It's All in Your Head

If you are a teenager, and if all teenagers think a lot about sex, what does that say about you? But, hey, thinking about sex isn't necessarily wrong. It's normal and natural to have a lot of thoughts and questions about something so powerful and mysterious. Yet if those thoughts shift to mental images of you and a boyfriend or girlfriend doing all sorts of unmentionable things, your curiosity has turned to lust. Curiosity is fine. Lust is a sin.

Sometimes our tendencies to lust can be initiated by certain things. And what causes some people to lust can draw yawns out of other people. So for each of the items listed below, indicate whether you admire it for its pure aesthetic beauty, despise it as an object of lust, or would rate it somewhere in between.

A THING _____ AN OBJECT
OF BEAUTY   OF LUST

The Venus de Milo (or Michelangelo's David)

A THING _____ AN OBJECT
OF BEAUTY   OF LUST

A friend's baby pictures (naked on a shag rug)

A THING _____ AN OBJECT
OF BEAUTY   OF LUST

Madonna's *Sex* book

A THING _____ AN OBJECT
OF BEAUTY   OF LUST

A real babe in a string bikini (or a hunk in a Speedo swimsuit)

A THING _____ AN OBJECT
OF BEAUTY   OF LUST

Naked tribespeople in *National Geographic*

A THING _____ AN OBJECT
OF BEAUTY   OF LUST

Lingerie models in the Victoria's Secret catalog

A THING _____ AN OBJECT
OF BEAUTY   OF LUST

Miss (Mr.) November from *Plaything* magazine

A THING _____ AN OBJECT
OF BEAUTY   OF LUST

R-rated movies (love stories)

A THING _____ AN OBJECT
OF BEAUTY   OF LUST

"Adult" movies on cable

A THING _____ AN OBJECT
OF BEAUTY   OF LUST

A nude model in a college art class

A THING _____ AN OBJECT
OF BEAUTY   OF LUST

A soap opera scene between two very good-looking people

STEP 1

Instead of the riddles, try this game. Form two teams. Each team is supposed to memorize a Bible verse. But every 15 seconds or so, tell one team to get up and run in a circle around the other, yelling the lyrics from a song of its choosing. After three minutes, see which team did a better job of memorizing its verse (have kids recite it one word at a time, taking turns). Tie this into the difficulty of concentrating when our minds are frequently interrupted by sexual thoughts. For more action in Step 2, skip the advice columns and have kids pantomime (for their teams to guess) the following ways in which some people try to get their questions about sex answered: watching a steamy video; sneaking into a theater to watch an R-rated movie; peeking at "skin" magazines in a convenience store; listening to jokes in the locker room; asking a parent; going to health class; checking out a library book. Then discuss which sources are most and least reliable.

STEP 5

To determine who answers the discussion questions in this step, have kids pass a foam rubber ball from person to person. Whoever is touching the ball when you finish asking a question has to answer it. Anyone who refuses to answer must recite the "Lustbusters Code" after you (see end of Step 5).

STEP 2

The smaller the group, the more reluctant kids may be to write down their own sexual questions and hand them in. It's pretty easy to guess who asked a question when there are just a few kids. So after using the advice columns, ask: **On a scale of 1 to 10—with 10 being the highest—how curious do you think most kids your age are about the following questions, and why?**

• **Where do babies come from?**

• **How can I stop thinking about sex so much?**

• **How can I keep from getting (or getting a girl) pregnant?**

• **What do people of the opposite sex look like naked?**

• **How far can I go without getting in trouble?**

Let kids suggest and rate other questions if they're willing.

STEP 6

Brainstorming can be hard when you have just a few kids and their brains aren't storming at the moment. Prime the idea pump by having kids list at least twenty things they could think about in a 10-minute period. Be sure to write the words "a sexual fantasy" somewhere on the list. Then ask what kind of positive, practical value could result from having thought about each item. Which "trains of thought" are a waste of time? What might we miss by spending too much time thinking about sex?

STEP 2

Trying to read the advice-column replies and answer the questions kids submit may take too long in a large group. Instead, form five teams. Each team answers the advice-column question from a different perspective: Team 1 is a doctor or psychologist; Team 2 is a nervous parent; Team 3 is a kid who thinks he or she knows all about sex but doesn't; Team 4 is a comedian; Team 5 is a pastor. After a few minutes, share and discuss results. Skip the submission of real sexual questions unless you're prepared to deal with them in depth at a future meeting.

STEP 5

To give more kids a chance to discuss the questions, break into small groups. Read a question (for example, **Why do you think teenagers think about sex so much?**) aloud; give groups one minute to discuss it, and then ask for reports. Work your way through the questions and the Repro Resource in this way.

STEP 3

Instead of doing the unscrambling activity, establish *why* it's important to filter out certain thoughts. Display several kinds of filters (oil, air, water, furnace, gasoline, etc.). See whether kids can guess what they filter out and what they leave in. Discuss the damage the filtered-out dirt, germs, or other impurities could have done if they weren't removed. Use this as an illustration of the practical value of keeping our minds clean to avoid damage (warped ideas and expectations about sex, gross images that keep coming back when we don't want them to, etc.) over the long haul.

STEP 5

The word *lust* sounds old-fashioned, even comical, to many kids today. If you're going to use it, define it first: **Lust isn't just any stray thought about sex that might flit through your mind. To lust is to set your heart on something, long for, covet it** (want to possess it even though it belongs to someone else). Also, kids may have heard Philippians 4:8-9 oversold as the "antidote" to "dirty thoughts." Instead of reciting the "Lustbusters Code," try a different tack: ask what is true, noble, right, pure, lovely, etc. about sex. For example, something true about sex: It's not all there is to life. Something right about sex: It's fine within marriage. Something praiseworthy: God's design of the reproductive system is pretty amazing.

STEP 3

The verse-unscrambling activity will be hard enough for kids who have heard the verses—impossible for those who haven't. Try this instead: Draw the outline of a human body on chalkboard or poster board. Have kids read the verses and add to the picture any body parts that are mentioned (mind [brain] and heart.) Explain that "heart" was used to refer to the source of emotions and motivations, the most personal inner part of ourselves. Using the picture, point out that God sees through surface qualities to the way we really are inside.

STEP 4

You may want to replace the 2 Samuel study with the shorter and simpler Genesis 39:6-10, the story of Joseph and Potiphar's wife (see "Combined Junior High/High School" option). If you prefer to stick with Amnon and Tamar, explain that in verse 13, Tamar is reminding Amnon that raping her could keep him from becoming king; her suggestion that David would let them get married probably was a desperation move, since such a marriage was illegal. Verse 16 refers to the fact that as an ex-virgin, Tamar couldn't be offered by her father as anyone else's bride-to-be. The ashes and robe-tearing in verse 19 were signs of mourning.

STEP 1

Instead of using the riddles, break the group into pairs. Have partners discuss approximately how old they were when they did the following, and how they felt about each event:

• learned how to tie their shoes;

• stayed overnight away from home;

• sent or received a valentine; and

• started wondering where babies come from.

STEP 6

Read Philippians 4:8-9 again. Hand out eight sheets of poster board to small groups or individuals. On each sheet should be written one of the qualities (true, noble, right, etc.) from the passage. Each person or group should come up with ten things that have that quality and that are present right now in your meeting place. This could include people, attitudes, actions, or things. Then share results. Make sure kids understand that God's gift of sexuality belongs on each list. Spend some time thanking God for the things on your lists.

STEP 4

After reading and discussing the events that took place in Tamar's life, talk about what might be different if the events had occurred in today's culture. Then ask: **Do you think God's attitude toward Tamar changed because of these experiences? Why or why not?**

STEP 5

Have group members form teams of four or five. Distribute paper and pencils to each team. Instruct each team to write a response to this statement: **Some say that "lust" is not as much a temptation for girls as it is for guys. If your team agrees with this statement, write down some suggestions for what you can do to help your guy friends. If your team disagrees with this statement, write down some suggestions for what you can do to help yourselves and your guy friends.**

STEP 2

Skip the verse-unscrambling activity and go directly to two Bible passages that deal specifically with the temptations felt by young men. Read Psalm 119:9-11 and ask: **Do you think it's tougher for a guy to "keep his way pure" than it is for a girl? Why or why not? If a guy were "living according to [God's] word," what would be his attitude toward sexual fantasies? Without the motivation shown in verses 10 and 11, how do you think a guy will do in a battle to control sexual thoughts? If you've tried hiding God's Word in your heart, what happened?** Then read I Timothy 5:1-2. Ask: **If all guys treated all girls "as sisters, with absolute purity," what would happen? How might this apply to the way a guy treats a girlfriend?** (He should respect her and stay away from sexual activity before marriage.) **How could it apply to the way guys think of the girls they see?** (Guys should think of girls as complete human beings, not sex objects; as people to be cared for, not used.)

STEP 5

They probably won't say it, but your guys may feel such hormonal pressure that most of the items listed on Repro Resource 6 could arouse them—unless they've been jaded by frequent exposure to the more explicit ones. Having to admit this to themselves may just make them feel abnormal. Consider skipping the sheet and spending more time at the end of the step discussing which stores, radio stations, TV channels, and other potential sexual stimulants guys should avoid if they want to make temptation-fighting easier.

STEP I

Bring a bunch of nylon stockings. Choose several "beauty pageant" contestants (both sexes) to parade before a panel of judges. Have all contestants wear the stockings over their heads, messing up their features. Ask the panel to choose winners in categories like Most Alluring, Most Likely to Rob a Bank, etc. Then ask whether wearing stockings over our heads would cut down on the number of "lustful" thoughts in the world. Would wearing baggier clothes help? If not, what do kids think is the answer to out-of-control sexual thoughts?

STEP 6

Provide a Polaroid camera, film, and a three-foot length of rope. Have kids pose in threes, with two kids using "mental floss" on the third—looking as if they're pulling the rope back and forth through the person's ears, cleaning out his or her brain. Encourage kids to ham it up, and to make the through-the-head illusion look as real as possible. Take enough pictures so that each group member gets one of himself or herself being "flossed." Have kids take the pictures home as a reminder of what you've discussed.

STEP 2

Bring a video camera, a flip chart, and a marker. Have kids put together a fake "health class film" called The *Birds and the Bees*, giving made-up explanations of where babies come from. (Examples: babies grow on trees; they come from vending machines; they're really dolls that have been exposed to radioactivity, etc.) Then play the video back to the group. Follow with a discussion on the kinds of sexual questions kids *really* want answered.

STEP 5

Set up a Nintendo or other video game and let kids play it for a round or two. Then liken the game to fighting sexual temptation. Have kids rename the parts of the game (weapons used, obstacles to overcome, traps, goal, etc.) to make it reflect the battle against out-of-control sexual thoughts. For instance, a weapon might be renamed "memorized Bible verses"; a trap might be labeled "too much time alone" or "watching old Madonna videos." Then have kids play the game with the new labels in mind.

STEP 1

For a shorter opener, replace Steps 1 and 2 with the following. Bring a package that you've put in a plain, brown wrapper and on which you've written "Adults Only" in large letters. Set the package at the front of the room and let kids ask yes-or-no questions until they guess what's in it (or until three minutes have passed). Then unwrap the package to reveal a jar of denture cleanser or another "senior citizen" item. Acknowledge that it's normal for kids to be curious about things that are for "adults only"—including sex. To save more time, skip the unscrambling activity in Step 3 and just read the verses.

STEP 4

For a shorter Bible study, see the "Combined Junior High/High School" option for Step 4. Or stick with 2 Samuel 13:1-22 and ask only the following questions: **Did Amnon really love Tamar? What should he have done about his fantasies? At what point did his thoughts turn to action? How might Tamar answer those who think sexual fantasies are no big deal?** To save time in Step 5, skip the discussion after the Repro Resource and jump to the summary (**Lust is one of the hardest emotions to cope with ...**).

STEP 2

After your group members give feedback on the magazine queries, tell them you will read old love letters of yours from the past. The love letters are actually from the Song of Solomon (Songs). On crumpled-up pieces of paper write portions of chapters 1-4. (Make gender changes where needed.) Begin each portion with "Dear_____." After reading nostalgically four separate letters, reveal to your group members that the letters are actually from the Bible. Explain that Solomon's description of his love has been used to describe Christ's love for the church.

STEP 3

Teaching that internal beauty is much more desirable than external beauty is key. A great way to do this is to post a picture of Mother Teresa and a picture of Madonna. Then ask: **Don't you think Mother Teresa is more beautiful than Madonna?** Group members will probably respond with statements like "Are you blind?" and "You need glasses!" That's OK. Ask them to explain their reactions. Then help them see that beauty is much more than sexiness and "looks." Sexuality is ultimately an attitude of the spirit, so that even if people choose a celibate lifestyle, they will be sexually fulfilled in Christ.

Have someone read aloud I Samuel 16:7. Then have each group member make two signs, one that says "Outward Beauty" and one that says "Inward Beauty." Then have group members tape each sign next to the appropriate picture. Madonna will probably receive the most "Outward Beauty" votes. But remind group members that the category that is important to God is "Inward Beauty." So Mother Teresa wins!

STEP 2

Younger kids may be at a loss as to how to answer advice column questions, especially those that deal with sexual specifics. Instead, cut the questions and answers apart, give each person at least one question and answer, and have kids mingle and match questions with answers. Then let kids give thumbs up or down on the advice contained in the ones they matched.

STEP 4

For younger kids, the story of Amnon and Tamar may be too long and may raise more questions than it answers. Instead, read part of the story of Joseph and Potiphar's wife (Gen. 39:6-10). Ask: **How does this story show that out-of-control sexual thoughts can be a problem for girls as well as guys? How could Mrs. Potiphar have reacted to Joseph's good looks instead of having fantasies about him? How did Joseph try to get Mrs. Potiphar's mind off fantasies and back to reality? How could we do the same thing when thoughts like these bother us? Mrs. Potiphar's thoughts just ended up frustrating her and driving Joseph away. How do our own sexual thoughts affect us and other people?**

STEP 3

Older kids may find the verse-unscrambling exercise "beneath" them, and three passages may not be necessary to convince them that God is interested in their thoughts. If you think that's the case in your group, look at two other passages instead: Matthew 5:27-28 and Romans 1:21-32. Concerning the Matthew passage, ask: **How do you think men felt when they heard this? How about women? Why do you think Jesus was as interested in thoughts as in actions?** (God knows our thoughts; thoughts often lead to action; God wants purity inside and out.) Regarding the Romans passage, ask: **How are lustful thoughts futile and foolish** (vs. 21), **degrading** (vs. 24), **and shameful** (vs. 26)? **How are wrong sexual thoughts part of the "bigger picture" of the way people relate to God?** (Many people have rejected God, so He has let them go ahead and live the way they want to. The includes having sexually immoral thoughts as well as the sins listed in verses 29-31.)

STEP 6

Instead of just encouraging kids to stop fantasizing sexually, challenge them to come up with specific ways to break such a habit. For example, what mental images could kids call up as "alarms" that go off when lustful thoughts are first detected? (A fire engine, a computer "bomb" icon, etc.) What mental "stepping stones" could kids take from fantasy to reality? (Remembering that a lusted-after girl is someone's daughter; imagining Jesus walking onto the scene, etc.) So that kids will share these suggestions for each other's benefit, make it clear that you're not asking what each person will do to combat his or her problem; you're asking for ideas that could help anyone.

DATE USED:

Approx. Time

STEP 1: *How Come?* _____
- ❏ Extra Action
- ❏ Fellowship & Worship
- ❏ Extra Fun
- ❏ Short Meeting Time
Things needed:

STEP 2: *Dear Abby* _____
- ❏ Small Group
- ❏ Large Group
- ❏ Mostly Guys
- ❏ Media
- ❏ Urban
- ❏ Combined Junior High/High School
Things needed:

STEP 3: *It's What's Inside That…* _____
- ❏ Heard It All Before
- ❏ Little Bible Background
- ❏ Urban
- ❏ Extra Challenge
Things needed:

STEP 4: *Horrible Thoughts…* _____
- ❏ Little Bible Background
- ❏ Mostly Girls
- ❏ Short Meeting Time
- ❏ Combined Junior High/High School
Things needed:

STEP 5: *Lust Busters* _____
- ❏ Extra Action
- ❏ Large Group
- ❏ Heard It All Before
- ❏ Mostly Girls
- ❏ Mostly Guys
- ❏ Media
Things needed:

STEP 6: *Worth the Wait (Part 3)* _____
- ❏ Small Group
- ❏ Fellowship & Worship
- ❏ Extra Fun
- ❏ Extra Challenge
Things needed:

Sex and Other God-Honoring Things

SEX MANUALS

EVERYTHING YOU ALWAYS WANTED TO KNOW ABOUT SEX *BUT WERE AFRAID TO ASK

A GUIDE TO BETTER SEX

THE ULTIMATE SEX MANUAL

HOLY BIBLE

A Beginner's Guide to SEX

IMPROVING YOUR SEX LIFE

When the fire is gone from your SEX LIFE

Sex & You

YOUR GOALS FOR THIS SESSION:
Choose one or more

☐ To help kids see why God demands sexual purity prior to marriage.

☐ To help kids discover a connection between sexual purity and spiritual purity.

☐ To help kids experience complete forgiveness for any previous sexual sin, and to commit to abandoning any sinful habits that have been developed.

☐ Other:_____
_____

Your Bible Base:

Numbers 25:1-15
Hosea 1—3
1 Corinthians 6:15-17

STEP 1

Common Bonds

(Needed: Pens, copies of Repro Resource 7)

OPTIONS

EXTRA **ACTION**

HEARD IT ALL **BEFORE**

FELLOWSHIP & **WORSHIP**

EXTRA **FUN**

SHORT MEETING **TIME**

URBAN

Divide into teams and hand out copies of "Three of a Kind" (Repro Resource 7). Ask group members not to look at the sheets until your signal. Before beginning, give them an example: **What do these three things have in common: birds, bats, and hospitals?** (They all have *wings*.)

Group members should work on the sheets individually or in groups to try to determine what each set of items has in common. The answers to the groupings on the sheet are:

(1) Kinds of snakes
(2) Things in banks
(3) Things with keys
(4) Words that come after "snow"
(5) Words found in recipes
(6) Things with blades
(7) "French" things
(8) Famous threesomes
(9) Things with rings
(10) Things with diamonds
(11) Things that have knots
(12) Tennis terms
(13) Types of sandwiches
(14) Types of cars
(15) Groups of animals (murder of crows, pride of lions, and school of fish)

After you've gone over the answers for the groupings on the sheet, give group members one more common bond to determine—a biblical one. Ask: **What do these people have in common: Rahab, Samson, and David?** If group members have trouble coming up with an answer, give them a clue by reminding them that this session is about sex. (All three were people who at one time gave in to their hormones and committed some serious sexual sins, yet who went on to do great things for God.) More people could be listed, but these three are all included in the list of "Heroes of the Faith" in Hebrews 11 (vss. 31-32). As you go through this session and compare sexual purity with spiritual purity, start with this reminder that God is quick to forgive sexual sin if people are willing to repent.

Don't Take My Wife—Please

(Needed: Copies of Repro Resource 8)

The purpose of this session is to compare sexual purity with spiritual purity. Throughout history, God has tried to help us understand His love and devotion for humankind by comparing His relationship with us to the relationship between a husband and wife. Such relationships are supposed to be marked by mutual trust, faithfulness, love, loyalty, and so forth. But God's people have repeatedly turned their backs on His love as they chased after other gods—many times even while continuing to receive His blessings. The Bible story that follows will show that while God does not always choose to act immediately when we are sexually (and spiritually) unfaithful, He doesn't take our indiscretions lightly. One time He tried to let us know how He feels when we are disloyal to Him by allowing one of His prophets to experience a bit of the same grief.

Hand out copies of "My Unfaithful Wife: I Think I'll Keep Her" (Repro Resource 8). This is a somewhat lighthearted look at the love life of Hosea (based loosely on Hosea 1–3). Assign a guy to read the Hosea part and a girl to read the Gomer part; have everyone else read the People part together. At the end, ask group members to complete the skit by offering advice on how to avoid sexual/spiritual unfaithfulness.

Then ask: **If God had called on you instead of Hosea, would you have done what He asked? Why?**

If you had committed yourself to someone you knew was likely to be unfaithful and did all you could to love the person, and he or she deserted you anyway, do you think you would ever take the person back? If not, why not? If so, under what conditions?

What do you think was God's point for having Hosea go through this hard experience? (It's hard to think in terms of "cheating on" God. But when we see the same thing take place between a husband and wife, we can better understand the pain, betrayal, and other feelings that are involved. And if we can learn from Hosea and Gomer, we need not make the same, or similar, mistakes.)

STEP 3

The Cozbi Show

O P T I O N S

LITTLE BIBLE BACKGROUND

MEDIA

(Needed: Bibles)

At this point, challenge your group members with some viewpoints that they're probably hearing from some of their friends. Ask: **Is sexual sin really that big a deal? We've already said that some of God's greatest heroes—including David and Samson—were sexually active outside of marriage. And in today's society, the majority of people have premarital sex. How bad can it be?**

Let group members discuss their opinions (and represent those of their sexually active friends). Encourage them to be as convincing as possible in trying to prove that maybe, just maybe, the expectations of Christian parents and leaders are a little too high and/or unrealistic when it comes to refraining from premarital or extramarital sex. Then have everyone read Numbers 25:1-15 individually. Discuss:

What did the Israelites do that got God so angry at them? (The first obvious answer might be their *sexual* entanglements with the Moabites. Even more important, however, is how easily the Israelites abandoned their own *religious* "commitments" when a little easy sex became available.) Point out that the Israelites had repeatedly been warned not to have *any* involvement with the heathen people in the land of Canaan. (See Deuteronomy 7:1-6, for example.)

Explain that sex was a part of "worship" by the Moabites and other people who did not follow God. They practiced fertility rites regularly. Then ask: **Why do you think so many of the Israelites were quick to abandon their worship of the true God?** If no one mentions it, point out that personal gratification is so important to some people that any kind of spiritual discipline only seems to get in the way. People are no different today than during this time in Israel's history. If we limit our attention to the here-and-now, it's easy to make the same kind of mistake the Israelites made. But our commitment to God is eternal, and the faithfulness we show now will be rewarded in eternity.

What do young people do today that may be similar to the worship of Baal in this passage? (In order to impress a date, Christians sometimes start drinking, get involved with drugs, go farther [sexually] than they are comfortable with, and so forth. In addition, they may also stop going to church regularly—either out of guilt or because their new romantic interests deprive them of the time and energy previously put into spiritual commitment.)

Do you think the solution to this problem was a bit severe in the case of Zimri and Cozbi? It may seem so to your group members. After all, if the same penalty was applied in today's society, our population would immediately dwindle to a small percentage of what it is now. But point out the brazenness of this couple who came into the Israelite camp—interrupting those who were mourning the situation.

Do you think God has "softened His position" on sexual sin in recent years? If not, why do you think it is so widespread today? (Scripture is clear that people who commit sexual sin will eventually face judgment. Yet God desires that we turn from *all* of our sins—sexual sins included—and experience His love and forgiveness [2 Pet. 3:9].)

[Note: This is probably not the right time to bring it up, but this is a good passage to recall when you're asked why God commanded the Israelites to annihilate the nations they encountered—women and all. While it seems cruel, God knew the weaknesses of His people. The Israelites were much too quick to abandon God when faced with the opportunity to participate in the sexual/religious practices of other gods.]

Representatives

(Needed: The name of each group member written on an individual slip of paper)

Explain that there is another reason why sexual activity is so related to spiritual things. To demonstrate, hand everyone a folded slip of paper that contains the name of a person in the group. Everyone present should have someone else's name. Then ask a number of opinion questions, and have people answer as if they were the person on the slip of paper. Here are some questions you could use:

- **What is one of your favorite sports?**
- **What would you say are your best characteristics?**
- **What do you think would be an appropriate nickname for you?**
- **When you face a conflict situation, are you more likely to run and hide, fight, or look for a compromise?**
- **Who do you think is the best-looking person in this group?**
- **Who in this group would you most like to date?**

OPTIONS

SMALL GROUP

LARGE GROUP

MOSTLY GIRLS

SHORT MEETING TIME

EXTRA CHALLENGE

• How would you describe your feet?

Try to have some fun with this, but not at the expense of someone's feelings. While you should expect some comical answers, don't allow group members to become cruel in their comments about the people they are representing.

Keep asking questions until it becomes clear who most of the group members are representing. Then discuss: **How did you like it when someone else got to answer personal questions on your behalf?** Were group members embarrassed? Angry? Frustrated?

How did it feel to represent someone else? Did group members try to be straightforward? Did they respond in an attempt to evoke a response from the person being represented?

Name some of the people or organizations that you actually "represent." (Schools, clubs, teams, bands, families, etc.)

How important is it to be a good representative of each of these groups?

Have someone read aloud I Corinthians 6:15-17. Discuss: **What does it mean that "[our] bodies are members of Christ Himself"?** (Each Christian has specific gifts and a responsibility to use those gifts for the good of the church as a whole [the "body" of Christ].)

How does it feel to know that you represent Jesus in everything you do? (It may be a bit overwhelming for many people. Yet it is also a tremendous privilege. While very few people in the group might be willing to be represented by another person, Jesus Himself trusts *us* with that responsibility.)

In the context of this passage, why do you think God has designated sex to be acceptable only within a marriage relationship? (The purpose of sex is to allow two bodies to become one. Without the commitment of marriage, sex divides rather than unites. And a Christian who engages in premarital or extramarital sex attempts to unite Jesus with the sinful world, which is not possible. The resulting dissonance then becomes a significant problem for the person.)

STEP 5

Wholly, Wholly, Holy

(Needed: Chalkboard and chalk or newsprint and marker)

OPTIONS

EXTRA ACTION

HEARD IT ALL BEFORE

MOSTLY GUYS

URBAN

JR. HIGH / HIGH SCHOOL COMBINED

EXTRA CHALLENGE

Your group members may or may not be experimenting with sex. But all of them are likely to relate to spiritual unfaithfulness. As they begin to discover how closely sexual and spiritual purity are related, their determination to strengthen one area should automatically strengthen the other as well.

Review: Previous sessions have dealt with several aspects of sex. The physical, emotional, and mental considerations of sexual involvements are fairly easy to understand. But the most important aspect of sex may be the most subtle and the most overlooked—the spiritual side of sex. No other human relationship is as important as the husband-wife union. It's the closest thing God can use to help us understand how we are to relate to Him. But if we do not honor our marriage vows to another person whom we can see, hear, touch, and even have sex with, we aren't very likely to remain faithful to our commitment to an invisible God.

The key to both sexual purity and spiritual purity is "holiness"—being "set apart" from any influences that would interfere with the relationship. Wrap up the session by allowing group members to brainstorm ways to be more holy (set apart) in their behaviors toward both God and other people. On a sheet of newsprint or a chalkboard, create two columns—with "God" at the top of one column and "People I Date" above the other. Then challenge group members to come up with as many suggestions as they can to ensure that their own behavior does not fall to the level of the rest of the self-centered world as they relate to God and others. After they compile their lists, see how many of their responses are true of the other column as well. For instance, their responses might include the following:

- Always put the concerns of the other person above your own (also true of God).
- Don't be bothered if people make fun of you for being a Christian (or a virgin).
- Good communication is a key to avoiding problems (prayer is important).

Acknowledge that remaining sexually pure in today's society is not easy. Neither is remaining spiritually pure. But God rewards both. And the sooner we determine to remain faithful, the better off we will be. Once we "cross the line" in either category, it is hard (and perhaps even painful) to restore the original relationship. It's *possible* (just ask Hosea and Gomer), but a lot of grief can be spared by making the right decisions to begin with and then sticking to those decisions.

STEP 6

Worth the Wait? (Part 4)

(Needed: The list you worked on in Sessions 1-3)

Close by listing additional reasons to save sex for marriage—this time based on a spiritual perspective. Three you might include are:
- Christians reflect Jesus in *all* of their actions.
- The faithful-to-one-person sexual relationship is a model for our spiritual relationship to God as well.
- Sexual promiscuity is a sin that interferes with one's spiritual growth.

Close the session in prayer.

NOTES

333
THREE OF A KIND

Each of the following "trios" has a common theme. For example, if the grouping were "Combs, saws, prehistoric tigers," the common bond would be "Things with teeth." See how many common themes you can find for the following trios.

1. **Garter, bull, coral**

2. **Money, rivers, snow**

3. *Florida, pianos, songs*

4. Man, peas, flakes

5. DICE, PEEL, BROWN

6. **Ice skates, lawn mowers, windshield wipers**

7. Horns, hens, fries

8. **Pigs, bears, wise men**

9. **Tree stumps, bathtubs, telephones**

10. Rings, baseball fields, deck of cards

11. Neckties, shoelaces, stomachs

12. Love, service, advantage

13. **Hero, club, submarine**

14. Mercury, Saturn, Galaxy

15. **Murder, pride, school**

MY UNFAITHFUL WIFE:
I Think I'll Keep Her

HOSEA: Hello. My name is Hosea.

PEOPLE: Who?

HOSEA: Hosea. I am a minor prophet … from the Old Testament. God spoke to me …

PEOPLE: That's nice (*yawn*) but we have to go now.

HOSEA: … and told me to marry a loose woman and make babies.

PEOPLE: Well, maybe we *can* hang around a while longer.

HOSEA: This is my wife …

GOMER: I'm his *lovely* wife, Gomer. And no cracks about the name, if you know what's good for you!

HOSEA: Now, dear, don't be rude to the nice people. Just tell your story.

GOMER: OK. We got married.

HOSEA: God *told* me to marry her.

GOMER: And I thought I'd heard 'em all! This guy had a lot to learn about women, and I was just the one to teach him.

HOSEA: We had three lovely children. We named the oldest boy "God Scatters." Our daughter's name is "Not Loved," and our youngest boy is called "Not My People."

GOMER: They're going to have a lot of fun when they start school. Personally, I would have named them "Bob," "Jennifer," and "Hezedekedediah." That's "He-*zed*-e-*ked*-e-*di*-ah." We'd have to have at least *one* biblical sounding name, I guess.

HOSEA: Those weren't *my* choices. God named them. Besides, there are some questions as to whether or not the kids are all mine! Anyway, God …

PEOPLE: Hold it! Back up! What was that?

HOSEA: Well, you see, for a while there I wasn't exactly the only man Gomer was seeing—even after we were married.

PEOPLE: You mean she was a …?

GOMER: Yes. Yes. Whichever name you want to use for it, that's what I was.

PEOPLE: Wasn't that, like, a problem?

GOMER: Of course, it was! For a while I didn't have the respect for Hosea that I should have had. I admit it.

HOSEA: That was the point. God was trying to show our nation something by using the two of us as an example.

GOMER: We were all acting like prostitutes—forsaking God and loving false gods.

PEOPLE: So what happened? It looks like the two of you are back together now.

HOSEA: We are.

GOMER: But it wasn't easy. After I left him and started sleeping around with other guys, I never figured he'd even *want* me again.

HOSEA: But God knew we still loved each other. I had to "buy" her to get her back. But, hey, we're together now and it was well worth the price.

PEOPLE: Did you make her come crawling back to you?

HOSEA: No. I wouldn't have wanted her back if I couldn't have forgiven her.

GOMER: So do you get it?

PEOPLE: Get what?

GOMER: The moral to this story! I'd hate to think Hosea and I went through all this suffering, only to have you nod off while reading through the Minor Prophets and miss the point.

PEOPLE: Of course we know the moral … but, uh, you can tell us anyway.

HOSEA: The moral is that God will not tolerate our unfaithfulness forever, yet He will readily take us back when we repent and turn to Him.

GOMER: And when we go putting other things before Him—especially sexual things—we're nothing more than spiritual prostitutes.

HOSEA: Take it from someone who knows.

GOMER: Hey! I *said* I was sorry.

HOSEA: Yes, dear. I was only joking. The two of us lived happily ever after. As for you listeners, you can too, if you'll only … (*Complete this sentence.*)

STEP 1

In place of the quiz, form two teams. Whisper the letter "Y" to each person, one at a time—except for two people, one on each team, to whom you whisper the letter "X." Kids must keep their letters a secret. Announce that you're going to have a human tug-of-war (with the rope held only by the two at the front of each line and the rest with arms linked around waists). Reveal that one unknown person on each team (the "X") is a "weak link." That person should participate normally until one team is on the verge of pulling the other across the finish line, when you'll shout, "X!" At that point each "X" should let go of the person (or rope) in front of him or her. Play several rounds, each time whispering "X" to someone on each team. Whichever team is ahead after a predetermined number of rounds is the winner. The winner will be determined by several factors, including the position (front or back) of weak links in each line. Use this to illustrate the fact that you can't be spiritually strong if you have a weak link in one area like sexuality.

STEP 5

Bring up four volunteers. Bind each person's wrists with a different material—one with rope, one with masking tape, one with yarn, one with a knot of toilet paper. See who can break the bonds first. Then ask: **Which of these bonds is most like the Bible's sexual rules? Why?** Note that we may feel restricted by God's rules, but He doesn't force us to obey Him. Obedience is to be based on our love for Him and on knowing that His rules are best for us; in that sense, His "bonds" are only as strong as our love for Him and our ability to see His love for us.

STEP 2

If you can't rustle up enough people to play the parts of Hosea, Gomer, and the People, you could have kids read the skit silently and then discuss it. Or skip the skit and have kids debate what punishment (if any) people should get for the following sexual sins: (1) living together before marriage; (2) rape; (3) watching an X-rated video; (4) publishing a pornographic magazine; (5) molesting a child. Then compare kids' verdicts with the wrath God shows in the Step 3 study.

STEP 4

Guessing who's representing whom won't pose much of a challenge if there aren't many in your group. Instead, display magazine photos of all kinds of people (from little kids to heavy metal musicians to grandmas to well-known politicians). Ask: **Which of these people would you want to stand in for you in the following situations: taking a college entrance exam; applying for a job; asking someone for a date; going to court to fight a traffic ticket? Why?** Then lead into the I Corinthians discussion.

STEP 4

Answering questions on each other's behalf may take too long with a large group, and guessing who's who will be tough if kids aren't well acquainted. Try an Elvis impersonators' contest instead. (You may want to get entrants signed up before the session to save time. If your kids aren't familiar with Elvis, choose a different celebrity.) Offer prizes in two categories: Best Vocal Impression and Best Physical Impression (lip-synching to an Elvis song you've brought). Discuss how you think "the king" would feel about being represented by his many imitators. Then move into the I Corinthians discussion about being a representative of Christ.

STEP 6

Have teams compete to create and shout out the best group cheers encouraging sexual abstinence before marriage. Examples: "Virgin, virgin, that's OK; virginity goes all the way … to marriage!" "Gimme an S! Gimme an E! Gimme an S-E-X! But first gimme a V! Gimme an O! Gimme those V-O-W-S!" "Purity, purity—fight, fight, fight! Save it for your wedding night!"

STEP 1

Kids may resist the idea that they have to talk about "spiritual stuff" to fully understand sexuality. Instead of using the "Three of a Kind" quiz, start with an activity that shows the practical value of knowing about a "dull" subject. Label seven bottles with the following: Na, NaCl, NaHCO$_3$, NaCN, NaF, C$_2$H$_2$FO$_2$Na, Na$_2$SiO$_3$. Display the bottles and ask: **All of these contain the element called sodium. Which would be safe to eat or drink?** After kids write down their guesses, reveal that only NaCl (table salt) and NaHCO3 (sodium bicarbonate, or baking soda) would be safe. The rest are dangerous: pure sodium (Na) explodes on contact with water, and the others are poisonous compounds containing things like cyanide and fluorine. **Just as you'd need to know something about chemistry to keep from killing yourself when faced with these choices, we need to know something about spiritual things when faced with sexual choices. Some expressions of sexuality are fine; others are spiritual poison. It takes a little study to know the difference.**

STEP 5

Kids may equate holiness with being boring and closeted away from real life. Help them see what it means to be set apart for God's purposes. Have three or four kids roll up their sleeves and dig with plastic spoons in a pail of mud to find a hidden marble. Whoever gets the marble wins. But the prize is a dish of ice cream, which must be eaten with the same spoon used to dig in the dirt. Point out how we "set apart" tools (like eating utensils) used for special jobs. Then pass out clean spoons and give everybody ice cream if possible.

STEP 2

Kids may be confused by the Hosea-Gomer story. Instead of using the skit, make a connection between sexual purity and spiritual purity with the following activity. Break the group into pairs. Start reading a story about a guy with an unfaithful girlfriend: **Scott and Caitlin had been going together for over a year. Scott was so in love, always attentive to Caitlin's needs and being a perfect gentleman. But one day he discovered the truth: Caitlin had been sleeping around the whole time. Half the guys in school were laughing at Scott behind his back. That afternoon Scott met Caitlin after school as usual and . . .** Have each pair come up with an ending and share it with the rest of the group. Make the parallel between this story and Israel's (and our) relationship with God.

STEP 3

Kids may wonder why it was so important for Israel to maintain its identity. Explain that God had chosen Israel as His people and made a covenant with them. Israel was surrounded by nations that worshiped false gods, and whose religions required everything from prostitution to killing babies as sacrifices. God wanted Israel to do things His way—for the Israelites' own good and to provide an example to the other nations of the way life was *supposed* to be.

STEP 1

On index cards, write the following amounts: $50, $500, $5,000, and $50,000. Make at least two cards with each amount, and make enough cards so that each group member will have one. As kids enter, give each person a card. Kids find the other(s) with the same dollar amount and form small groups. Each group must plan a wedding for its oldest member, spending no more than the amount on its card. The oldest member gets to make the final decisions and should explain his or her reasons. Then have each group discuss: **Which kind of marriage is more likely to stay together: one with a cheap wedding or one with an expensive one? If money has nothing to do with it, what do you think keeps husbands and wives faithful to each other?**

STEP 6

Bring a guitar or other accompaniment, plus a songbook that includes "I Have Decided to Follow Jesus." Remind kids that sexuality is just one area in which our actions show how we really feel about Jesus and His commands. Sing the existing verses of "I Have Decided"; then have kids make up new ones. Some of these should reflect a commitment to follow Jesus in the sexual choices we make. Example: "Because I love Him, I'll wait for the wedding."

MOSTLY GIRLS

MOSTLY GUYS

EXTRA FUN

STEP 2

To make Repro Resource 8 more appropriate for your group of girls, rewrite it so that Gomer is talking to her neighbors, explaining what happened in her marriage. Have her describe her husband, Hosea, and his attitudes and actions. In rewriting the skit, you can use most of the words already written for Hosea to say.

STEP 4

After the discussion, give everyone another slip of paper that has the word "God" written on it. Have each girl write down at least two things God might say about having her as His spokesperson and representative. Ask group members to consider the risk God is taking by asking us to be His representatives. Ask: **How might people learn about God and His sexual standards through you?** Ask volunteers to share some things God might say.

STEP 2

Can't do the skit? If you can't get a guy to play Gomer, try this instead. Designate one side of the room as "Perfectly Happy" and the other side as "On a Rampage." Have guys move back and forth between the poles as you read this "love note" addressed to them: **Oh, I miss you so much while I'm away at camp this summer.** (pause) **I can almost see your handsome face —**(pause) **but not quite, because I lost your picture when Chad and I went canoeing.** (pause) **Chad isn't as sweet as you are, of course.** (pause) **But he's better-looking.** (pause) **Still he's not as muscular as some of these guys up here.** (pause) **They keep asking me out, but I say no—**(pause) **unless it's a weekend night.** (pause) **I wish you were here so I could give you a big kiss.** (pause) **But since you aren't, I'll have to settle for Jeremy, Luis, and Jean-Claude.** Then compare guys' feelings to those God might have over the spiritual unfaithfulness of people.

STEP 5

The idea of being 100 percent sexually pure and holy may seem hopeless to guys, some of whom have tried unsuccessfully to stamp out sexual thoughts or break habits like masturbation. Encourage them by emphasizing the idea of making steady, step-by-step progress in purity and holiness—getting stronger by resisting temptation and getting forgiveness when they fail. Use the following to illustrate. Have kids try to "broad jump" 15 feet, a task at which they're unlikely to succeed. Then let them jump 15 feet on one foot in as many steps as it takes—a much easier way to get there.

STEP 1

Start with Thumb Tag. Form two teams. One team colors its thumbs with blue washable markers; the other team uses red. At your signal, each team tries to leave its thumbprints on the hands of kids on the other team. Kids may touch only hands. After three minutes, examine hands. Anybody left unmarked by the other team wins. Point out that just as kids tried to remain untouched by each other, we need to stay untouched by sexual sin because of the Person whose team we're on.

STEP 6

Wrap up the meeting by staging a "wedding reception" mini-party. This can be as simple or as complicated as you like, but it would be good to include a cake, wedding-bell decorations on the walls, and some recorded music in the background. Remind kids that this is a party celebrating the "marriage" of every Christian to Christ.

STEP 3

Bring a video camera that has a time-lapse feature. Set it up on a tripod, let it run in time-lapse mode, and see whether kids can sneak into the room, perform a task of your choosing, and sneak out without the camera catching them. The task will depend on the interval of time your camera waits between shots; the longer the interval, the more complex the task should be. After kids try it, play the tape to see whether they escaped detection. Discuss the futility of trying to get away with something sexual without God noticing, which is apparently what the Israelites tried to do in Numbers 25.

STEP 6

Wrap up with either of the following. (1) Borrow a wedding video from a couple in your church. Cue it up to the part with the vows, the minister's pronouncement, and the happy couple leaving. Ask: **How is a wedding both very serious and very happy? How is that like becoming a Christian? If we took vows to become Christians, what do you think they might be like? Why do you think we don't?** (2) Listen to and discuss as many wedding songs as you can locate—anything from old standards like "I Love You Truly" to newer favorites like Noel Paul Stookey's "The Wedding Song." What do they say about faithfulness? How much of each song could apply to one's relationship with Christ as well as one's relationship with a husband or wife?

STEP 1

Replace Steps 1 and 2 with a shorter opener. Bring enough cans of yellow and blue Play-Doh or other modeling dough so that each person can have a golf-ball-sized lump of one or the other. Form pairs; give one kid in each pair a lump of yellow, and the other kid a lump of blue. Have a race to see which pair, using only the hands holding the dough, is able to first (and thoroughly) combine the yellow and blue to make green. After determining the winner (and awarding a prize if you like), ask kids to separate the colors into yellow and blue again—an impossible assignment. Note that in the same way it's impossible to keep our relationship with God separate from what we do sexually, and vice versa.

STEP 4

Skip the representing-each-other activity. Read the I Corinthians passage and use the questions following it. In place of Step 5, apply the marriage metaphor with the following wrap-up. Have each person create two time capsules—letters in sealed envelopes. One should be addressed to a future marriage partner, the other to Christ. Both should express whatever promises of faithfulness the person is willing to make at this time. Save the letters and send them to the kids a year from now.

STEP 1

Here are some other "three of a kind" groupings you might consider using:

• Candy wrappers, cans, glass bottles (Things for the trash—not the ground)

• TLC, DMC, BBD (Music groups)

• Jordan, Barkley, Ewing (Basketball players)

• Elevator, 20+ floors, people (Things in a high-rise building)

• Tracks, cars, underground (Things associated with a subway)

• Truth, King, Mandela (Great black leaders)

For extra points:

• Umoja, ujima, imani (Things associated with Kwanzaa, the African-American holiday)

STEP 5

Distribute paper and pencils. Point out that a famous man, Karl Barth, once described sexuality as the "God-like" in us. Explain that he was talking about those positive "sexy feelings" which are given by God and are most appealing in our personalities. These can be used to bring joy to others and glory to God. Have each group member write a list of ten things God would describe as "sexy" about him or her. However, group members may name only one item that concerns their outward appearance. Afterward, ask for volunteers to read what they've written. Then discuss the areas in our lives in which holiness and sexuality converge. Emphasize that sexuality is not simply "acts of sex," but a pursuit to obtain a "Christ-likeness" within.

STEP 2

The Hosea-Gomer story may go over the heads of younger kids. Instead, make the point that you can't separate your relationship with God from sexual relationships, pretending that one doesn't affect the other. Bring a doll house with furnishings (borrow one from a young girl or an older woman who's into collectibles). Cover the opening to one of the rooms with paper, so that kids can't see it. Let kids admire the other rooms. Then tear off the paper and reveal the last room—which you've filled with "gross" stuff like rubber bugs. Use this as an illustration of how some people let God clean up every "room" of their lives except the one involving sexuality.

STEP 5

Younger kids will have a tough time coming up with ways to be holy. Skip the two-column approach and ask questions like these to help them brainstorm ways to be "set apart": **If you had a computer, what would you want to keep it away from so that you could really use it?** (Computer viruses, heat, cold, water, lightning storms, clumsy people, etc.) **If you had a car, what would you keep it away from so you could use it?** (Rust, vandals, thieves, accidents, potholes, bad gasoline, etc.) **What might God want to keep you away from so that He can really use you?** (People who tell you not to believe in Him, daydreams or guilt feelings that preoccupy you all the time, hobbies that keep you too busy, dangers that might hurt you, etc.) **What sexual temptations and activities might God want to "set us apart" from so that He can really use us?** (Fantasies that keep us from thinking about Him, habits that make us feel too guilty to talk to Him, videos and magazines that encourage those fantasies and habits, sexual relationships that draw us away from Him, etc.

STEP 4

Follow the I Corinthians passage by discussing the following imaginary situation. **A new NC-17 movie has just come to town. It's called The Secret Life of Jesus, and it portrays Jesus as having sexual encounters with most of the women who followed Him. The movie's most notorious scene shows Jesus and His disciples going into a brothel and having sex with prostitutes. Most people in your church are angry about the movie, but not sure what to do about it. How would you feel about such a movie? Why? What would you want to do about it? How is this like the I Corinthians passage? If you were God, what might you want to do about Christians who, through sexual immorality, "take the members of Christ and unite them with a prostitute"?**

STEP 5

Challenge kids to go beyond discussing holiness and to make a personal commitment. Bring copies of the traditional wedding ceremony (your pastor should have it) and pass them out. Using this as a model (or departing from it if kids want to), have group members write "wedding vows" expressing their commitment to be faithful to Jesus. Each person should write one or two sentences. Then put the vows together, photocopy them, and read them aloud as a group. Encourage kids to take the copies with them and to look at them again this week.

DATE USED:

Approx. Time

STEP 1: *Common Bonds* _____
- ❏ Extra Action
- ❏ Heard It All Before
- ❏ Fellowship & Worship
- ❏ Extra Fun
- ❏ Short Meeting Time
- ❏ Urban
- Things needed:

STEP 2: *Don't Take My Wife…* _____
- ❏ Small Group
- ❏ Little Bible Background
- ❏ Mostly Girls
- ❏ Mostly Guys
- ❏ Combined Junior High/High School
- Things needed:

STEP 3: *The Cozbi Show* _____
- ❏ Little Bible Background
- ❏ Media
- Things needed:

STEP 4: *Representatives* _____
- ❏ Small Group
- ❏ Large Group
- ❏ Mostly Girls
- ❏ Short Meeting Time
- ❏ Extra Challenge
- Things needed:

STEP 5: *Wholly, Wholly, Holy* _____
- ❏ Extra Action
- ❏ Heard It All Before
- ❏ Mostly Guys
- ❏ Urban
- ❏ Combined Junior High/High School
- ❏ Extra Challenge
- Things needed:

STEP 6: *Worth the Wait (Part 4)* _____
- ❏ Large Group
- ❏ Fellowship & Worship
- ❏ Extra Fun
- ❏ Media
- Things needed:

Being Sexual without Being Sinful

YOUR GOALS FOR THIS SESSION:
Choose one or more

☐ To help kids see that, while being "sexual" is a natural part of life, there are certain limits that should be self-imposed at this point in their lives.

☐ To help kids understand that no matter how much they know about sex, it's what they do about it that matters most.

☐ To help kids who are already guilty of sexual sins experience complete forgiveness and get a new start.

☐ Other:_____
_____

Your Bible Base:

1 Kings 11:1-13
Proverbs 7:6-27
John 8:1-11

STEP 1

Object Lesson

(Needed: A variety of objects of assorted shapes, sizes, and weights)

Have group members sit in a large circle and pass an object (like a tennis ball) from person to person. Explain that if someone drops the object, he or she is out. If the drop occurs during a hand-off from one person to the next, both people are out. When this happens, tighten the circle and continue playing with the remaining people. As group members begin to get a bit bored (or smug) from handling the single item, begin another item (like a bowling ball) going in the opposite direction. At regular intervals, keep adding new objects (a single hair, a lawn chair, an egg, etc.).

Group members should soon discover that while any of these things are easily managed individually, they can cause significant problems when combined or when they appear unexpectedly. Trying to deal with sexual issues is somewhat similar. As young people try to deal with all the aspects of sexuality—physical, emotional, mental, and spiritual—the challenge may seem overwhelming. The purpose of this session is to help your young people put together a practical plan for how to deal with the sexual issues in their lives.

STEP 2

Let's Make a Deal

(Needed: A mixture of inexpensive "gift" items, both gag gifts and nice ones)

Call for some volunteers and let them participate in a quick game of "Let's Make a Deal." Provide one person with an attractively wrapped item and see if he or she would be willing to trade for what's "behind the curtain" (or "in the sack," "under the table," etc.). If the person trades, offer the item he or she gives up to someone else who will then have similar options.

In each case, make sure to provide the person with his or her best possible choice *to begin with* (whether or not he or she can even tell what the item is at the time). Anyone who trades should unknowingly be trading down in value. Have some fun with creative gag gifts. But later, at an appropriate time, make a serious point: A person's virginity is a very special thing that should not be traded (or given) away lightly. It is a thing of value that should be cherished. Given in the context of marriage, it is replaced with intimacy, and genuine love can continue to grow. Given prior to marriage, however, it is lost forever. Only too late do many people discover that the exchange of their virginity for a short-lived "loving" relationship is a bad trade.

STEP 3

Opinion Poll

(Needed: Calculator)

Ask the following questions and have group members respond. Record their answers and come up with an average for each question. You will probably need a calculator.

- **What percent of people your age do you think are unaware of how sex works—the actual physical act of sexual intercourse?**
- **What percent do you think don't really know about the physical risks such as pregnancy, AIDS, other sexually transmitted diseases, and so forth?**
- **What percent would you say, as they begin to feel sexual urges, really take into account the feelings of the other person as much as their own?**
- **What percent would you say continue a lasting relationship with the first person they have sex with?**
- **What percent do you think look beyond the actual sexual act and anticipate the emotions that are likely to be felt afterward—confusion, worry, guilt, shame, uncertainty, etc.?**
- **What percent would you say think about sex too much?**
- **What percent do you think have some kind of personal, religious, or moral standard that prevents them from participating in sex?**

OPTIONS

EXTRA ACTION

LARGE GROUP

URBAN

JR. HIGH / HIGH SCHOOL COMBINED

- **Of the people you know who have had sex, what percent would you say are more satisfied because they did?**
- **Of the people you know who have had sex, what percent would you say were pretty much aware of most of the physical, emotional, mental, and spiritual aspects of sex, yet went ahead and became sexually active anyway?**

Discuss the results of your opinion poll. Are any of the answers surprising or shocking? Do any of them need to be challenged? Were any of your group members surprised by any of the others' answers?

Explain that when it comes to dealing with sex, most people are probably knowledgeable of the "how-to" part. Many are also aware of the risks and potential consequences. Yet in spite of all the knowledge and the awareness, they go ahead and have sex.

Ask: **Why do you think so many people choose to have sex in spite of all they know?** (They get caught up in the heat of the moment. They are so eager to experience the feeling that they ignore the facts. They are swayed more by someone they like than by their own convictions.)

**STEP
4**

Like an Ox Going to the Slaughter

(Needed: Bibles)

Call for one male and one female volunteer (people involved in drama, if possible). Explain that you are going to narrate a passage and you want them to pantomime the action of the script. It begins with the guy, and the girl comes in soon thereafter.

Read aloud Proverbs 7:6-23, giving your actors time to respond to what you are reading and allowing them to create the proper motions and facial expressions. After you have finished reading the passage, let your actors take a bow. But then finish by reading verses 24-27. Ask: **Do you think this is an accurate portrayal of young men who allow themselves to be seduced by more "experienced" women?**

Explain that this advice was given by Solomon. Then see how much your group members can recall about Solomon. They should be aware that he:

- was the wisest man of his time (I Kings 10:23).
- was the wealthiest man of his time.
- was the person chosen by God to build the temple.

O P T I O N S

LITTLE BIBLE BACKGROUND

MOSTLY GIRLS

MOSTLY GUYS

SHORT MEETING TIME

JR. HIGH / HIGH SCHOOL COMBINED

• had good common sense in addition to "smartness" (as attested by his handling of the "Whose child is it?" case [I Kings 3:16-28] and his encounter with the Queen of Sheba [I Kings 10:1-13]).

If you read through I Kings 10:14-29 and see everything Solomon had, it's hard to imagine that *anything* could destroy such an empire of wealth and wisdom that he had accumulated. Yet something did.

Have group members read I Kings 11:1-13. Then discuss: **Do you know what a "concubine" is?** (A woman who was lawfully married to a man, yet didn't have the full title or benefits of a regular wife. Concubines could be sent away and their children excluded from an inheritance by simply awarding them a small gift.)

Was it wrong for Solomon to have concubines? (Even though God had established a monogamous husband-wife relationship, many men during Old Testament times had more than one wife, including concubines. This was never God's ideal.)

What was Solomon's real problem? (He was attracted by women whom God had specifically forbidden him to get involved with.)

Do you think God's restrictions were unreasonable? (Not at all. Solomon fell right into the trap that God had warned about. He abandoned his faith in God—the very thing that had allowed him to accumulate his wealth and wisdom—and began to worship the gods of his many wives. The worship of some of these gods even included sacrificing children to them, so this was no small offense.)

Why was Solomon's sin so significant? (For one thing, it shows the power of sex to cause an otherwise intelligent person to forsake everything he has to get more and more involved in sensual pleasures. For another, since Solomon was an influential and powerful person, he established the worship of these foreign gods in his own land—exposing the whole nation to spiritual, as well as physical, prostitution.)

What was the result of Solomon's sexual entanglements? (The united kingdom of Saul and David would be divided. Solomon's own son would not inherit the power and influence that Solomon had accumulated. And perhaps worst of all, Solomon would be remembered more for his final failure than for all of his unprecedented accomplishments.)

Point out that if Solomon could be brought to ruin by not being able to control his sexual activities, none of us is immune.

Too Late to Wait?

(Needed: Bibles, pens, copies of Repro Resource 9)

Explain: **We need to be practical in our approach to sex. We need to know about all the aspects of sex—physical, emotional, mental, and spiritual. But it takes more than knowing about these things. We must act on what we know. As difficult as it might be, we need to use common sense. For example, try to determine what practical, commonsense options are appropriate in each of the following situations:**

(1) After only three dates, Sean and Francis have gone from hand holding to some pretty serious fondling of each other.

(2) Sally really likes Dave, but doesn't want to have sex. Dave likes Sally too, but he really wants to have sex.

(3) Ken and Debbie haven't yet gone "all the way," but they've done a lot more than Debbie is comfortable with.

(4) Bob and Lisa have gone all the way. But now they realize they can't handle the pressure that sexual activity creates, and they don't know what to do.

OPTIONS

Group members should see that in many of these cases, the options boil down to one of two. The people involved must either: (1) commit to slowing down and finding non-sexual things to do together, or (2) stop dating altogether. Otherwise, the escalation of sexual desire and experimentation can get out of control. Saving sex "until the time is right" never works unless the "right time" is mutually determined to be "on our wedding night." To ignore the practical outcomes of sexual feelings and decisions is to invite temptation and trouble.

Hand out copies of "Any Questions?" (Repro Resource 9). This sheet will encourage group members to raise any questions that may not have been dealt with yet. If time permits, deal with their questions at this time. If not, schedule a discussion at a later meeting. But remember that the sooner your young people find good answers to their questions, the sooner they will be able to make wise decisions regarding their sexual behavior.

One question that group members may be a little hesitant to ask is: "What if it's too late for me to remain a virgin? What if I've already gone too far?" In response, read aloud John 8:1-11. It should need little comment. But two things are very clear:

(1) *Sexual sin can and will be forgiven.* God understands our strong feelings. He doesn't want one sin to separate us from Him forever. So if sexual sin has taken place—regardless of the magnitude—we should confess it to Him and experience His full forgiveness.

(2) *Sexual sin must be eliminated.* God forgives our "sins of passion," yet He is serious about our not allowing such behavior to become a lifestyle. When we experience His freeing forgiveness, we should, from that point on, try to avoid any further entanglements with sin.

Provide a time of silent prayer so group members can confess any such recent sins. Then challenge them not to overlook the importance of a fresh start. You might also let them know that you are available at any time to help them think through and talk through any hard decisions they need to make.

STEP
6

Worth the Wait? (Part 5)

(Needed: Copies of Repro Resource 10, copies of the list you worked on in Sessions 1-4)

Hand out copies of "Worth the Wait? Definitely!" (Repro Resource 10), as well as copies of the list your group has compiled. Challenge group members to keep the list(s) in a place where they will be seen frequently. And encourage your young people to continue to add to them. As they think of new reasons to save sex for marriage, let them share their observations at future meetings and make this an ongoing project.

[Optional ending: If any time remains, have a few more volunteers play "Let's Make a Deal." Because of the first game, the tendency of your group members should be to hold on to what you give them the first time. But this time if anyone is willing to trade, make sure each successive swap is better than the previous one. The first lesson was that virginity should not be quickly traded away. But use this final demonstration to show that God never expects us to give up something without providing us with something better. When we "take a pass" on the opportunities for sexual encounters that come our way, we can experience His full peace, love, joy, and more. In addition, we have clean consciences, and can look forward to eternal rewards. "Sacrificing" for God is never a bad trade when we look at the long-term results.]

O P T I O N S

HEARD IT ALL BEFORE

FELLOWSHIP & WORSHIP

MOSTLY GUYS

EXTRA FUN

MEDIA

EXTRA CHALLENGE

ANY QUESTIONS?

Most people have a lot of questions about sex. Some answers are found very quickly.
Other answers seem to escape us for a long time. You may have found answers to many of
your sexual questions, but perhaps you're still hoping to have a question or two answered.
Look over the questions below and circle any that you're not sure you know how to answer.
Also add any questions that you have, but that you haven't gotten around to asking yet.

IF I DON'T HAVE THE SAME SEXUAL URGES THAT SOME OF MY FRIENDS TALK
ABOUT, AM I ABNORMAL?

IF I'VE ALREADY GOTTEN INVOLVED SEXUALLY, ISN'T IT TOO LATE TO WORRY
ABOUT HOW I ACT FROM NOW ON?

IF I RULE OUT SEX AS AN OPTION, HOW CAN I PROVE THAT I LOVE SOMEONE?

IF I SAVE SEX UNTIL MY WEDDING NIGHT, HOW WILL I KNOW WHAT TO DO?

HOW DO I HANDLE THE PRESSURE BEING PUT ON ME TO HAVE SEX—WITH-
OUT COMPLETELY DESTROYING THE RELATIONSHIP?

WHAT IF SOMEONE OF THE SAME GENDER SEEMS ATTRACTED TO ME?

_____

_____

_____

NOTES

WORTH THE WAIT? DEFINITELY!

As a relatively normal teenager, you're going to hear a few "logical" reasons from some of your friends why it's "perfectly OK" to go ahead and have sex whenever you're ready. But here's a list of twelve even better reasons why you should save sex for marriage. (And this is just a starter list. Feel free to add other reasons as you think of them.) The next time you start feeling a little pressure to give in, consult this list (and if possible, also consult a good Christian friend or counselor).

Why Should We Save Sex for

Marriage?

1. All risk of premarital pregnancy (and its many complications) is eliminated.

2. Any risk of the sexually transmitted HIV (AIDS) virus disappears.

3. The risk of other sexually transmitted diseases (syphilis, gonorrhea, etc.) is gone.

4. We never have to worry about "getting caught." Rather than living with guilt, shame, and other horrible feelings, we can eventually experience the full pleasure of sex with complete peace of mind.

5. We offer our future spouses a first-ever, one-of-a-kind experience, and give him or her complete loyalty.

6. When sexual entanglements are removed, our current relationships will be stronger (and probably longer).

7. We find much more efficient uses for our mental time and energy, rather than thinking so much about our sexual encounters.

8. Our priorities remain clear and we are able to focus better on schoolwork, jobs, and other important areas of life.

9. Abstinence is a source of creative power. Rather than allowing lust to overwhelm us and be channeled through sexual encounters, our powerful emotions can be expressed more appropriately through songs, poems, plays, and so forth.

10. Christians reflect Jesus in all of their actions. Sexual unions make us (and Him) look particularly bad.

11. The one-to-one sexual relationship in the context of a loving and committed marriage is a model for our spiritual relationship with God.

12. We cannot grow spiritually if we have recurring sexual sin in our lives.

NOTES

EXTRA **ACTION**

SMALL GROUP

LARGE GROUP

STEP 3

In place of the survey, play "Time Bomb." Have kids stand in a circle. Set a wind-up kitchen timer on one minute or so and put it in a lunchbox or similar container. Kids must pass the "bomb" around the circle as quickly as they can; whoever's touching it when it goes off is out. Repeat until you've eliminated all of the kids. (If your group is too large for this, just have five or six kids play the game while the rest of the group watches. Either way, play until all participants are out.) Ask how waiting for the bomb to go off is like having premarital sex despite the risks. Then talk about how kids take risks sexually even when they supposedly know what's going on, thinking the consequences (pregnancy, AIDS, etc.) won't happen to them.

STEP 5

Have several volunteers compete in a 50-yard dash. The winner is the first person who crosses the finish line *and* reaches a complete stop within five feet of crossing the line. Have half the non-runners watch the finish line and half watch the "stop" line. After declaring a winner, discuss how hard it was to run as fast as you could, yet try to stop quickly. Tie this into the fact that the further you go sexually, the tougher it is to stop.

STEP 1

Since a small group can't sit in a large circle, replace the object pass with a "driver's test." Have kids sit in a row, side by side, with a few feet between chairs. Sit behind kids, as if they were in the front seat of a car and you were in the back. Then give instructions (turn right, accelerate, stop, etc.). Kids respond with hand signals, verbal "vrooms" and screeches, etc. But they must do the *opposite* of what you tell them. Anyone who doesn't do the opposite is out. Then discuss the fact that some kids who know the sexual "rules of the road" from the Bible still insist on doing the opposite.

STEP 5

Kids may be reluctant to hand in their sexual questions on the Repro Resource, knowing you probably can guess whose sheet is whose. Try these approaches: (1) Cut the questions from the sheet; give a set to each person. Pass around a box with a slot in the top and let kids put in any of the questions that interest them (sort of a secret ballot). (2) For additional questions, give each person a turn at a typewriter to type a question and put it in the question box (so that handwriting won't be recognizable).

STEP 2

To allow more group members to participate, replace "Let's Make a Deal" with the following. Before the session, cut two-inch-square samples of all sorts of gift wrap that's meant for specific occasions. Cut each square so that it's hard to tell what the whole pattern is. Glue each sample to an index card and write a number on the card. Display the cards on the walls around your meeting place. Give each person paper and pencil to record his or her guess as to what occasion each type of paper is for. The one with the most correct guesses wins. Then show the group the larger pieces of wrap that you cut the samples from so that they can see the whole pattern. Use this to illustrate two points: (1) just as each type of wrap was for one special occasion, so is sex (the occasion being marriage); and (2) when we're concentrating on a small part of the pattern (whether it's wrapping paper or the right-now urgency we feel about sex at a given moment), it's hard to see the big picture.

STEP 3

Recording individual survey responses and averaging them may take too long in a large group. Instead, mark percentages from 0 to 100 (in increments of 10) on a roll of butcher paper and hang it along one wall. Have kids respond to each question by standing under the number that reflects their answer. Draw a star on the paper where most of the kids are bunched (or make a rough visual estimate of the average and draw the star there). Have kids sit down so they can see the stars and discuss their answers.

STEP 5

Some kids may have heard many times that God forgives all kinds of sins, but can't bring themselves to believe that He'll forgive theirs. Have small groups make "wanted" posters for Rahab (wanted for prostitution—see Joshua 2 and Hebrews 11:31); David (wanted for adultery and conspiracy to commit murder—see 2 Samuel 11); Moses (wanted for murder—see Exodus 2:11-15); Paul (wanted as Saul for conspiracy to commit murder—see Acts 7:54-8:1). Discuss what happened to these people and how God forgave and used them despite "big-time" sins, sexual and otherwise. Explain that God is ready to forgive us if we repent. We're "wanted" by Him for a loving, personal relationship.

STEP 6

Try one more time to get jaded kids thinking with "Recorder Roulette." Before the session, record statements like these on audio tape with a five-second pause after each: "Boy, are you lucky—only God knows what you did." "You figured sex was okay because you were in love, but you just got dumped." "Sorry, you've tested HIV-positive." "Nobody got pregnant this time." "Ready or not, the two of you are going to have a baby." "The good news: It's not AIDS. The bad news: It's herpes." At this point in the session, explain that premarital sex is like Russian roulette—it's always risky. Have volunteers, posing as sexually active kids, come up one at a time to push the "play" button on the recorder to hear the results of their latest encounter. Push the "stop" button after each statement. Then discuss the "It'll-never-happen-to-me" myth.

STEP 4

Instead of the Solomon story, try something simpler: James 1:21-25. Use questions like these to spark discussion: **When you see the phrase "moral filth," what do you think of?** (We may think of sexual sin, but other sins qualify, too.) **What are some sexual "evils" that are "prevalent"** (vs. 21) **today? How common do you think these things are among Christian teenagers? Why? Why would someone listen to God's instructions about sex, yet do nothing about them? If people's sexual sins somehow showed on their faces, what do you think most kids would see in the mirror? What's the difference between hearing a sermon and looking "intently into the perfect law"? How could we keep from forgetting what we've heard here about sex?**

STEP 5

Explain the background of John 8:1-11, the story of the woman caught in adultery. Note that both the man and the woman had sinned; but the religious leaders must have let the man escape. They also misquoted the Old Testament law; execution had to be by stoning only if the woman was a virgin and was engaged, and in that case both the man and woman were to be executed. The leaders asked Jesus a trick question, trying to get Him in trouble with Roman law (the Romans didn't let the Jewish people perform executions) or Jewish law. Note also that Jesus didn't just say "That's OK" to the woman; He told her to stop sinning.

STEP 1

Before the session, get a jigsaw puzzle with 25 to 50 pieces. Put it together on a sheet of stiff cardboard. Put another piece of cardboard on top of it and turn the whole thing over. Write the names of group members all over the back of the puzzle, breaking names up (half a name on one piece, half on another). Repeat names as often as needed to fill up the puzzle. Then take the puzzle apart and put it in the box. At the meeting, have kids put the puzzle together, using only the names for reference. Then discuss how we often feel alone in facing sexual pressure, but need to remember that (1) we all face similar problems, (2) we can pray for and encourage each other, and (3) we can remember we're not the only ones who believe in saving sex for marriage.

STEP 6

Read Romans 11:33–12:1. Discuss what it means to offer our bodies as living sacrifices. Ask: **Why are we to do this?** (As worship, because of God's greatness described in 11:33-36.) Have each person cut a human figure from a sheet of paper. As kids do so, they should think about their willingness to give their bodies to God for His use. Let them show the degree of their willingness by having them place (or not place) their cutout figures in a "recycling bin" (any container that you provide). Point out that God wants not just our knees for kneeling or our mouths for singing, but all of us—including our sexuality.

STEP 4

Instead of using a guy-girl skit for Proverbs 7:6-23, ask two girls to present the passage. Have one read the verses as a narrator/observer from the window of her house; have the other pantomime the actions of the woman described in verses 10-23. Finish the presentation by reading aloud verses 24-27.

STEP 5

After discussing the four situations, ask your group members to talk about the pressure they feel to have sex, and/or to keep talking about whether you have or will have sex. Ask: **Where is this pressure coming from?** Work together as a group to make a list of the possible sources of the pressure. Include on the list a boyfriend, guy friends, girl friends, the media, and things you read. Talk about why it might be important to someone to give in to these pressures.

STEP 4

Pantomiming the Proverbs "seduction" will be either impossible or hard to take seriously if you have no girls; if you have just one or two girls, they may feel unfairly singled out. Instead, just take turns reading the passage. Then ask questions that help guys update the passage to include situations they face today: **Out of all the cases in which teenagers have sex before marriage these days, what percentage do you think are "start-ed" by the girl? By the guy? In what percentage do the guy and girl have equal responsibility? If most girls aren't giving guys this kind of invita-tion, why do so many guys think they're entitled to have sex? In what ways are some movies, TV shows, ads, and music giving guys the same message as the woman in this passage? How could premarital sex cost you your life** (vs. 23) **physi-cally? Emotionally? Spiritually?**

STEP 6

Guys may feel they won't become real men until they go through the "rite of passage" of having sex. Form small groups and have them come up with different ways of "proving" one's manhood without having sex. Ideas could be serious or funny. To help them along, ask: **What if people in our culture felt you weren't a real man until you changed a diaper? Until you led someone to accept Jesus? Until you lifted your father over your head?** You may want to point out that Jesus was a real man—and He never had sex.

STEP 1

Bring two identical, fairly complex board or card games that few if any kids in your group are familiar with. Form two teams. Half the kids on each team get to see the instructions but not play; the other half get to play but not see the instructions. Players may ask yes-or-no questions to try to discover the rules from the non-play-ers. The first team to complete a round of the game, following the rules, wins. (You'll need a judge, someone who knows the game, to watch each team to make sure the rules are followed.) Tie this into the fact that one has to know the rules and follow them to play the game. It's not enough to just know rules or just fool around with the game pieces. Similarly, we need to know God's sexual instructions and follow them—not just know them and ignore them.

STEP 6

Have a mustard-eating contest. Set out three large bowls of the stuff and ask for volunteers (or get volunteers before they know what they'll be eating). Contestants must keep their hands behind them and use only their mouths. Allow two minutes; chances are that kids won't be able to eat much without getting really tired of it. After rewarding the winner (perhaps with a jar of mustard), ask how contestants felt after the first mouthful or so. Then note that sex, like mustard, is great in the right context (sex in marriage, mustard on a hot dog). Out of context, though, it can be boring and even unpleasant. Wrap up by serving hot dogs—with mustard.

STEP 2

Instead of playing "Let's Make a Deal," watch coming attractions from the beginning of a couple of movie videotapes. Analyze how the clips were arranged to make the movie look more exciting, scarier, or funnier than it might really be. If anyone has seen the movie, ask how accurate the coming attractions are. What was left out? Have kids been disappointed by any movies after seeing ads or clips? Compare this to the "buildup" that premarital sex is given on TV and in movies—versus the reality of giving up one's virginity.

STEP 6

Bring a rap accompaniment tape. Form six groups or pairs. Assign each group or pair to rewrite two of the twelve reasons on Repro Resource 10 so that they become phrases in "The Let-It-Wait Rap." Then have kids take turns performing their parts of the rap for each other. Consider having the whole group perform the rap at a later date for your entire church or for your junior high group.

Here are a few ideas to get you started:

"Yo! Listen everybody to something great—

Twelve hip reasons to let it wait

'Til you're married—yeah, that's the plan

It's God's design for every woman and man

Reason one is plain to see

It'll keep you from unwanted pregnancy."

STEP 1

Replace Steps 1 and 2 with a short opener. Before the session, tape "Wet Paint" signs all over your meeting place. Plant one or two group members in the room who have paint on their hands or faces. Make sure your helpers show off the paint as kids enter. See who ignores the evidence and touches the paint. Use this example of evidence-ignoring to lead into the Step 3 survey. Instead of recording and averaging survey responses, save time by asking for one response to each question and letting others disagree during discussion if they wish.

STEP 4

For a shorter Bible study, see either the "Combined Junior High/High School" option or the "Little Bible Background" option. In Step 5, break into four small groups or pairs. Have each group or pair discuss just one of the situations (Sean and Francis, etc.) and give a one-minute report to the other groups.

STEP 2

Conclude this step with a short study of one or more of Jesus' parables. Point out that virginity is as much a beauty to God as sex during marriage. Both are traits of the kingdom of God. As such, some of the parables of Jesus can adequately describe the validity and beauty of virginity. Among the parables you might consider using:

• The Pearl of Great Price (Matthew 13:45-46)

• The Hidden Treasure (Matthew 13:44)

• The Mustard Seed (Matthew 13:31-32).

STEP 3

Here are some alternate questions you can use to make the survey more urban-specific.

• **What percent of the people in this group would you say are having sex?**

• **What percent of your peers would (or do) go to the school nurse for condoms?**

• **How many teenagers do you know who have died from AIDS?**

• **How many of your peers have a child already?**

• **What percent of the kids in your high school would you say are actively gay?**

• **What one thing would reduce teenage pregnancy forever?**

• **How many of your peers have a sexual disease, but continue to have sex?**

• **What percent of your peers would approve of the arm-implant method to prevent young ladies from becoming pregnant for five years?**

• **What percent of the kids in your school are virgins and proud of it?**

These aren't all "percentage" questions, so you'll have to adjust the activity accord-ingly.

STEP 3

Younger kids may find it hard to answer the survey questions. Instead, turn them into a mystery to be solved. Before the session, write the following five clues on separate slips of paper: "Fred knows how the physical part of sex works." "Fred knows the physical risks such as pregnancy, AIDS, etc." "Fred knows that people often feel guilty, worried, and ashamed after having premarital sex." "Fred believes it's wrong to have premarital sex." "Fred knows kids who have had sex and who then split up." Hide the clues throughout your meeting place (don't make them too tough to find). Say: **Fred is a teenager who recently started having sex. Why he decided that is a mystery. Look around and see if you can find some written clues that might help us solve the mystery.** After kids find and read the clues aloud, point out that there must be a missing clue; otherwise, why would Fred ignore everything he knows and believes? Lead into the discussion in the last two paragraphs of Step 3.

STEP 4

Kids may be confused by the example of Solomon, not to mention his concubines. Instead, study the temptation of Jesus (Matt. 4:1-11). Ask what appeals the devil used (physical appetite; testing God by taking unnecessary risks; getting power and recognition). **How does sexual temptation appeal to us in the same way?** (By using our normal sexual desires; by convincing us that we won't have to suffer consequences; by offering power over people by making them "conquests," giving us recognition as being sexy or grown up, etc.) Encourage kids to remember that the same enemy who tempted Jesus is behind our temptation today.

STEP 1

If the basic first two steps aren't brain-oriented enough for your group, substitute the following. Before the session, cut from newspapers and magazines a few dozen "cents-off" coupons for groceries, fast food, household items, etc. Put them face down on a table in your meeting place. To start the session, have several kids come up one at a time and take two coupons each. Each person must explain in one minute why one of the coupons he or she drew is objectively more valuable than the other. Some choices may be easy, but many won't. For example, is it better to get 75 cents off a bottle of aspirin or 25 cents off a candy bar? What if you never have headaches, or you're on a diet? Challenge kids' choices and allow other group members to do so. Then point out the many factors involved in seeing the real value of one coupon over the other. In the same way, the pleasure of sex now may seem more valuable than the rightness of sex postponed—but it's a lot more complicated than that.

STEP 6

Using the Repro Resource, have kids rank the 12 reasons to show which are most important and convincing to them personally. For example, someone who is most concerned with the risk of AIDS and not at all with the creative power of abstinence might write a "1" by #2 and a "12" by #9. Share results as kids are willing.

DATE USED:

Approx. Time

STEP 1: *Object Lesson* _____
- ❏ Small Group
- ❏ Fellowship & Worship
- ❏ Extra Fun
- ❏ Short Meeting Time
- ❏ Extra Challenge
Things needed:

STEP 2: *Let's Make a Deal* _____
- ❏ Large Group
- ❏ Media
- ❏ Urban
Things needed:

STEP 3: *Opinion Poll* _____
- ❏ Extra Action
- ❏ Large Group
- ❏ Urban
- ❏ Combined Junior High/High School
Things needed:

STEP 4: *Like an Ox Going…* _____
- ❏ Little Bible Background
- ❏ Mostly Girls
- ❏ Mostly Guys
- ❏ Short Meeting Time
- ❏ Combined Junior High/High School
Things needed:

STEP 5: *Too Late to Wait?* _____
- ❏ Extra Action
- ❏ Small Group
- ❏ Heard It All Before
- ❏ Little Bible Background
- ❏ Mostly Girls
Things needed:

STEP 6: *Worth the Wait (Part 5)* _____
- ❏ Heard It All Before
- ❏ Fellowship & Worship
- ❏ Mostly Guys
- ❏ Extra Fun
- ❏ Media
- ❏ Extra Challenge
Things needed:

Unit Two: The Drug Free Challenge

"Why Not?"

by Stephen Arterburn

There are two important questions today's Christian teens must answer every single day. "Why wait?" and "Why not?" Why wait? deals with waiting for sex until marriage. The Why not? question goes something like this: If drugs and alcohol make me feel good and if everybody else is doing it, why not? Both questions are very enticing to a young person looking for a rite of passage and a sense of belonging. Any youth worker or parent not prepared to address these questions is missing an opportunity to connect with a teen and perhaps help him or her avoid years of heartache.

Through campaigns like *True Love Waits, Thru the Roof,* and *Why Wait?,* youth workers have focused large amounts of time and energy with great success to equip and motivate their students to wait until marriage for sex. The same cannot be said about the second question. It is probably more of a stigma on today's high school campus to have never tasted alcohol than it is to be a virgin. The average high school student may have three times as many opportunities to try drugs or alcohol as they do opportunities to have sex. Yet, many youth workers often give their students a quick "Just Say No" pep talk and think they've prepared them to face the real world. It's time that youth workers begin to pour large amounts of time and energy to equip and motivate today's teens to be drug free.

You know that students' needs are complex. They won't be helped by quick fixes. They are hungry for real answers to real questions. As you strive to provide them, you can keep two things in mind. First, rely on the insights and ideas in this book. This is not just another "Just Say No" pep talk. It's an important work that features a team effort from a number of seasoned youth ministry veterans. But second, remember that the most important thing you can give your students is something you can't find in any book—your own story. Use the following two pages to help you prepare to talk to your teens about your own experience.

We encourage your work on the "front lines" with students. You will never know the full impact of your work. You may be the only person to discuss this important subject with a teenager. You may be the only person to show love for hurting teens—and that may be the very thing that leads some of your students to say no to drugs and alcohol and yes to Jesus Christ. You will never know the tally of your work. Do not give up on a frustrating and sometimes difficult problem. You can and will make a difference.

An Important Note: Working with Parents

There is only so much you can do for your students. The most important job is for the parents. Many studies show that the key factor in whether a teen says no to drugs and alcohol is whether they have a close, emotional bond with a parent. It is the parent, not the church or school, that must play the key role in kids making wise decisions. The greatest thing you can do to combat drugs and alcohol is to encourage parents to love their kids. *Feel free to photocopy the following three pages and send them out to your students' parents.* This important information will help you partner with and encourage parents.

Talking to Teens about Drugs and Alcohol

The best way to gain credibility in the area of drugs and alcohol is to tell teens that you know how tempting it is to want to experiment. Curiosity and a strong desire to experience the unknown lead many teens to try alcohol and drugs. Do not downplay that urge. Rather, relate to it and acknowledge that it would be easy for anyone to give in.

Your Story

There are really only two options you can take in a discussion on this temptation. You either have to explain why you succumbed to the temptation yourself and the effect of it, or you can talk of how you refused to succumb and the way that made you feel. There is a third option and many take it, but lying about your past is never recommended.

Let's look at how you would approach alcohol and drugs if your only option was to tell how you gave in to peer pressure. The following are some concepts to stress when relating your story:

1. It was not all it was cracked up to be.
2. It was not worth breaking the law just to be able to feel part of a group.
3. The act was done out of weakness, not strength.
4. The decision to drink and/or try drugs was a symptom of a character weakness that manifested itself in other areas.
5. You admire others who do not need a substance to feel better about themselves.

If you are able to tell how you resisted peer pressure, talk about:

1. How you felt about yourself.
2. The admiration others had (and have) for you.
3. How the strength to say no carried over and helped you in other areas of your life.
4. Other things that were more tempting or just as tempting and how you handled them.
5. How the students can follow your example.

Risks and Rewards

Once you have entered the discussion, there are two concepts that need to be addressed: risk and reward. Talk with teens about the rewards (or benefits) that they believe they might obtain if they tried alcohol or drugs. The list may include such things as:

1. Feeling part of the group.
2. Feeling grown up or mature.
3. Experiencing something new.
4. The accomplishment of getting away with something.
5. Feeling intoxicated.
6. Relief from emotional pain.
7. Feeling more comfortable with friends.

These are some of the reasons teens try alcohol and drugs. Talking about these reasons won't make them seem any more appealing. In fact, discussing them takes some of the power away from them. It's especially helpful if teens realize that they are not the only ones who feel that way. Tempting desires are less alluring when we know that others have felt the same way or desired the same things.

After discussing the appeal or reward, risk needs to be addressed. It is in this area that you can provide insight that many teens often overlook. Clarifying the risks for teens can be a powerful deterrent. When discussing risk, be sure to include the following:

1.   Risk of being caught.
2.   Risk of being punished.
3.   Risk of getting hooked or addicted.
4.   Risk of feeling worse about yourself.
5.   Risk of losing control and getting hurt.
6.   Risk of stepping outside of God's will.
7.   Risk of hurting someone else.
8.   Risk of leading someone else down the wrong path.
9.   Risk of becoming "numb" and unable to handle pain or tough problems.

Help teens name the risks and explore all the dimensions of each one. Ask teens to share the consequences they have seen in the lives of those who chose to drink or use drugs.

The Rewards of Saying No

You can discuss the many rewards of not using drugs or alcohol. These include:

1.   Self-discipline
2.   Self-respect
3.   Self-control
4.   Following God; seeking His will
5.   Character development
6.   Being seen as a leader
7.   Respect from other others

You can essentially sum up all the rewards of abstaining by discussing the following: Whenever anyone drinks or takes drugs, he or she does it to feel good. It might make him or her feel more comfortable with a certain group of peers, or it may be simply because the chemical causes one to feel good physically. But making decisions as a mature person requires that you go beyond what makes you feel good now and choose what will make you feel good about yourself later. Beyond this, mature Christians consider what is right and wrong. Not only do they want to feel good about themselves, they want to feel right about themselves. Only in doing the right thing can we feel right about ourselves . . . and what a feeling that is!

Stephen Arterburn is the cofounder of the Minirth Meier New Life Clinics. He wrote Drug Proof Your Kids *with Jim Burns.*

Drugs and Alcohol, A Parental Eye-opener

As parents we have a responsibility to care for the health and well-being of our children. Sometimes it seems there's a fine line between being an observant, responsive parent and being paranoid. Here are some signals to help you determine whether your son or daughter may have a drug or alcohol problem. Some of the patterns described could point to other struggles your teenager might experience. Either way, the symptoms should not be ignored. They're all unhealthy and a wise parent will pay close attention.

1. **Mood swings** beyond the normal ups and downs of adolescent transitions. Look for extremes, both high and low, that appear unconnected to visible circumstances or events in your teen's life.

2. **Problems at school.** Dropping grades, disinterest in sports or other activities, and, of course, skipping school or missing classes are all signals that should be taken seriously.

3. **Choosing unhealthy friendships.** Be careful not to judge teenagers who look or dress differently too quickly, but realize that friendships with kids who abuse drugs and alcohol can make it very tough for your son or daughter to stay committed to their standards.

4. **Habitual dishonesty.** Adolescents who abuse drugs and alcohol have no choice but to "live a lie." Often the habit becomes so familiar that they lie or distort the truth even when it's not necessary.

5. **Isolation and secrecy.** Teens who disengage from their families to spend most of their time alone in their room and those who become inappropriately defensive when asked about their plans or activities may very well have something significant to hide. Beware when kids go straight to their rooms when they arrive home.

6. **Violence, vandalism, and delinquency.** A tendency to be destructive, angry, and violent is often connected with drug and alcohol abuse. Note any cuts and bruises that may indicate having been in a fight and take very seriously any brushes your son or daughter may have with the law.

7. **Stealing.** Illegal substances are expensive and most students don't have the kind of cash it takes to support a drug or alcohol habit. Watch for things missing around the house or for items in your adolescent's possession that may not belong to them.

8. **Drugs or alcohol missing.** Keep a close watch on your medicine cabinet if it contains prescription drugs that could be abused. The same principle is true for your refrigerator, liquor cabinet, or wine cellar. Too many teens have learned to drink or abuse drugs in the lonely convenience of their own homes when no one was paying attention.

9. **Physical symptoms.** These may be very obvious but for some reason parents often choose to deny or ignore physical symptoms. Glazed eyes, insomnia, hallucinations, slurred speech, alcohol breath, needle marks, and the smell of marijuana smoke on clothing cannot be rationalized away.

10. **Stashed drugs and alcohol.** Finding bottles, baggies, drug paraphernalia or unusual powders and substances in drawers, pockets, backpacks, or hiding places must be addressed. Be prepared for excuses and explanations (see #4) but recognize that these sins are serious and must be confronted.

Facing the awful reality that our kids may have a serious problem is not easy for most parents. You may want to enlist the help of a counselor, pastor, or youth worker if you feel that you need to confront this issue in your family. Whatever you do, don't belittle the problem by assuming that it's just an adolescent phase or rite of passage. It IS a big deal and must be treated as such.

Marv Penner • Chairman, Department of Counseling • Briercrest Schools Seminary, Saskatchewan

Publicity Clip Art

The images on these two pages are designed to help you promote this course within your church and community. Feel free to photocopy anything here and adapt it to fit your publicity needs. The stuff on this page could be used as a flier that you send or hand out to kids—or as a bulletin insert. The stuff on the next page could be used to add visual interest to newsletters, calendars, bulletin boards, or other promotions. Be creative and have fun!

You've seen the stats. You've heard the stories.
You know what drugs and alcohol can do to your body—
you know what they can do to your life.
But you also have questions. Real questions.
Like: What's wrong with experimenting a little? and Why should I miss
out on the fun? Get some real answers to your real questions.
Find out what The *Drug Free Challenge* is all about.

Who:

When:

Where:

Questions? Call:

Life is tough. **How Do You Cope?**

The Drug Free CHALLENGE

Ever feel like you're
Missing the Party?

But I Don't Want to Miss Out on the Fun!

YOUR GOALS FOR THIS SESSION:

Choose one or more

- [ ] To help students realize that experimenting with drugs and alcohol has both physical and spiritual consequences.

- [ ] To help students understand that there are several ways to view the "fun" of drug and alcohol use.

- [ ] To help students understand that being filled with God's Spirit is ultimately more satisfying than being temporarily filled with drugs and alcohol.

- [ ] Other:_____

_____

Your Bible Base:

Ephesians 5:15-20
Ecclesiastes 2:1-11
Galatians 5:22-25

STEP 1

Drug and Alcohol Effects

(Needed: pens and paper)

Before you dive into a series on drugs and alcohol, one of the first things you'll need to do is see what your students know about these drugs' effects. Break into teams of two or three and hand out paper and pens. Give teams the category "drug effects" and two minutes to list as many kinds of effects drugs, both legal and illegal, have on humans. After the two minutes are up, have teams read their lists to the group one answer at a time. Cross off any answers that any other team also listed. Award teams one point for each answer that no other team came up with.

What are some positive effects drugs have on us? (Prescription drugs heal us, control pain, etc.)

What are some negative effects drugs have on us? (Impaired judgement, addiction, put us and others at risk.)

A drug is a substance that affects your body, either positively or negatively. But keep in mind that drugs are not always pills. Alcohol, tobacco, and nicotine are also classified as drugs.

Why are some people drawn to drugs and alcohol? Does it make their life better or worse?

Be sure to differentiate between legal and illegal drugs for your students. Also remind them that although alcohol is legal, it cannot be legally consumed until they turn 21!

Drugs and Alcohol Talkstarter

(Needed: copies of Resource 1, pencils.

Hand out copies of "Drugs and Alcohol Talkstarter" (Repro Resource 1) and pencils. Discuss the talkstarter questions one at a time. Every student can follow along by filling out his or her own sheet. No student should feel **obligated** to answer out loud, but the talkstarter is designed with provoking questions to engage your students in lively discussion. Listen to all of your students' points of view, even if they differ from your own or from the Bible. *There will be time to discuss these issues in light of the Bible's ultimate authority. But first it's important to communicate that everyone's opinion matters.*

To conclude, say: **We live in a world that says, "If it feels good, do it!" As a result, many people see nothing wrong with drugs or alcohol. They think, "What's wrong with experimenting a little bit if it makes me feel better?" But what should our response as Christians be? If we really do know Jesus personally, should we expect drugs and alcohol to meet our needs? How much fun do they offer? Is what God offers better?**

You Won't Want to Miss This!

(Needed: Bibles, copies of Repro Resource 2, pencils)

Break into three groups. Assign each group one of these passages: Ephesians 5:15-20, Ecclesiastes 2:1-11, Galatians 5:22-23.

The Bible is severe and consistent in its warnings against pursuing pleasure more than pursuing God. Note in Galatians 5:21 that drunkenness is clearly one of the results of pursuing pleasure over God and is called sin (see also Romans 13:13-14.) Although many of the hard, narcotic drugs that are common today are not

addressed, use of hard drugs, because of the "highs" it produces and the addictive consequences can easily be put into the same category as drunkenness.

Give groups five minutes to study their group's Bible passage. Tell them to be on the lookout for what it is that God has to offer Christians that's better than the temporary fun of drugs and alcohol.

Give each group of students copies of the "Insight Cards" (Repro Resource 2), pens, and a few minutes to fill them out. Encourage the students to weigh the pros and cons of what they know about drugs and alcohol, and God's promise for a fulfilled life. Have them put the cards away (you will discuss them again during step 4.)

Then, give the groups a few more minutes to prepare a presentation or roleplay that advertises the benefits of their Scripture passage.

The Ultimate High

(Needed: copies of Repro Resource 2 used in Step 3, pens, newsprint, marker)

Our culture does a great job portraying drug and alcohol use as something fun, relaxing, even sophisticated. But often, those promises are hollow. Only God can meet our needs that drugs and alcohol only temporarily cover up. Create a commercial that portrays your Bible passage and God's promise. It can be a dialogue between two friends or a catchy jingle. You decide!

After the students have presented their ads, have them stay in their groups. Ask volunteers to share what they wrote on their "Insight Cards" in Step 3. Use the newsprint and markers to make a list of their responses. Now refer back to the list of drug effects your students identified during Step 1.

Let's review. What are some "fun" reasons people use drugs and alcohol? Refer back to the Talkstarter.

How do these compare to the benefits of following God?

Conclude by saying something like: **Jesus is the Ultimate High. When we worship Him in the Holy Spirit, we experience to a fuller, more satisfying degree everything the "partyer" is looking for but will never really find in drugs or alcohol.**

O P T I O N S

EXTRA
ACTION

HEARD IT ALL
BEFORE

LITTLE
BIBLE
BACKGROUND

FELLOWSHIP &
WORSHIP

MOSTLY
GIRLS

MOSTLY
GUYS

EXTRA
FUN

SHORT MEETING
TIME

URBAN

STEP 5

Customized Challenge

(Needed: index cards and pens)

Pass out index cards and pens. Tell students to bow their heads and listen while you read this list of challenges. You don't have to use the exact challenges below. Customize the following to the needs you know your students have:

- **Are you using drugs and alcohol regularly? My challenge to you is to be honest with God. Admit your struggles to Him. If you're willing to change, tell Him that. Also, tell a trusted adult what you're going through. I'm willing to talk to you after the session.**

- **Is drug or alcohol use an off-and-on struggle for you— you wouldn't say you're a regular user, but sometimes you might have a beer or something at a party? My challenge to you is to get into an accountability relationship. Find a friend—maybe someone who has struggled in this area in the past but is doing better now—who can somehow show you what it means to be "filled with the Spirit." Commit to meeting with him or her by phone or in person for at least 15 minutes each week to share and pray for God's strength.**

- **Maybe you know in your head all the things we talked about today but you still *feel* like you're missing out on the fun. I challenge you to spend some time doing some fun things that are healthy for you. Make a list of all the things that you enjoy doing that don't involve drugs or alcohol. Then decide to do one or two this week. Thank God for the opportunity to enjoy yourself in a healthy way.**

- **Finally, if you're growing in the Lord and this is not an area of struggle for you, ask God to help you continue to yield your life to the work of his Holy Spirit. Pray that you will experience the real joy and power of God's "abundant" life.**

Ask students to choose a challenge and write it down on an index card. Encourage students to share what they wrote with at least one other person this week.

Drugs and Alcohol Talkstarter

1 **In your school, what percentage of the students do you think use drugs?**

0%   10%   20%   30%   40%   50%   60%   70%   80%   90%   100%

What percentage do you think drink alcohol?

0%   10%   20%   30%   40%   50%   60%   70%   80%   90%   100%

2 **Why do you think so many students try drugs and alcohol?**

____ They want to see what it feels like

____ They think it's cool

____ Their friends do it

____ They want to get high

____ They don't realize what they're doing

____ They need something to help them cope with life

____ They want to escape from reality

____ Other:

3 **Which of the following statements do you agree with:**

____ I believe drug and alcohol use, if done only once in a while, probably won't have an effect on you.

____ I believe it's OK to drink socially (at a party or at dinner), as long as you don't get drunk.

____ I believe that drug and alcohol use is usually a symptom of deeper issues.

____ I believe that you can't have a social life if you don't go to parties where drugs and alcohol are being served.

____ I believe that any use of illegal drugs or getting drunk is a sin.

____ I could hide drug and alcohol use from my parents.

4 **Which of the following drugs do you think are OK for a teenager to try?**

____ Tobacco (nicotine)   ____ Alcohol

____ Heroin   ____ Anabolic steroids

____ Aspirin   ____ Methamephetamines

____ Model-airplane glue   ____ Cocaine

____ Marijuana   ____ Other:

____ Coffee (caffeine)   ____ None of the above

Adapted from the "Drugs Talkstarter" and "Alcohol Talkstarter" in the *One Kid at a Time Mentor Handbook* by Miles McPherson with Wayne Rice (Cook Ministry Resources). Used by permission.

InSight Cards

When I consider the
"benefits" of following God, I think:

When I consider the
"benefits" of following God, I think:

When I consider the
"benefits" of following God, I think:

When I consider the
"benefits" of following God, I think:

When I consider the
"benefits" of following God, I think:

When I consider the
"benefits" of following God, I think:

Left Out

Stuck home, Friday night . . . that's OK . . . I'll make the best of it.

See, it's just me and God, and I got my Bible here. What could be more fun than this, right? *(Sits down to read his Bible.)*

(Standing up abruptly.) Fun . . . Fun? Who am I kidding?

I should've gone to that party. That's the life right? All the rest of the guys, they're not worried about their bodies—they don't miss a few little brain cells. They're certainly not concerned about what God has to say.

(Pretending he's at the party) Hey, everybody, the life of the party's here! Check me out! *(Pretends to guzzle a beer.)* That's my second beer. C'mon, give me another one. I'm starting to get a buzz.

(Not pretending anymore) I know, I know. That could never really make me happy. How could I feel good about my relationship with God the morning after I partied? What would I tell my Christian friends?

But that's what gets me so mad sometimes, God! I can't win! It seems like the people who don't know You get to have all the fun! It doesn't seem fair.

Sometimes I think You just want me to live a boring life.

(Sitting back down, grabbing the Bible.) I'll just sit here with my halo on. I'll play the angel.

Stuck here on a Friday night. I got my Bible right here. I don't need anything else . . . right?

Dear Abbey

Dear Abbey,
I've been invited to a party where I know people will be drinking beer. A lot of my friends will be there. I don't want to drink but I like hanging out with everybody. Should I go to the party if I don't drink anything? Or should I just avoid the temptation altogether?
Signed,
Party Pooper

Dear Party Pooper,
I tell my students that "a plane takes off best against the wind." What do I mean by this? Two things. First, Jesus was right in the thick of things all the time. I try to teach my kids that they need to be actively involved in witnessing to their friends in real, authentic ways. This might mean that they go to the parties because that's where kids are. Also, I believe that kids who are at these parties and intoxicated and drugged up are at their most vulnerable. And I don't mean that this is an opportunity to manipulate them; rather I believe that these kids have a clearer glimpse of who they really are. And this glimpse shows them that they are miserable, hurting, lonely, depressed, and so on. When a Christian teen befriends this kid at a party in a loving, non-condemning way, the opportunity of true witnessing can occur.

Dear Abbey,
It's not always easy to stay focused on my walk with God. When I'm at church or at home, it's easier. But when I'm around my friends who party, God seems to slip my mind. What can I do?
Signed,
Backslider

Dear Backslider,
Be spiritually prepared. Read the Word, pray, attend Bible study and church. Two, have a partner. Someone who's is praying for you, edifying you and is going to ask the hard questions. Three, forewarned is forearmed. Know the enemy and know what you're up against. Tempting situations are going to happen, but don't be caught off guard.

Dear Abbey,
When I'm offered a can of beer or a drag on a cigarette, what can I say that won't make me sound like a loser?
Signed,
Closet Jesus Fan

Dear Closet Jesus Fan,
This question needs to be addressed, handled, and answered WAY before you actually get asked the question. I believe boundaries need to be firmly decided upon and drawn in a person's life. It's healthy and I know kids want and appreciate such.

Dear Abbey,
I've never had a drink of alcohol in my life. I've never smoked a cigarette. I've never tried any narcotic drugs. And I have a reputation around school of being a "goodie-goodie." I hate that. I'm trying to make smart decisions and I get labeled like that. What can I do about it?
Signed,
Goodie 2 Shoes

Dear Goody 2 Shoes,
Laugh. Understand the big picture. You've got something other people don't. Remember and believe that you are called by God to a higher purpose and a higher calling.

STEP 1

Split your group into five-person survival teams. Tell the teams that their goal is to get their entire team to the "drug-free zone" within a certain time limit. The drug-free zone (an outside location) should be a good distance away from the initial meeting location. The problem is that certain members of their team are handicapped. One is deaf (give them earphones), two are blind (blindfolded), one is unconscious (require him or her to be motionless throughout the activity), and only one member is completely healthy. Tell groups they will receive one million dollars for each team member that makes it to the drug-free zone under the time limit (12 minutes). While teams attempt this dangerous mission, make life more difficult for them by pelting them with enemy "bombs" (soft playground balls or paper wads, for example). Discuss: Did you ever feel like leaving someone behind? Why was it important to work as a team and not leave anyone behind?

STEP 4

Ahead of time, label three tennis balls "thought," "feeling," and "counsel." Have students stand in a circle and toss the balls in a repeating pattern. Randomly call out "stop." The three students who are holding balls at that time must should shout either a thought or feeling about drugs or alcohol use, or counsel that they might give to someone contemplating using drugs. Encourage students on their turn to share some thoughts and feelings they wrote on their Insight Cards in Step 3.

STEP 1

Start your group by telling students you have some extra cookies (or other favorite food or candy) in your office that you would like to share with them. As you pass out the treats, take one yourself, and give some to the other students, but run out while several students are left empty-handed. Vaguely apologize for not having enough, then continue to enjoy your goodies. Keep the gag going as long as you're comfortable with it, but finally break out extra cookies and explain you were trying to make a point. Talk about how food can be similar to people and their quest for drugs or alcohol. Ask your students how they felt when they either received or didn't receive a cookie.

STEP 3

Ahead of time, record commercials or get clippings from magazines that glorify drug and alcohol use. As you display and discuss what the ads communicate to people, say: **We are now going to make our own commercial advertising how God can help with everyday struggles.** With a camcorder and a TV hookup you can now have fun making your own ad. Assign volunteers to play roles on the commercial crew (parts will depend on size of your small group). Give your group a few minutes to brainstorm and then video the live commercial based on the verses studied in Step 3. Of course you will have some laughter and mess ups, but this will only add to the fun! After you have completed the video get your students looking forward to next week by saying you will be debuting the edited version of the new commercial.

STEP 2

Ask for three volunteers to come up front. Give one person an empty beer can, another a pack of unopened cigarettes, and the third a bottle of pills (aspirin—just for effect). Say: **Okay, we know the media paints a picture of drinking and smoking as something sophisticated, cool, and mature. Our three volunteers are going to have one minute to try to be as persuasive as possible as they "sell" you on the benefits of their product. At the end, you will decide who did the best job by an "applause meter."** Encourage volunteers to do a quick skit off the top of their heads. Give a prize to the student who receives the loudest applause. Use the discussion questions at the end of Step 2.

STEP 5

Many large groups have small group programs. If you don't have one yet, you might consider investigating what it would take to start one. Present the challenge as directed in Step 5. Then break down into small groups; ideally there will be one adult leader in each group of six to eight students. Students can share with their group what challenge they are targeting for their own life. This does two things. 1) It facilitates accountability—no student should have to walk through the tough issues surrounding drugs and alcohol without being able to tell others what's going on. 2) It may prevent some struggling students from slipping through the cracks.

STEP 2

Tape three or four current TV beer ads that most students will be familiar with, or cut print ads from magazines or newspapers. (You might also collect cigarette ads.) Evaluate whether the ads depict the true picture of alcohol or tobacco use or glorify it. Discuss: **How does this ad say your life will change if you smoke these cigarettes or drink this brand of alcohol?** Then have students create and perform a roleplay showing the devastating "down sides" of alcohol or drug abuse. Prompt them to depict scenes of violence, family brokenness, lost opportunities, alcohol-related accidents, and so on all of which are clearly associated with substance abuse. Students can present their findings as a "freeze frame" or "live action."

STEP 4

Divide students into groups of three. In each group, tell the student with the biggest Bible he or she gets to be "Pat." Of the two left, the one with more hair gets to be "Christian" and the remaining person gets to play "Abbey." Take a look at the Repro Resource 4, "Dear Abbey." Instead of using this as written, use the letters as examples of scenarios Christian could roleplay, for example, Christian could play someone who is tired of being called a "goodie, goodie." Pat should answer Christian's questions with, you guessed it, "pat" answers—your church kids will know them all well. Abbey should give an answer that is not pat and predictable. Ask Christian what it felt like to get these answers to his or her deep dilemmas.

STEP 3

If you think your group is interested in more of the benefits God bestows on Christians, try this. Give each small group a portion of Ephesians 1:1—3:21. Read Ephesians 1:3 aloud, telling students that the book of Ephesians lists a couple dozen blessings (benefits) that are showered on Christians. For example, 1:4 says that God chose us before the creation of the world. The next verse says He has adopted us into His family. Have your groups search their portions and list or underline as many blessings as they can find. Then, list their results on a chalkboard or newsprint and discuss the meaning of each blessing; or go ahead with the original suggestion to make creative presentations of the findings featuring bumper stickers, jingles, or a talk show dialogue. Be sure to point out just how incredibly fortunate we are to have a God who gives us so much.

STEP 4

For best results, sit in a circle. Take a look at the Repro Resource 4, "Dear Abbey." Instead of using this as written (for example, as a series of "Dear Abbey" letters), use just the letters as examples of questions students ask about drugs and alcohol. Read aloud the letters hypothetical teens wrote in to "Abbey." Tell students to take turns sharing their responses to the question. If you want, compare students' answers included on the resource.

STEP 2

Encourage students to get into groups of three or four with people they don't know very well. Say: **Advertising and the media do a great job depicting the positive aspects of a lifestyle that include drugs and alcohol. People who drink are often portrayed as sophisticated, fun-loving, relaxed, and mature. Take the next five to seven minutes and put together a collage of ads, pictures, and words that would convince someone of the benefits of alcohol/drug use.** Pass out newspapers and magazines which include alcohol and cigarette ads, large pieces of poster board, glue sticks, scissors, and thick markers. Let each group make a collage as directed. If time permits, have a spokesperson from each group share a persuasive presentation about the benefits of a lifestyle that includes drugs/alcohol according to their collage.

STEP 4

Worship, at its best, is like a party where all the participants get drunk on the Holy Spirit. One of the best ways to help students who feel like they're "missing out" on the fun of drugs and alcohol, is to teach them how to worship well. Sing songs that celebrate following Jesus. Let students share how grateful they are for Jesus in their own words. Share reflective thoughts about what Jesus means to you. Do what you can to create a festive atmosphere.

MOSTLY
GIRLS

MOSTLY
GUYS

EXTRA
FUN

STEP 1.

Have the girls brainstorm fun ideas that are alternatives to the parties where chemicals are involved. Get girls brainstorming right away. For example, make your own pizza at the local pizza joint. Build a mega-sundae. Rent a stupid but fun video and have people come dressed as their favorite character. Discuss: **You've probably heard people say before that parties are more fun when there's drugs and alcohol available. It seems like people think drugs and alcohol make everything more fun! What do you think? Can you have just as much or maybe more fun without using drugs or alcohol?**

STEP 4

Before passing out copies of the Repro Resource 4, "Dear Abbey," read the letters (not "Abbey's" response), and ask students what advice they might give. if they were responding to the letters. Then pass out copies of the resource and discuss what students think of Abbey's answers.

STEP 1

Guys love to remember the gross, the loud, the stupid, or awesome prank they pulled on someone. Give your guys just a few minutes and ask them to share the gross, loud, stupid, and funny highlights of their previous year. Give a can of something gross (like Spam) or some stupid prize to the guy who tells the best story. Your transition to the lesson could go something like this: **I obviously missed out on some of the nasty and smelly stuff you guys did recently. It sounds like a lot of fun. Would your friends think this was fun? What would other people consider more fun?**

STEP 4

Step 4 starts off by comparing the way athletes separate their bodies and minds for their physical goals with the way Christians should separate their minds, bodies, and spirits for their goal to live for God. This is an idea guys can really relate to. Expand on this idea. Ask guys who participate on sports teams to share what past or present sacrifices they have made or are making due to their training. Pass out pens and paper. Ask students to list things that they need to separate themselves from to live for God. Then have them list all the things they can think of to do in "training" for God that will help them both have fun and be spiritually "fit."

STEP 1

Most kids are aware that just messing around with drugs doesn't guarantee that you will become a hopeless addict. Because they are kids, they feel invincible and live by the motto "It'll never happen to me." You can bring to light the idea that using drugs is a crap shoot with your life—"Russian roulette" with little to gain and much to lose. Discuss: **Out of all the teens who experiment with drugs, how many do you think will have no serious consequences? How many do you think will get seriously messed up? How do you know who will get messed up and who won't?** (No one can know.) Have students take turns rolling one die. Congratulate each student that rolls a six—they have just become one of the lucky ones who get "messed up" by drugs. To symbolize this, "mess them up" with shaving cream, an egg, or a pie in the face. Tell students "1 in 6" is a number you pulled out of your hat—there's no hard evidence to support it. But the point is: **Why would you want to take that chance?**

STEP 4

Some things are not compatible. A mind controlled by the Holy Spirit and a mind controlled by drugs are like oil and water. You can't mix them together. A person makes a choice when they stand at the crossroads of drug use: to have God control their minds or allow their minds to be controlled by a substance. Have some fun illustrating this by using a cup of cooking oil and a cup of water (use a bit of food coloring to brighten it up). Dump both into an empty glass jar. Stir it, shake it, and the two still separate. Christians and chemicals are not compatible.

STEP 1

Take your video camera to a mall or teen hangout and interview as many teens as you can—or better yet, coach some of your students to do the interviews. Ask teens if you can interview them, be honest and upfront about what you're doing, and thank them for helping. Try to get 5-10 minutes of tape time from a wide variety of students. Use questions like: **How common is drug use at your school? What drugs have you used? What drugs do you think are OK for teens to use? Are there any drugs you should never take? Why? Do you think whether or not you believe in God should affect whether or not you take drugs or drink alcohol?** After the video, discuss what your students think of the answers given.

STEP 2

On the Repro Resource 3, "Left Out," a typical Christian teen is stuck home on a Friday night and feeling "left out." Prepare an actor to perform this monologue in front of the camera. The video will automatically engage students and keep away the giggles and heckling.

TIP: The following tip is effective not just for the monologue above, but for any time you film interviews. Think in terms of three cameras. Any time you can, between questions and comments, stop and move to a new position. Although you have only one camera, it will seem like you have more.

STEP 2.

Instead of breaking into small groups, use Repro Resource 1 as a guide for your discussion and let students answer with their bodies. For questions 1 and 2, set up a spectrum in your room—point to one end of the room and call it "100%" and call the other end "0%"; tell the students to answer in terms of a percentage of students by where they stand in the room. For questions 3 and 4, have students stand up when they agree with a statement and sit down for when they disagree.

STEP 3/4 - INSIGHT CARDS

Instead of introducing the "Insight Cards" (Repro Resource 2) at the end of Step 3, use this resource to help focus and streamline the entire step. Instead of reading Scripture and then making a creative presentation, simply give students a few minutes to read all the Scripture on their own and write down their "insights" as directed in Step 3. This activity will lead more fluidly into Step 4.

STEP 4

Keep students in the groups they did their Bible studies in and announce that they are now to pretend that they are a council of urban Christian educators about to embark upon starting a Christian high school which will be an area-wide magnet school for drug abusers (believers and new converts). By using one of the Scriptures which was given during the earlier activity each group will do the following: 1) Name the Christian high school; 2) Define which two drugs addictions the school will focus on; 3) Create a motto for the school from Scripture; 4) Design a curriculum of eight classes (two per year) which will help the addict and heal his or her soul. Give students a few minutes to brainstorm, then have each group describe the school they designed to the entire group.

STEP 5.

As a festive closer, have what R&B gospel musician Kirk Franklin calls "A Holy Ghost Party!" This can be a small or big party and can be at the end or take the majority of your meeting time. Include light food and snacks, Christian music, and some games. The purpose is to celebrate the power of God's Spirit (our Comforter) who helps us overcome all addictions (physical and moral) even though there are tough episodes. Finally, a "Holy Ghost Party" must include at some point a reading and reflection of Acts 2 which describes the first experience with the Holy Spirit at Pentecost. Be sure to reflect that the persons at the first celebration had real problems and addictions in their lives, but that it was the power of the Spirit at Pentecost who gave them victory over sin through Jesus Christ our Lord.

COMBINED

STEP 2

Play with four students at a time (all girls or all boys). Have contestants circle up and each grab one end of two pieces of rope so that the rope connects all four of them in a circle. Contestants are eliminated if they touch the trash can or let go of the rope. Keep eliminating girls until only one is left. Repeat the same process with the guys. Afterward, lead a discussion comparing the circles formed with the ropes with circles of friendship you experience. Both are difficult, and at times students get eliminated from the circle. Ask: **What kinds of things are we eliminated from because we're Christians? Why do we eliminate ourselves from drug and alcohol use? What are the advantages?**

STEP 5.

Instead of praying as a group, capitalize on the peer pressure that both junior and senior highers face through the positive peer pressure of prayer and accountability. Break into groups by school. This provides more natural opportunities for accountability, as well as potential similarity of temptations (for example, the new temptations of junior high school or the big school Friday night football party). Within their school groups, ask students to partner off to pray for each other and encourage them to serve as positive peer pressure for each other when they see each other at school or extracurricular events. If someone is the only student from a certain school, pair him or her with an adult leader or with another student who is also the sole student from their school.

EXTRA CHALLENGE

STEP 3

Read the story of Matthew in Mark 2:13-17, Matthew 9:9-13, and Luke 5:27-32. Make two columns on newsprint and have students shout out to you things Matthew stopped doing when he converted and began to commit himself to following Jesus. Next have students shout out to you things that Matthew started doing—the things that Jesus was doing in His life for example. The most obvious example is the incredible opportunity Matthew had to follow and learn from Jesus. Compare the two lists. **For Matthew, the price of giving up his old way of life for God's purposes was well worth it because he had a higher purpose for his life than just doing what he wanted for his own gain. Matthew knew that his love relationship with Jesus would never end—it would lead to eternity in heaven. If we trust Jesus for our sins we can be assured of the same thing.**

STEP 5

Bring in some cards with blank insides. For best results, use cards with fruit on the front. Using Galatians 5:22-25 as a guide, help students identify which of the fruits of the Spirit seem to be most lacking in their lives. Tell them to, as a seed of faith, write a "fruit card" to someone else. For example, if they are in need of peace, they might send a card to someone blessing them with the peace of God. You and your students may be surprised at the results.

PLANNING CHECKLIST

DATE USED:

Approx. Time

STEP 1: *Drug and Alcohol Effects* _____
- ❑ Extra Action
- ❑ Small Group
- ❑ Mostly Girls
- ❑ Mostly Guys
- ❑ Extra Fun
- ❑ Media
Things needed:

STEP 2: *Drugs and Alcohol Talkstarter* _____
- ❑ Large Group
- ❑ Heard It All Before
- ❑ Fellowship & Worship
- ❑ Media
- ❑ Short Meeting Time
- ❑ Combined Junior High/High School
Things needed:

STEP 3: *You Won't Want to Miss This!* _____
- ❑ Small Group
- ❑ Little Bible Background
- ❑ Short Meeting Time*
- ❑ Extra Challenge:
Things needed:

STEP 4: *The Ultimate High* _____
- ❑ Extra Action
- ❑ Heard It All Before
- ❑ Little Bible Knowledge
- ❑ Fellowship & Worship
- ❑ Mostly Girls:
- ❑ Mostly Guys:
- ❑ Extra Fun
- ❑ Urban
Things needed:

STEP 5: *Customized Challenge* _____
- ❑ Large Group
- ❑ Urban
- ❑ Combined Junior High/High School
- ❑ Extra Challenge
Things needed:
* combined steps

Coping with Life in a Cop-Out Culture

YOUR GOALS FOR THIS SESSION:

Choose one or more

☐ To help students learn that using drugs and alcohol is copping out, not coping—it only leads to more problems.

☐ To help students understand that Jesus can give them the power to cope with life's struggles.

☐ To equip students with healthy coping strategies, such as spending time in God's Word, praying, and leaning on the support of Christian friends.

☐ Other:_____
_____

Your Bible Base:

Hebrews 4:15-16
Philippians 4:6-7
James 1:2-5

Don't Get Buzzed

(Needed: cut-up copy of "Coping Cards" (Repro Resource 5), timer, buzzer or bell)

Cut up one copy of Repro Resource 5 and put the cards in a bag. Divide into two teams and tell teams to choose one clue-giver. Have the first team's clue-giver choose a card from the bag. Once he or she silently reads the "clue word" and the "off-limit list," he or she must hand you the card. Start the timer and give the clue-giver 30 seconds to get his or her team to name the clue word. The clue-giver can use any combination of words, phrases, and sentences to give his or her team clues except for any of the words—or any form of the words—on the off-limit list. If the clue-giver says anything illegal or goes over the time limit, "buzz" him or her out with your buzzer or bell. Rotate clue-givers until all the cards are used. Award one point for each correct answer and congratulate the winning team.

Did you catch what all of the clue words had in common? (Each clue word names a "coping mechanism," or a way of dealing with life's problems.)

Remind students what all nine coping mechanisms were. **Which of these coping mechanisms do you think are most popular among people your age? Why? Which of these do you think are the least popular ways of dealing with problems? Why?**

Besides the ways mentioned on these cards, what other ways do people try to cope with their problems?

Turn to the person next to you and share two ways you typically cope with your problems.

STEP 2

Coping Quotes

(Needed: copies of Repro Resource 6 and 7)

OPTIONS

FELLOWSHIP & WORSHIP

MEDIA

SHORT MEETING TIME

JR. HIGH / HIGH SCHOOL COMBINED

For best results, sit in a circle. Pass out copies of Resource 6. It has a slightly different format than the talkstarter used in Session 1. It will cause students to think a little more about what they want to say. But you want to establish the same discussion guidelines. Establish an atmosphere where every student knows his or her opinion is valued. Read each quote about drug and alcohol use one at a time. Then have students share either a thought, feeling, or Bible verse that applies to the quote.

What's the difference between coping and copping out?

Copping out is running away from or burying your problems. Coping with your problems means not being afraid of pain when life is painful. It's sticking it out. It's facing life head on, even when that's not the easiest thing to do. Why do you think so many people have a hard time coping with life?

Do you think most people who depend on drugs just decide one day, "Hey, I think I'll get addicted to alcohol or strung out on drugs because I don't know any better way to deal with life"? What do you think happens instead?

To help students process this question, pass out the case study on Repro Resource 7. Read this true story about Reed aloud and discuss: **Reed had a tough family background. Do you think he did a good job coping with his problems or did he cop out? Why?**

What are some things Reed could have done to help him cope with his problems in healthy ways?

STEP 3

A Better Way to Cope

(Needed: Bibles)

O P T I O N S

Divide into three groups and assign each group one of these three passages: Hebrews 4:15-16; Philippians 4:6-7; or James 1:2-5. Each of the three passages contains a type of "problem" we all face, along with a promise from God in response to that problem. You might introduce this study by saying something like: **If we don't use drugs and alcohol to cope with life, what should we do? Let's see what the Bible has to say.** Give groups a few minutes to list the problem addressed and the promise God gives to help us cope with the problem. Have each group appoint a spokesperson to share their group's answers. Encourage students to take notes on the other presentations.

Here are some possible answers for you to guide your students toward:

- **Group 1: Hebrews 4:15-16**
  The Problem: Temptations; any time of need.
  The Promise: We will receive mercy and find grace to help in our time of need.
- **Group 2: Philippians 4:6-7**
  The Problem: Things that cause us to worry or become anxious.
  The Promise: God's peace will guard our hearts and minds in Christ Jesus.
- **Group 3: James 1:2-5**
  The Problem: Trials of many kinds.
  The Promise: Trials make us mature and complete. If we do not understand the purpose of our trials, we are to ask God and He will give us understanding.

At this time, summarize the difference between relying on God's promises to cope with life and relying on drugs and alcohol. For example, you might say: **God is not a drug. He doesn't promise to dull our pain. He's not an escape from tough times. He simply promises to walk with us through our struggles. The Bible is very upfront about the fact that life is tough. Tough times happen. The Bible also tells us that, as Christians, we don't have to turn to drugs or alcohol or anything else to help us cope when life gets tough. God is enough. God can help us get through our problems.**

The PRAY Strategy

(Needed: leather strings, beads with the letters P, R, A, and Y on them [optional]).

You'll need four station leaders who are adults or mature students. Choose leaders who can lead their station by example. Use the directions below to prepare your leaders ahead of time. Designate four areas in your room as your "stations."

Small groups should rotate and spend about five–seven minutes at each station. At each station the leader should: 1) talk briefly to define his or her station and give details about how he or she uses the particular strategy to cope with life, and 2) use the discussion questions below to facilitate a practical follow-up discussion.

Optional: Prepare each leader with enough beads for each student. The beads should say the letter of each station on them. At the end of rotating through the stations, pass out leather strings. Help students put their beads together to make bracelets that remind them to PRAY.

STATION 1: **P**RAYER—Prayer is an effective coping mechanism when we understand that God wants us to express our real, honest emotions about our struggles. Prepare the station leader to share in detail how he or she talks to God with honesty and emotion.

Discuss: **Does prayer help you cope with your problems? Why or why not? Do you have any questions about prayer in general? Do you have any questions about how to be honest with God about your emotions and struggles?**

STATION 2: **R**EADING THE BIBLE—Reading the Bible is an effective coping mechanism when we bring an open heart and listen to what God has to say to us. Prepare the station leader to share in detail how he or she listens to God through Scripture reading.

Discuss: **Does reading the Bible help you cope with your problems? Why or why not? Do you have any questions about reading the Bible in general? Do you have any questions about how to hear what God wants you to hear when you study the Bible?**

OPTIONS

EXTRA ACTION

SMALL GROUP

HEARD IT ALL BEFORE

LITTLE BIBLE BACKGROUND

FELLOWSHIP & WORSHIP

MOSTLY GIRLS

EXTRA FUN

MEDIA

SHORT MEETING TIME

URBAN

JR. HIGH HIGH SCHOOL COMBINED

EXTRA CHALLENGE

STATION 3: **A**CCOUNTABILITY—Building accountability friendships involves getting together with friends who are also committed to God and keeping one another on track. Prepare the station leader to share in detail how his or her own accountability friendships help him or her cope with tough times.

Discuss: **Do your friends help you cope with your problems? Why or why not? Do you have any questions about accountability friendships in general? Do you have any questions about how to build the kind of accountability friendships that will support you and help you cope?**

STATION 4: **Y**OUTH GROUP—Committing to the youth group is an effective coping mechanism because God can use the group to provide support, encouragement, and spiritual direction. Prepare the station leader to share in detail how his or her own youth group provided these benefits.

Discuss: **Does the youth group help you cope with your problems? Why or why not? Do you have any questions about how you might take some steps toward the youth group so that the youth group might help you cope with your struggles?**

Bring the group back together. Summarize the lesson. For example, you might say something like: **Maybe drugs and alcohol are a real temptation for you. Or maybe anger, denial, busyness, or depression are more common in your life. Whatever unhealthy coping devices you may use, recognize that they are walls that keep you from experiencing the real peace and faith that God promises. When life gets tough, please remember to PRAY. Put that strategy into action by praying, reading the Bible, building accountability friendships, and committing to the youth group.** Close in prayer, thanking God for His help in our times of struggle.

Coping Cards

Smoking Cigarettes

Off-limit List:
smoke, cigarettes, nicotine, tobacco, drag

Procrastinating

Off-limit List:
procrastinate, put off, avoid, wait

Using Alcohol

Off-limit List:
alcohol, drinking, partying, beer, bottle

Worrying

Off-limit List:
worry, stress, anxiety, panic, fret

Overeating

Off-limit List:
eat, food, pig out, stuffed, a lot

Get Busy

Off-limit List:
busy, action, do, work, hurry

Spacing Out

Off-limit List:
space, veg, daydream, nothing, sit

Pity Party

Off-limit List:
pity, sympathy, sorry, depressed, beat up

Coping Quotes

1. Share a thought, feeling, or verse...

"Most teens who use drugs and alcohol are just immature and insecure. Drugs are their way to escape the pressures of adolescence."

2. Share a thought, feeling, or verse...

"My life stinks! I drink a lot because drinking helps me get through life. When I'm drinking, I don't have to think about all my problems."

3. Share a thought, feeling, or verse...

"Everybody needs something to get through life. Some people overeat. Some people have to complain to everybody about every little thing. My thing is I use cocaine. It's no big deal. I'm no worse than the guy who's addicted to watching TV. It's what I use to get through life, one day at a time."

4. Share a thought, feeling, or verse...

"If my parents knew that I was smoking weed, they'd be ticked. But they're hypocrites. They smoked when they were my age—in fact, they did a lot worse things than I did! I've got my whole life to be serious. I just want to have a good time while I'm young. What's wrong with that?"

5. Share a thought, feeling, or verse...

"I haven't had a job in two years. I'm living out of a paper box these days. If I can bum some loose change off a yuppie downtown tonight, I'm gonna go get me some more crack as fast as I can. I need my high so bad right now I'm shaking. If anyone tells you drugs help you cope with life, tell him he's a dope."

Case Study: Choices

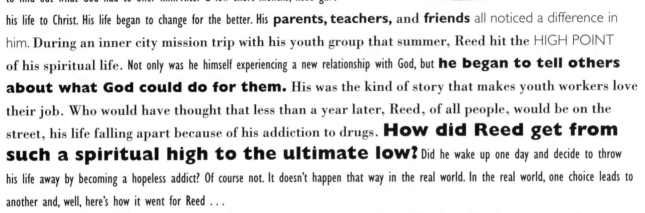

Reed didn't come from a **"churched"** background. **He was a skater,** and somewhat of a rebel— **often in trouble at school and at home.** When he moved from San Antonio to Colorado, he started attending the small youth group I led. He sometimes caused more than his share of trouble there, too, but he was a **GENUINE "seeker."** He was interested in spiritual things; he wanted to find out what God had to offer him. After a few short months, Reed gave his life to Christ. His life began to change for the better. His **parents, teachers,** and **friends** all noticed a difference in him. During an inner city mission trip with his youth group that summer, Reed hit the HIGH POINT of his spiritual life. Not only was he himself experiencing a new relationship with God, but **he began to tell others about what God could do for them.** His was the kind of story that makes youth workers love their job. Who would have thought that less than a year later, Reed, of all people, would be on the street, his life falling apart because of his addiction to drugs. **How did Reed get from such a spiritual high to the ultimate low?** Did he wake up one day and decide to throw his life away by becoming a hopeless addict? Of course not. It doesn't happen that way in the real world. In the real world, one choice leads to another and, well, here's how it went for Reed . . .

As we returned home, within the next couple of months, **Reed's family began to have problems.** They stopped going to church, considered divorce, and argued all the time. During this time, Reed began to experience problems with grades, teachers, and other authority figures. Over the next several months, **Reed began to slowly and inconspicuously withdraw from his friends and his youth group.**

Reed couldn't stand to be around his house and could not get along with his parents. He started hanging out with new friends, friends who seemed more **"real"** and who seemed to be able to relate to what he was going through. Reed's new friends did drugs and Reed started using soon after. Reed did not choose the friends because of their habits, he adopted their habits because they became his friends! As Reed's youth pastor, I CONFRONTED HIM and WARNED HIM about how important it was for him to stay connected to other Christians through the youth group. *But Reed just distanced himself further from the youth group and eventually stopped going altogether.*

Reed came over one night and **told me how he had started using drugs.** He said he **couldn't stop.** My heart broke. I knew he did not plan to take this road, but **each little choice he had made to cope with the pain and disappointment he was feeling had led him further down this path.** I had no special formula or message I could pull of of my hip pocket to help him. I was just truly broken for him. I prayed for him. **Reed eventually got kicked out of school.** He's now been in trouble with the law for stealing to support his drug habit. He's lost most of his chances for ever getting a degree. He's emotionally separated from God, family, friends, and church. **He can't hold a job *and continues to use drugs.***

I can honestly say that Reed never **"intended"** to take this road. **He didn't say "I think I will try dope this week."** Drugs were never the way Reed **decided** to cope with his problems. **The mess his life is in now is a result of many small choices.**

STEP 1

Have students circle up and face clockwise. Introduce this terminology: "Go" means walk in the direction you are facing. "Stop" means freeze! "Turn" means make a half turn (180°) and freeze. "Jump" means jump, make a half-turn, and freeze. "Twizzle" means jump, make a full (360°) turn, and freeze in either the cope position (hold your arms up like a muscle man) or the cop out position (cover your head with your arms). Get students warmed up by calling out the above directions in random order. Then add this wrinkle: Each time you stay stop, read one of the the "coping mechanisms" off Repro Resource 5 and yell "Twizzle." Students decide whether the item read was an example of coping or copping out and get into the appropriate position. Each round, have a few students share why they chose to pose how they did.

STEP 4.

Use Step 4 as written with these variations: Have students partner up. Blindfold one student in each pair. The unblindfolded partner must guide the other from one station to the next. He or she can only touch the partner's one open palm with his or her own palm and must make up a set of signals (for example, pull down for stop, pull left to turn left, and so on). While traveling from station to station partners should discuss what they just learned at the previous station. Rotate which partner is blindfolded at each station. At the end of the activity, add these comments: **Think what would have happened today had your guide not been present and you had to navigate the room blindfolded. That's sometimes the way we try to live life—we go our own way without Christ, our guide! No wonder we end up lost. But Jesus promises to walk with us and guide us if we trust Him.**

STEP 3

For a fresh approach to God's promises to help us through life, write the Bible references listed in Step 3 on a chalkboard, white board, or somewhere else where students can see them. Next, call out a life situation. Students race to look up the verses and give the promise that corresponds to the life situation. For example, you would say, "Problem: Facing trials or struggles in your life." Students would then search the references listed on the board. The correct answer, er, question, would be, "What is James 1:2-5?" After each round, discuss: **What is promised in this verse? How can you cope with life by living out what this verse says?**

STEP 4

Instead of setting up four stations, give each student a blank sheet of paper and have them write the "PRAY" acronym vertically down the left side of their page. Discuss what each letter stands for in detail. Use the activities and discussion questions included in the PRAY stations but go through them as a group. Encourage your students to be honest and discuss their questions, doubts, and personal experiences with each aspect of the PRAY strategy. When you get to the accountability section, instead of just saying accountability is important, consider assigning accountability partners for the upcoming week and challenge your students to hold each other accountable to put the PRAY strategy in action. Conclude by telling students that next week you will ask: 1) Who put PRAY into practice and how? and 2) Who followed through and talked to their accountability partners?

STEP 1

For an activity that will get more students involved, clear a large playing area—preferably in a gym or outside. Have all students line up at one end of the court. Have your adult leaders stand around center court. Say: **When I say go, your goal is to get to the other side of the court (field, etc.) without being picked up off the ground by one of your leaders. You are "out" if you are picked up and both feet leave the ground and the person (or people) picking you up yell, "American Eagle!" When that happens, you become one of the people trying to pick up the runners for the rest of the game until everyone has been grabbed.** Have students run back and forth until all have been picked up. For obvious reasons you might want to run two separate games—one for girls and one for guys.

STEP 3

You can adapt the Bible study in Step 3 for a large group in several ways. First, divide your students into groups of no more than four and assign them all of the passages in Step 3. Or, you could have each small group discuss the verse's significance with their own small group.

STEP 3

This option will require you to take some risks and it may raise more questions than it answers. (Jesus often did that.) Use Step 3 as directed but add an important element of discussion: The three passages listed in Step 3 will be familiar to church kids. Ask students to recall times when they didn't find the connection between the problem and the promise to be quite that simple. Start with the Philippians passage—it may be the least threatening, then move to the James passage, and finally to Hebrews. Discuss the factors that may have contributed to the promises not working. For example, maybe students misinterpreted the promise, or they were not willing to wait for God's answer, or perhaps they didn't take the issue very seriously. Help students see what a real, honest walk with God is—not always having all the answers but trusting and growing closer to God all the time.

STEP 4

Put your students in four small groups as the original idea suggests, but instead of having them rotate through the stations, assign each group just one of the four steps. Groups should prepare and produce a 30-second TV commercial that promotes the specific step they've been assigned. Either have the students perform their commercials "live" or videotape them and watch them on a TV/VCR unit.

STEP 1

Use Step 1 as directed, then debate these questions: **Is it harder to cope with life today than in Jesus' time? What were the pressures faced by young people in Israel all those years ago? How did they cope? Were they faced with the temptation to drink or do drugs? Did they live in an easier time or were they somehow stronger than people today?** The fact is, life was every bit as difficult then as now. Don't allow anyone in your group to cop out by claiming it's harder to cope now. The Bible's prescription for coping, which is what this session is about, is totally sufficient to deal with modern trials.

STEP 4

Impress upon your group that the PRAY strategy includes the steps students need to take to reach the source of the power to succeed: God. In other words, it is God who brings victory over drugs and other issues, not us. Each of the steps in the PRAY strategy is designed to help a student achieve a healthy, vibrant relationship with the One who can destroy the power of temptation and addiction. Without this relationship, the motivation to live a godly life and the ability to do so are not there. This is a good time to present the way of salvation if there are students in your group who may never have given themselves fully to Him.

STEP 2

Instead of using the "Coping Quotes" activity, divide students into small groups of four to six students. Tell them to discuss more personal, in-depth questions that will help breed deeper fellowship, like: **What's one problem you're going through right now that's tough to deal with? What do you "feel" like doing in response to the problem? How are you really coping with the problem? What can this group do to help you learn and grow from your struggles?**

STEP 4

After working through the PRAY stations, gather students in a circle on the floor. Turn the lights down low. Read the following prayer and encourage students to personalize, reflect on, and meditate on the words: **Lord, there are times when I try so hard, but still fail, and times when I feel so discouraged I want to quit. There are times when I feel betrayed by my friends and hurt by my parents. There are times when I haven't remained pure and the guilt weighs heavy on me. There are times when I feel like giving in, giving up, and checking out. But then I remember the scars on Your brow, the stripes on Your back, the nails in Your hands, and the spear in Your side. And I remember . . . You've been there. And You're here to help me in my time of need. Thank you, Lord, for loving even me.** While students remain in a reflective mood, read Hebrews 4:15-16. Close by singing several songs that deal with trusting God such as: "You Are My Hiding Place" or "Thy Word."

MOSTLY GIRLS

STEP 1

Here are two additional ways girls sometimes cope with life. Put these two on index cards and add them to the list of coping mechanisms on Repro Resource 5 for use in the "Coping" game:
• Clue word: Under-eating. Off-limit List: diet, skipping meals, starving, purging.
• Clue word: Escaping. Off-limit List: shopping, TV, talking on the phone, video games.

STEP 4

This session would be great to use as a springboard for further discussion in the context of an overnighter or day away. Use Step 4 as directed, then invite the girls to help you plan a "Girls Night Out," an overnighter held either at the church or a retreat center. In the last few minutes of the meeting, girls can offer their suggestions and input but many of the following suggestions will require your leadership and direction outside of the meeting time. Ideas: Design different activities geared toward helping the girls have a healthy self-image both internally and externally. Possible ideas are: have a "mini-spa" where a physical trainer talks about the benefit of keeping in shape, for example, how being physically fit reduces a person's stress level and how girls have a healthier worldview when they are physically active; bring in a makeup artist to teach how to do facials/manicures and see if they can bring in samples. Also, bring in a local counselor (preferably female and Christian) who specializes in working with teenage girls and have her talk about how to develop healthy coping strategies.

MOSTLY GUYS

STEP 1

Although guys definitely use the coping mechanisms listed in Resource 5, there are a couple of other mechanisms you might want to add to the list that are specific to guys. Put these on index cards and add them to the list from Repro Resource 5 for use in the "Coping" game:
• Clue Word: Burying It. Off-limit List: bury, forget, dead, tomb, casket. (This issue refers to the idea that guys don't want others to know they are struggling, so they bury the issue by acting like nothings wrong.)
• Clue Word: Too Cool. Off-limit List: cool, cucumber, happening, above it. (This issue refers to the idea that guys will put on airs as if they are above the fray of life's problems. Guys don't like to look weak, especially not around other guys.)

STEP 3

One of the most prevalent problems teenage guys face is lust. Use Step 3 as directed, but add this discussion as well: Have your guys look up Matthew 5:27-28. Include this in your discussion of problems—the problem here, of course, is lust. Then talk about God's promise. Read 1 Corinthians 10:13. Ask guys to put this verse in their own words.

EXTRA FUN

STEP 1

Ask your students to come up with some really DUMB things that people do that get them in trouble or mess up their lives. Pass out index cards and ask students to write down a dumb thing on each card. Each example should start out with "You could . . ." (Example: You could take a swing at a cop.) Collect all the cards and put them in a container. Then, have your students brainstorm a list of problems that people face from time to time, write each on a slip of paper, and deposit in a container. For example: a broken heart, failure to make the team, rejection by friends, feeling left out or insignificant, and so on. Now, match the problem from one container with the dumb example from the other. Could be very funny and sometimes very accurate! Discuss: **What are some healthy ways to deal with your problems—instead of just picking a foolish idea out of a hat?**

STEP 4

When others encourage us, we often can handle situations that would otherwise really mess up our minds. Here are a number of ways you could provide opportunities for students to encourage one another:
• Have students create and give cheers for one another (example: Ra, Ra, Roo, Roo, there's no one like Mary Lou. A great big smile and warm hello makes you want to stay and never go!)
• Have students write encouraging letters to one another. Ask them to incorporate the biblical promises studied in Step 3.

STEP 2

It's OK to have a lot of fun while making a serious point! First, brainstorm with your "actors" some typical ways teenagers cope with their struggles today. List five or six good ones. Next, figure out how you and your group can depict these in one or two minute vignettes. Practice for a few minutes. Get your camera cued and then have the students act out the vignettes one at a time. When you're done, set up the TV so that these can be shown to the whole group. Stop after each individual vignette and discuss each one.

STEP 4

Again, brainstorm with your students some healthy, appropriate ways to cope with difficult drug-related situations. After coming up with five or six, determine how these can be acted out on camera. Then, act it out and videotape it for your group. That night, show to your group these more appropriate forms of handling these situations. You can stop after each one and discuss it. To end this segment, read Hebrews 4:15 together.

STEP 1

Instead of waiting for all the students to arrive to play "Don't Get Buzzed," begin by drawing on a chalkboard or piece of newsprint pictures and symbols to represent as many coping mechanisms as you can think of. Begin by drawing those listed on Repro Resource 5. Let students compete to be the first to guess what you're drawing. Use the discussion questions at the end of Step 1.

STEP 2

The "Coping Quotes" activity is a good idea but it may take up too much time. Instead, start Step 2 by reading as dramatically as you can the story of Reed ("Choices," Repro Resource 7). Use the discussion questions at the end of Step 2.

STEP 4

Instead of spending the time to divide into groups and walk around to different stations, present the information, activities, and discussion questions for each station.

STEP 1

The city has many pressures which can lead teens to use drugs abuse. Illustrate this by asking for a volunteer who can take the pressure of a big group squeeze. Have all students squeeze-in on the volunteer for five seconds. Be sure teens know that when the five seconds are up they must immediately break up the squeeze. Next, ask for three students who want to protect the volunteer during the next squeeze. Have the three volunteers circle themselves as a barrier around the student to be squeezed. The role of the three volunteers is to keep the group pressure off of the student in the middle. Again, have everyone "Squeeze!" for five seconds and head back to their seats. Discuss: **Was the first or second squeeze tighter? Why?** Finally, relate the activity to the fact that all Christians have an assurance of full pressure-protection from God. God doesn't remove the negative aspects of life's pressure, but He keeps it from overtaking us.

STEP 4

City teens constantly need to justify why Christianity is right because of the public skepticism true believers face. Another way to do this activity is to simply have students justify the importance of each station and to give five hip-pocket justifications as to why a believer should be dedicated to each.

STEP 2

After using the "Coping Quotes" activity as directed, make a list of all the people who they know who have "copped out" of their problems by using drugs and alcohol. For example, students could list friends, family members, musicians (Elvis Presley, members of the Rolling Stones, Kurt Kobain), celebrities (John Belushi, Kelsey Grammar, Robert Downey Jr., Robin Williams), and professional athletes (Steve Howe, Michael Ervin, Leon Lett, Tony Phillips). In as many situations as you have time for, discuss how using drugs and alcohol simply made the abusers' problems worse, not better. This activity can replace the reading of the "Choices" story (Repro Resource 7).

STEP 4

To help make this step more engaging for a combined group of junior and senior highers, end the fourth rotation right after students move to that fourth station. Explain that you've chosen to end it early because you've got an even better idea. You want each group of students to make up either a funny or serious drama about the station that they're in right now to help the rest of the students understand the role that station plays in healthy coping. Every student gets to be involved. Give each group eight–ten minutes to design their drama and then ask each group to perform their drama sketch before the rest of the group.

STEP 3

Begin the Bible study by asking: **What is the difference between a pinball and a car? How is "trying to cope" like living like a pinball? If we were to truly live for God, how could that be like driving a car?** Supplement students' answers by saying: **If Christ is firmly on the throne of our lives, we won't have to just "cope" in the same way others do; we can see circumstances as tools in God's hand to shape us in His image. We can be like the car—driven and propelled to reach our goal, and not like the pinball—bounced around by gears and levers.** Read 2 Corinthians 11:16—12:20 together. Discuss: **How would Paul react to the drug use in today's culture? How was Paul a "conqueror," much more than merely a "cope-er"? What behavior or attitude will have to change in your life to make you a conqueror? What problem would you like to conquer in your life?** Leave students a few minutes of silence to ponder the last two questions on their own.

STEP 4

Go through the PRAY stations as directed, but refer back to the Bible study above and instead of calling PRAY a coping strategy, call it a conquering strategy. After the PRAY stations, gather together and close together by praying for one another. Challenge students to be honest about their answers to the question: *What needs to change in your life for you to become a conqueror?* When a student shares, encourage the rest of the group to respond by praying for him or her right there on the spot.

DATE USED:

Approx. Time

STEP 1: *Don't Get Buzzed* _____
- ❑ Extra Action
- ❑ Large Group
- ❑ Little Bible Background
- ❑ Mostly Girls
- ❑ Mostly Guys
- ❑ Extra Fun
- ❑ Short Meeting Time
- ❑ Urban

Things needed:

STEP 2: *Coping Quotes* _____
- ❑ Fellowship & Worship
- ❑ Media
- ❑ Short Meeting Time
- ❑ Combined Junior High/High School

Things needed:

STEP 3: *A Better Way to Cope* _____
- ❑ Small Group
- ❑ Large Group
- ❑ Heard It All Before
- ❑ Mostly Guys
- ❑ Extra Challenge

Things needed:

STEP 4: *The PRAY Strategy* _____
- ❑ Extra Action
- ❑ Small Group
- ❑ Heard It All Before
- ❑ Little Bible Background
- ❑ Fellowship & Worship
- ❑ Mostly Girls
- ❑ Extra Fun
- ❑ Media
- ❑ Short Meeting Time
- ❑ Urban
- ❑ Combined Junior High/High School
- ❑ Extra Challenge

Things needed:

But It's Not That Easy to "Just Say No"

YOUR GOALS FOR THIS SESSION:

Choose one or more

☐ To help students realize that there is no quick fix to stay drug free in today's world.

☐ To help students understand that God can give them the power to stay off drugs and alcohol.

☐ To challenge students to develop real-life strategies and action plans to help them stay off drugs and alcohol.

☐ Other:_____

_____

Your Bible Base:

I Corinthians 10:13
Romans 7:19-20; 8:1-4
Hebrews 4:15-16; 12:1-3

Quick Fixes

(Supplies needed: random items, paper bag, copies of Repro Resource 8)

Cut out copies of Repro Resource 8 and put the "Problem Cards" into a paper bag. Choose four volunteers. Each volunteer should pick a "gadget" (one of the random items you brought in—anything from a stirring spoon to a football) and a Problem Card. Instruct volunteers to create a 30-second commercial proclaiming how their gadget can fix the particular problem on their card. Judge the best presentation with an "applause meter." Give one of your gadgets away as a prize.

Can you think of any examples in real life where people try to apply "quick fixes" to tough problems? (instant weight-loss pills, get-rich-quick schemes, instant muscle drinks, *Cliff Notes*.)

Let's take the problem of staying off drugs and alcohol. Is that an easy problem or a hard one?

What kinds of "quick fixes" do you hear to the problem of drugs and alcohol? Do these quick fixes usually work? Why or why not?

Wouldn't it be great if all we had to do to stay "drug free" was get the right "gadget"? Unfortunately, real life doesn't work like that, does it? For example, there's no magic wand that will help you stay off drugs, is there? Staying drug free in the real world is much more difficult.

Get Real?

(Needed: two copies of Repro Resource 9, for actors)

Prepare two actors ahead of time with copies of Repro Resource 9. Encourage them to memorize and rehearse the mini-drama.

You can introduce the drama by saying something like: **What's your experience been in terms of saying no to drugs and alcohol? Here's one scenario for you to consider.** Cue your actors to perform the drama, then discuss:

Was this a realistic conversation? Why or why not?

Do you like what Dave had to say when he was offered drugs? Why or why not?

Would you have said anything different than Dave in handling the situation? If so, what?

What would be the hardest thing about being in Dave's situation or any other situation in which you are offered drugs or alcohol?

Conclude by saying something like: **On any given weekend, it can seem like "everybody's doin' it"—like all your peers are drinking, partying, or using drugs of some kind. Is it realistic for you to go through high school without getting caught up in the party scene at some point? It may be difficult. But it's not impossible. Let's see what the Bible has to say.**

Three Groups and a Bible

(Needed: index cards, pens, Bibles, cut-out copies of Repro Resource 10)

Recruit three adult volunteers or mature students to lead each group. Use the directions below to prepare your leaders in advance to lead a short activity and a brief follow-up roleplay in their groups. Set

up three areas in your room for each group. Divide your students into three small groups.

Each group should spend five minutes interacting with their Bible passage and then use the rest of the time preparing their roleplay for the group.

Group 1—*What students read:* 1 Corinthians 10:13.
What students do: Write down on index cards times when they believe God provided for them a "way out" of a tempting situation dealing with drugs and alcohol.
What students roleplay: Give each student a copy of the roleplay card from Resource 10 that deals with their group's Bible passage. Give them five minutes to create and present a roleplay based on the card.

Group 2—*What students read:* Romans 7:19-20; 8:1-4.
What students do: Write a short letter to God on index cards describing any struggle they're having or have had with drugs and alcohol, and asking Him for the power to win that struggle. (If drugs and alcohol is not a problem, students may write a letter to God discussing some other issue they struggle with for which it is difficult to say no.)
What students roleplay: Give each student a copy of the roleplay card from Resource 10 that deals with their group's Bible passage. Give them five minutes to create and present a roleplay based on the card.

Group 3—*What students read:* Hebrews 4:15-16.
What students do: Write a paraphrase of the verse; in other words, put the verse in their own words. In this station it is particularly important that the leader be ready to offer his or her explanation of the verse. Equip the station leader to close this station by emphasizing the fact that Jesus understands the temptations we go through; He had complete victory over temptation, and that means all of us can go to Him to receive help when we are struggling with drugs and alcohol.
What students roleplay: Give each student a copy of the roleplay card from Resource 10 that deals with their group's Bible passage. Give them five minutes to create and present a roleplay based on the card.

Keep the groups where they are, but have them send up their drama teams to present their Bible passage and roleplay.

www.drug.free

(Needed: overhead projector, overhead pens, transparencies)

Keep your students in the same three groups from Step 3. Have your groups create a concept for a web site that can be used to help their peers be drug free. As they develop their concepts, hand each group overhead pens of different colors and an overhead transparency.

Explain: **Your job now is to take what you have learned from your Bible passage and your roleplay and design the home page for a web site. Your web site's address is up to you. Just make it practical and attractive. You will present the page to the rest of the group in seven minutes. Have fun!**

After each group has shown their home page on the overhead projector, discuss: **Why should your friends care about God's help to stay drug free? How can you talk to them about it?**

Prayer Cards

(Needed: index cards, pencils)

Pass out index cards and pencils. Asking for prayer from peers is a huge step for most teens. But if you can begin to teach students to pray for one another, there's no better way to build community in your group.

Give students a few minutes to write down a prayer request about a situation dealing with drugs and alcohol. For example, students might write: *I need help to know what to say when someone offers me drugs* or *I need help to know what to do when students call me a loser for not doing drugs.* Encourage students to put their names on the cards, but do not require it. Collect the cards, then distribute them randomly. Challenge students to make a two-week commitment to pray once a day for the person whose card they received. Close your time by leaving a few minutes for students to pray silently for the person whose card they have.

Quick Fix Cards

Problem #1
Always Losing Things

You keep losing things like your car keys, wallet/purse, homework, little brother, Bible, jacket, etc.

Problem #4
Headaches

It never fails. Every time you sit down in English class, you get a splitting headache.

Problem #2
Embarrassing Noises

You have a habit of making uncontrollable and obnoxious noises at the most embarrassing times.

Problem #5
Can't Remember Names

You keep forgetting names of people you know.

Problem #3
Broken Stereo

Your stereo broke and you need something to fix it.

Problem #6
Breaking Up

You need help breaking up with your girlfriend/boyfriend.

Everybody's Doing It!

STEVE: Are you coming to the party tonight?

DAVE: Yeah, I'll be there.

STEVE: It seemed like you had a good time last week.
Were you drunk or what?

DAVE: No. I just had a couple of beers. I don't think I'll
even drink tonight.

STEVE: How come? Everybody's doing it.

DAVE: I'm a Christian. I made a mistake last week. I'm
suppose to have higher standards.

STEVE: *(still not quite getting it)* Well, how about pot? I've got
a sample for you, if you want. You'll have a great time
with this tonight!

DAVE: Thanks Steve, but I don't think so. I like to hang out
with everyone, but I just don't want to get messed
up with drugs or alcohol.

STEVE: You won't get messed up. Heck, I've been doin' drugs
and getting drunk all through high school . . . and look
at me! *(smiling, like he's doing great)*

DAVE: *(sarcastically positive)* Yeah, look at you. Well, I have to
go. See ya' next week.

STEVE: What about the party tonight?

DAVE: Like I said, see ya' next week.

STEVE: Okay, but it's your loss.

DAVE: I don't think so, Steve. I just don't think so.

Roleplay Cards

I Corinthians 10:13

WE HAVE GOD'S POWER TO RUN FROM TEMPTATION:

God will always provide a way of escape. Roleplay a situation where someone is offering you drugs or alcohol. The pressure to give in is high, but you simply say "No!" and walk away.

Romans 7:19-20, 8:1-4

WE HAVE GOD'S POWER TO HELP US WHEN WE STRUGGLE:

Despite your resolve to stay drug free, it's impossible without God's help. Roleplay a situation where a friend invites you to "hang out" at a party where there will be drugs. You respond by choosing to do something fun, somewhere else.

Hebrews 4:15-16

WE CAN ASK FOR HELP, AND GOD'S POWER, WHEN WE SEEK IT:

Trying to handle a serious struggle drug or alcohol on your own just won't work. Roleplay a situation where a person struggling with drug use finally goes to a respected peer or adult and seeks his or her advice and help.

Internet Threads

JESSI345:   Mad...hey, what's up?

MADDOGJD: Not too much here, you?

JESSI345:   I dunno...I was invited to this party.

MADDOGJD: That's kewl, so what's the problem?

PSALM23:   What kind of party is this Jessi????

JESSI345:   Well...a lot of my friends are gonna be there, so I wanna go...but I know there's gonna be drinkin too, and I'm not into that.

MADDOGJD: DRINKIN! Right On!

CUTIE6234:   That's a tough issue. My personal belief is it's not wrong to drink unless you get drunk.

PSALM23:   Yeah, but it's against the law if you're under age. How old are you?

JESSI345:   I'm 17. Well, I'm not sure if I wanna go and hang out...or what?

NUHTCASE: Anyways, so this guy at school stuck a joint in my face the other day and I hardly even knew him.

ARIELLE: Really? That goes on at my school all the time, too.

WILDMAN4U: I'm not into any of that. I've told a lot of people no at my school. Now I got a reputation as a goodie goodie.

ARIELLE: Doesn't that make you feel like a loser????

WILDMAN4U: Yeah, sometimes.

NUHTCASE: I hate that. It's like...you do it or your a loser. I wish there was something else I could say.

ANGEL1285:   I'm tired of the drinking and smoking at my school. It's like people don't have anything better to do.

BEARCLAWZ: If they want to drink or smoke...you should respect their decision.

ANGEL1285:   I think they're all losers.

MARKOPOLO: I'm not a loser...I'm a good Christian...most of the time. But when I get around my friends who party, God seems to slip my mind.

ANGEL1285:   You make it sound like they make you drink or something??? If you were really a good Christian, you wouldn't let God slip your mind. I don't.

STEP 1

Choose one student to be the communicator and give him or her a piece of paper with a design on it. Without showing the group the design, the communicator must effectively describe the design so that the rest of the class can duplicate it on their own papers. This activity would make a good lead-in to the discussion at the end of Step 1.

STEP 5

Give each student a medium-size stone, a pen, a piece of paper, and a rubber band. Tell students to write out an ending to this sentence: "When it comes to drugs, alcohol, or the whole party scene, I need prayer for _____." Have students fold up the note, wrap it around the stone with the rubber band, and throw the stone and note into a pile in the center of the room. Say: **The house that you live in is built upon a rock solid foundation. The foundation is made up of thousands of tiny stones that make it strong. It is the same way with prayer! Our foundation is made up of thousands of tiny stones that make it strong. It is the same way with prayer! Our everyday prayers are like tiny stones that make up the foundation of our lives. Also . . . when we pray for someone else we are helping them build a strong and solid foundation.** Have your students grab a stone from the center of the pile, making sure that they don't grab their own. Challenge them to place the stone in their room at home where they can see it. The stone will be a reminder that they are to pray once a day for the person whose note was attached.

STEP 1

As you probably know, putting students on the spot in a small group is a dangerous proposition. Students can feel extremely awkward and the activity can quickly backfire on you. Instead, have students pair up and charge them to come up with as many examples of "quick fixes" as they can in three minutes. After three minutes, have pairs read their lists. Give pairs one point for each item listed that did not appear on anyone else's list. To transition to the rest of the lesson, tell the group you will throw out a saying and they should throw back at you what problem the slogan is meant to be a "quick fix" for "Just Say No." Students will of course know this refers to turning down drugs. Use the discussion questions at the end of Step 1.

STEP 4

Instead of having several groups create several web sites, have your group of students create an Internet search engine. A search engine is similar to a telephone book, except it groups web sites by function and/or topic giving you a quick and easy way to access whatever sites you're searching for. Have your students create directories and topic listings for their directory of drug-free sites. Then, have them create the name, look, and web address of their search engine. You'll find that your students already have the ability to access and organize several pieces of information to help them and their friends be drug free.

STEP 1

Ahead of time, prepare an overhead transparency, screen transparencies, and marking pens for each team. Write 10 things that have to do with "fixing," each on one index card (for example, wrench, screwdriver, duct tape, calculator, glue, plumber, math teacher, and so on.) Divide into two teams. To begin, each team sends one contestant up front. Show contestants one of the cards, then have them try to draw a picture of that object on the transparency. The first team to guess the word wins that round. Post judges close to each team so they can determine which team guesses the drawing first. Then rotate drawers. Use the transition comments at the end of Step 1.

STEP 3

Have students remain seated and pass out pens and paper. A single teacher can teach the group about the four Scripture passages (see Step 3). Or you might wish to have three different teachers handle the teaching in a "tag-team" approach.

STEP 3

Your students are probably ready to put some of their wisdom and experience into practice. Move them into three groups (or multiples of three if your group is large), and ask them to imagine that they are leading a voluntary attendance Bible Study in a Juvenile Detox Center with a group of adolescents who genuinely want to kick their drug or alcohol habit. Have each group prepare four or five discussion starting questions on their passage of Scripture. Encourage them to add any other related passages that might be helpful.

STEP 4

Take a fresh approach to get students' attention. Pass out copies of Repro Resource 11, "Internet Threads." Most of your students will be familiar with what "chat rooms" are on the Internet. But you may need to explain the concept to others. Chat rooms are a way of having electronic conversations with people from across the world who, via their computer and phone line, arrive at the same electronic address. During the course of the conversation, what one person types and sends on his or her computer shows up on another person's computer screen. Repro Resource 11 contains three of these electronic conversations. The addresses, or names, have been changed. Discuss with students: **If you were on the Internet right now, what would you write back? Why?** If time permits, let students write out their advice on Repro Resource 11 and let volunteers share what they wrote.

STEP 3

Hebrews 4:15 tells us that our Savior was tempted in every way, just as we are. Students may question whether or not Jesus faced the exact same pressures to use drugs that they face. Did Jesus' schoolmates try to con Him into using the latest designer drugs? There is no such record in Scripture, but there is a text that reveals how Jesus dealt with a different temptation. Matthew 4:1-11 gives a detailed account of Christ's temptation. There are many lessons to be learned here, including the importance of following faithfully wherever God's Spirit leads, the reality of Satan's involvement in temptation (including substance abuse), and the need to use the Bible as a weapon against temptation. Take a moment to read the passage aloud and discuss these points with your class.

STEP 5

Some of the anonymous prayer cards may reveal that one or more students have done drugs and are in trouble. Point out that sins—even substance abuse and addiction—can be forgiven by God. He stands ready to do so as we confess (see 1 John 1:9). At the conclusion of the activity, allow your class a minute of silent prayer during which they can take their sins to God. Close the prayer by thanking God for providing forgiveness to all who ask. Tell your class that you are available to meet with anyone who needs help or advice. Encourage your students to call you if they don't feel comfortable approaching you now. You must be ready to offer help and support to anyone who seeks it. If you do not feel qualified to deal with an addicted student, be sure you know the names of people and organizations who are.

STEP 2

This idea may challenge your students out of their comfort zones a little but the end result is always more positive fellowship. Instruct students to get up and find one person they don't know very well. Encourage them to walk around the room with that person—movement can help eliminate some awkwardness. Throw out general questions about drugs and alcohol that students can review while they walk. For example: **On a scale of 1 (easy) to 10 (very hard) how hard is it for you to say no to alcohol or drugs if they're offered to you? Do you believe relying on God alone can be enough to resist the temptation to experiment with drugs and alcohol? Why do you think so many teens are so tempted to experiment with drugs, smoking, and alcohol?**

STEP 5

This step works best if you work with a team of adult volunteers. If that's not the case for you, you might ask a few adults in your church to come to the meeting specifically to make themselves available to pray for students. To close the meeting, ask students to pause wherever they are and reflect upon what the Lord may be speaking to them about in regard to drugs and alcohol. If you can, have a song leader lead the group in several worship choruses and instruct students to sing or pray quietly. Then, make a general invitation to your students to get up and ask one of the adults to pray for them. Dismiss after all have had a chance to be prayed for.

STEP 2

Choose one student to be "Oprah," others to be guests on the show, and the rest to be audience members. Have Guest #1 play the role of a hard-core partyer who has no intention of giving up her lifestyle. Have Guest #2 be a "goodie-goodie" who stays at home crocheting tea cozies (whatever those are). Guest #3 is a recovering partyer who became a Christian and is honest about how hard it was to give up that life. Guest #4 is a Christian who is really attracted to the party lifestyle and is seriously thinking about going to a party this weekend and getting drunk. Let the audience ask questions and interact with the guests. "Oprah" needs to know how to facilitate this kind of discussion and how to draw it to a positive conclusion. At the end, have the girls debrief their reactions/experience. **Did anything happen that made you think differently about the topic of drugs and alcohol? Guests, how did you feel playing roles that did not fit you?**

STEP 5

Pass out index cards and pens. Have girls write down any questions they have about drugs anonymously and put these in a hat. Then pass around the hat and instruct students to draw a card that is not their own. Students should research the problem/question in the upcoming week and come back with an answer. Example: "I have a friend who confides in me that he thinks chewing tobacco won't hurt him because he's not smoking. What do I tell him?"

STEP 1

Divide into three teams. Have one team design and present a 30-second commercial for a powdered protein drink guaranteed to turn weaklings into muscle men overnight! Have a second team design and present a 30-second commercial for a no-fail, get-rich-quick money-making scheme. Have the third team design and present a 30-second commercial for any "miracle" product students can dream up that can solve any number of problems they can think of. Use the discussion questions at the end of Step 1.

STEP 3

Supplement the activity by adding a fourth group specifically geared to the needs of your guys: *What guys read:* Matthew 4:1-11. *What guys do:* Write a short "critique" letter to Jesus on how He handled temptation; write the letter in a style and voice similar to that you would use to encourage and congratulate a close friend. *What guys roleplay:* Have a few guys act out ways they can use Scripture and follow Jesus' example to overcome temptation.

STEP 4

Use this discussion starter to get the students to think of several light-hearted ways to respond to drugs and alcohol.
• You could . . . crack a joke. Brainstorm funny one-liners students can say when they're offered drugs and alcohol. Humor is a good way to lighten up a tense and tempting situation.
• You could . . . do a whole bunch of things a lot more fun than drugs and alcohol. Every student should know what puts him or her into the "fun zone"—what activities they enjoy and get pleasure out of. The more healthy and fun activities students are involved in, the less they need drugs and alcohol for a good time.
• You could . . . laugh at yourself. Students who are self-confident enough to see the big picture and simply laugh when they get labeled "goodie-goodie" and "prude" are in good shape.
• You could . . . laugh at the "druggies." The idea that a substance could offer you more than God could? Now that's funny!

STEP 5

Clothes carry messages. Kids often show their allegiance to an idea, sport, music group, or place by the designs on their T-shirts. Pass out paper and pencils and have your students create designs that would give the message that drugs are for losers. Have them come up with a number of ideas and sketch out the images. Let them know they don't have to be great artists—they just need to get the concept across. Post all the suggestions and vote on which the class would be most likely to wear. Turn over the winner to a kid in the class who is an artist and turn the concept into final art and ultimately T-shirts for the group.

STEP 1

Have fun with the "quick fix" gadget idea in Step 1 by putting the same concept on video. Grab five gadgets from your house, give each gadget a funny name, and determine how these gadgets can be used to fix some significant or completely corny problem. Then videotape five students advertising these gadgets. For example: Call normal stereo headphones "Dr. Eric's Ear Cleaning System." Talk about how Dr. Eric has developed a method by which your ears can be deep cleaned in a painless, effective way. (The content does not have to be great because your students will get a kick out of watching their peers come up with these goofy commercials.) The options are endless! Conclude by using the discussion at the end of Step 1.

STEP 4.

Here's a great way to include mom and dad into your youth ministry. Set up interview with parents of the kids in your youth group. Be sure not to tell the kids what you're up to! Here's what you do: First, before each interview, videotape (to music) a specific question your students have about drugs and alcohol. For example, print up and videotape for 30 seconds the question, "Should Christian teens go to parties where alcohol is being served?" Then, interview two or three parents and their answers to this question. Do this for five or six questions. Stop the tape after each section and discuss it with your students. The following are good questions to use: What should I say when I'm being offered drugs? How did you deal with drug usage when you were in high school? How can I stay focused on God in tempting situations? What can I do about being labeled a "goodie goodie"?

STEP 1

Instead of having an activity ready for students when they arrive, gather as much "Just Say No" paraphernalia as you can. Network with your local government and community organizations. You shouldn't have a problem getting groups to give you items once you tell them what it's for. When students examine the materials, discuss: **How is the slogan "Just Say No" helpful to you? Does it encourage you in any way? How? Does it seem like a quick fix or a true solution to a tough problem? What is a quick fix? What's an example of a realistic strategy for handling a tough problem?**

STEP 3

If you don't have time to go through all the discussion and activity involved in the groups, give students "power packets" instead—give them tangible reminders of the power of God that's available to them. Once you get done studying the verses listed in Step 3, pass out items like:
• A masonry nail to remind students of the cross and that God uses His power to serve us because of His great love for us.
• A mustard seed to remind students that even faith the size of a mustard seed can be powerful in God's hands.
• A carabiner, used in mountain climbing, to remind students that they are connected to God at all times—God carries them when they start to fall; and there is no challenge too great that they can't tackle it and conquer it with God's help.

STEP 2

While alcohol is the most popular gateway drug in our *country*, some *cities* recognize that many teens are skipping alcohol completely and going straight to the more harmful drugs. Instead of starting with alcohol then moving onto marijuana and eventually harder drugs like crack cocaine, some city teens are getting their first highs from cocaine. If this is your situation, alter the reading of Repro Resource 9 to reflect the drug which is most problematic in your community—alcohol may be the least of your problems.

STEP 4

"Dear Crabby" is a spin-off of the popular advice column "Dear Abbey" —but the writers who write "Dear Crabby" don't want help with the problem; they're writing just to voice their opinions and to be crabby. As such, the challenge is to give advice which has the best chance to get "crabby" teens to respond responsibly. Read the letters below. Students can respond by writing out their advice in the form of a newspaper column or simply stating it verbally to you.
• CRABBY #1: When I go to parties I get drunk off of beer with my friends. But my youth group is always dissin' my drinking. I don't see anything wrong since Jesus turned water to wine. Why should I stop?
• CRABBY #2: I'm no loser if I take a drink so not to offend those givin' it. Yeah, so what if I go to church? The rest of the people at church are just like me. Jesus hung with sinners too. Why should I stop?
• CRABBY #3: I've given up trying to walk focused with God. Some people are cut out for that. But as long as I go to church after a party, it all cancels out. Why should I stop?

STEP 2

Step 2 asks students to discuss what a realistic encounter with drugs might look like at their schools or with their friends. Junior and senior high students, of course, come from different worlds. Use this option to help the two groups learn from one another. First ask for the junior highers to share their answers to the discussion questions in Step 2; write these answers on the left side of a whiteboard. Then ask the senior highers for their answers; write these answers on the right side of a white board. Add these questions: **Based on these answers, what are some of the differences between junior high and senior high? Junior highers, what did you learn about life in high school? Senior highers, what did you learn or remember about life in junior high?**

STEP 3

Modify Step 3 to make the groups more applicable to students (especially young or somewhat sheltered junior highers) who have not been that close to tempting situations involving drugs and alcohol. For Group 1, have students write down a way that God provided a "way out" of any tempting situation—whether or not it specifically dealt with drugs and alcohol. For Group 2, have students write letters that ask for God's power in the area of their lives they need it most—whether or not it specifically has to do with drugs or alcohol.

STEP 3

In addition to or in place of the Bible study in Step 3, assign students to read John 16:33, Acts 14:21-22, Romans 5:3-5, Mark 4:17, Romans 8:35-39, Galatians 6:11-12, Acts 20:22-24, 2 Corinthians 6:3-10, and Colossians 1:24-26. Discuss: **Why do you think early believers went through so much persecution and affliction? Is it reasonable for us to assume that we may face similar situations? Why? How do most Christians today think and feel about suffering and being persecuted for God? How could these verses help remind us, even encourage us, to stand strong for God and say no to drugs and alcohol even if it means being persecuted?** Conclude your study by saying something like: **In North America, most of us want a painless Christianity. We want the best of both worlds: a godly walk and the closeness with worldly friends. That's not always possible and there are times you will have to draw the line. You will have to choose to take your stand, even if that means some friends reject you.**

STEP 5

Read Romans 8:35-39. Ask: **What are you willing to die for?** Don't be surprised if many teens say they would die for God because it's the "right" answer. But don't be afraid to push your students further. **If we say we're willing to die for God, why do we have such a hard time living for Him?** Write the following on a chalkboard or piece of newsprint: He died for me. _____ will live for Him. Challenge students to write their name in the blank as a symbol of commitment in front of their peers.

DATE USED:

Approx. Time

STEP 1: *Quick Fixes*   _____
- ❑ Extra Action
- ❑ Small Group
- ❑ Large Group
- ❑ Mostly Guys:
- ❑ Media
- ❑ Short Meeting Time
Things needed:

STEP 2: *Get Real?*   _____
- ❑ Fellowship & Worship
- ❑ Mostly Girls
- ❑ Urban
- ❑ Combined Junior High/High School
Things needed:

STEP 3: *Three Groups
and a Bible*   _____
- ❑ Large Group
- ❑ Heard It All Before
- ❑ Little Bible Background
- ❑ Mostly Guys
- ❑ Short Meeting Time
- ❑ Combined Junior High/High School
- ❑ Extra Challenge
Things needed:

STEP 4: *www.drug.free*   _____
- ❑ Small Group
- ❑ Heard It All Before
- ❑ Extra Fun
- ❑ Media
- ❑ Urban
Things needed:

STEP 5: *Prayer Cards*   _____
- ❑ Extra Action
- ❑ Little Bible Background
- ❑ Fellowship & Worship
- ❑ Mostly Girls
- ❑ Extra Fun
- ❑ Extra Challenge
Things needed:

Glazed Eyes, Hangovers, and, Uh...Really Great Prayer Times

YOUR GOALS FOR THIS SESSION:
Choose one or more

☐ To help students realize that use of drugs and alcohol hinder their spiritual walks.

☐ To help students understand that a Christian's body is the temple of the Holy Spirit.

☐ To challenge students to take the Drug Free Challenge—a commitment to honor their bodies as temples of the Holy Spirit, in particular by staying off alcohol, cigarettes, and narcotic drugs.

☐ Other: _____
_____

Your Bible Base:

1 Corinthians 6:19-20
Ephesians 1:13-14

Drug Runners

(Needed: blindfolds, obstacles such as tables, chairs, etc.)

Set up your classroom or another room as a simple obstacle course. Break your students into pairs and hand out one blindfold to each team. Give teams two minutes to come up with a team name and decide who will fill the following roles of either the Runner or Director. Explain to your students that their goal is to work together to plan a strategy to make it through the obstacle course. After you give them a couple of minutes to strategize, instruct the Directors to blindfold the Runners. This now leaves only the Director's voice to guide the Runner. But, tell the groups that once the Runner starts on the course, no one is allowed to touch him or her. All directions must be given orally. In addition, if a Runner touches an obstacle on the course, he or she is out and must leave the course. Of course, if several teams are doing the course at the same time, there will be several conflicting voices making it harder for the Runner to do what their Director says!

After a few tries, see how many groups were able to execute their plans to make it through the course successfully. Even if some of the pairs still aren't finished, end the game and bring the group back together. Interview a couple of Runners with questions like the following:

What was the best part of being a Runner?
How did you listen to your Director?
How did things change once you put the blindfold on?
Now interview a couple of Directors.
How did you like being in control?
Was it easy or hard to direct another person?
How were you able to avoid the obstacles?
Conclude by saying: **Obviously, we all face things that hinder us in life. Some things are put in our way. Other things we put in our own way! Drugs and alcohol can be like this. As your pair found out, life may be hard enough without all the obstacles we put in our bodies that hinder us! God's way is better.**

Human Graffiti

(Needed: newsprint or butcher paper, markers, copies of Repro Resource 12)

Prepare a body outline on newsprint before class. Have an adult or teen lay down on a long piece of newsprint or butcher paper and trace his or her outline onto the paper with a marker. Tape this outline to a wall in your room. It should be in a place where all students can see it. Hand out copies of "Drug Info Sheet" (Repro Resource 12). This sheet contains some facts primarily about the physical effects of drugs and alcohol. This is information students have probably heard before in one form or another. It's important, though, that students *interact* with this information. For the "Human Graffiti," students will draw symbols of the physical effects of drugs on a newsprint outline of a human body.

To start the activity, choose volunteers to take turns reading one section at a time from the "Drug Info Sheet." Allow the readers to symbolize the physical effects of the drug or drugs discussed by making marks, words, or "graffiti" of some sort on the newsprint outline. For example, if a student reads that "Marijuana can cause lung damage, impair mental skills, and cause an acute panic or anxiety reaction," the reader might then mark red X's or other graffiti where the lungs, brain, and other affected parts of the body on the figure outline. The more disorderly the markings, the better. Not all the information on Repro Resource 12 translates easily to a specific place to "graffiti," but in such cases you can discuss the psychological and spiritual effects. When you get done reading the "Drug Info Sheet", your newsprint figure should be significantly "vandalized."

Discuss: **How good does the human body look after drugs and alcohol have gotten a hold of it? Do you want your body to look something like this? What is the purpose of our bodies? Are we to drive them hard and fast until we die, or are we to take care of them? Do drugs and alcohol help us do that?**

OPTIONS

EXTRA ACTION

FELLOWSHIP & WORSHIP

MOSTLY GIRLS

MOSTLY GUYS

MEDIA

JR. HIGH / HIGH SCHOOL COMBINED

Who, Me a Temple?

(Needed: Bibles)

Students should have a pretty good reminder in front of them of the physical effects of using drugs and alcohol. Now it's time to talk about the spiritual consequences. Choose students to read 1 Corinthians 6:19-20 (even though these verses come from a passage specifically dealing with sexual sin, the principle can appropriately be applied to drug and alcohol use) and Ephesians 1:13-14.

What does it mean that Christians are "temples of the Holy Spirit"? (God lives inside us in the person of the Holy Spirit.)

Why does God choose to have the Holy Spirit live in us? (He gives us the Holy Spirit to help us in the ways that Jesus helped the disciples when He was with them on earth.)

What does the Holy Spirit do for us? (Guides us into God's truth; gives us power to do God's work on earth; convicts us of sin.)

What does it mean to be a "temple"? (A temple is a dwelling place.)

So what does it mean that our bodies are "temples of the Holy Spirit"? (God's spirit lives in us constantly. We are the dwelling place of the Holy Spirit.)

So let's make the connection. Drugs and alcohol and the temple of the Holy Spirit. What can we learn from the passages we've just read?

Since we are temples of the Holy Spirit, what difference should that make in the way we treat our bodies?

Look at the newsprint poster up here. Imagine for a moment that you are God. Imagine this newsprint poster was the actual body of a Christian—imagine it was the dwelling place of the Holy Spirit that you have sent to help your children. How do you think you might feel about seeing such damage to this body?

The Bible says your body is the Temple of the Holy Spirit. That means when you take drugs into your body, you bring the Holy Spirit along with you. Would you take a six pack into church and drink it during the sermon? Would you snort cocaine during worship? Then why would you put drugs into your body when you know that God values you and your body this much?

Testimonials

You will need to recruit two mature teens or young adults who are willing to talk about their past experiences with drugs and alcohol. Your guest speakers can give their testimonials in one of two formats.

- If your speakers are not experienced talking to teens, they may need some help telling their stories. You would do well to interview your guests. Know their stories ahead of time. Ask questions that will help them, such as: **When did you first start using drugs? How did that affect you physically? How about spiritually? What happened then?** If possible, prepare them with a list of the questions you will ask ahead of time.
- Or, you may choose to get the students involved in a question and answer format. Guests should give their testimony in a "nutshell" form and then field questions from your students. Use this second format only if you're confident that your group will show interest and ask plenty of questions of your guest speakers. Be prepared with questions of your own, just in case.

Regardless of the format you use, look for speakers that get beyond cliches. You want real people talking to real people. This is a great opportunity for students to hear some of the spiritual effects that drugs and alcohol can have on a person. Pray for your speakers and support them as they talk to your students.

The Drug Free Challenge

(Needed: cut-out copies of Repro Resource 13, pens)

OPTIONS

Students who take the Drug Free Challenge make a commitment to abstain from certain drugs and alcohol. Think through how you want to present this challenge. We encourage you to challenge your group to abstain from alcohol, cigarettes/tobacco, and narcotic drugs (like methamphetamines, cocaine, and marijuana). Have students write out their commitments in their own words and include only the specific things they are ready to commit to.

Optional: On Repro Resource 13, we've included both a Drug Free Certificate and a Commitment Card. Use whichever you think will work with your students. To prepare the Certificate, copy it onto heavy, formal-looking stock paper and cut it out. There is one line for students' own signature and three for whichever accountability partners they wish to include—parents, peers, youth leaders, and so on. To prepare the Commitment Card, copy the boxes at the bottom of the resource on heavy or regular paper and cut them out. There is less room for students' own words, but the cards are small enough that students can keep them in their wallets or purses.

To lead your students through their commitments, tell them the commitment you're making. Next, give students a chance to complete their sheets. Make sure no one feels pressured to make a commitment. Before closing, allow volunteers to share what they wrote.

Close your time by praying that God will give your students the power they need to honor their commitments.

Note: Many students may need a trusted adult to talk and walk with through their decisions. They will need an adult's wisdom, support, and encouragement. Be willing and ready to support them in their commitments.

Drug Info Sheet

Marijuana is not a "hard" drug like cocaine. I can't get addicted.

Is this "hard" enough? Consider the facts: marijuana will damage your lungs, impair your brain's ability to think like a normal person, may cause a severe panic or anxiety reaction, and can lead to severe problems with your hormones, especially for teenagers. What's more, marijuana almost never stops with marijuana. It's called a "gateway" drug because it often leads to use of even more dangerous drugs. Thousands of teens in North America ARE addicted to marijuana.

It's my body. If I feel like smoking, I'll smoke. If I want to drink, I'll drink.

If you smoke, you slowly destroy your lungs, your teeth, and your ability to function without nicotine. Over 10 thousand people die of lung cancer related to smoking every year. If you drink excessive amounts, you'll destroy your liver, kill brain cells, and risk becoming an alcoholic.

Smoking cigarettes helps me relax.

Nicotine, the active drug in cigarettes, doesn't help the normal body relax. In fact, it gives healthy bodies a quick rush. But when your body gets used to the rush caused by nicotine, it starts to depend on it. It gets to the point where you can't relax without nicotine.

"I took some pills at a party one time. I think they were amphetamines. It was a pretty cool high. Nothing bad happened to me. I don't see what the big deal is. I'll probably try it again."

If you start messing around with amphetamines or other "uppers," it's not a matter of **if** something bad will to your body but when. Prolonged use can cause headaches, blurred vision, dizziness, sleeplessness, and anxiety. An amphetamine injection creates a sudden increase in blood pressure that can cause death from stroke, very high fever, or heart failure. Over a long period of time, you'll probably suffer from hallucinations and paranoia. Long-term use may also lead to malnutrition, skin disorders, ulcers, and various diseases that come with vitamin deficiencies.

I drink because everybody else does. It's how we "party." It's how we celebrate.

Aren't there better ways to celebrate than by killing brain cells, damaging sexual organs, causing possible hangovers, sacrificing your integrity if you can't be honest with your parents, friends, and others, and risking the possibility that you might get so into "partying" that it will rob your energy for other pursuits?

I know cocaine and crack are dangerous. But that's a risk I'm willing to take. I like the high too much to stop.

Enjoy the high while it lasts because you're heading for some low spots if you don't stop, including: confusion, slurred speech, anxiety, serious psychological problems— like the inability to function in school or hold down a normal job!

I'll never get addicted. I know what I can handle.

Be careful how much you trust yourself. It starts like this: you start liking the high you get from a drug, then you start needing it, then you find that you need something stronger to get a high, then before you know it—before you've ever planned for it to happen—you're fully addicted. It's a physical fact. No one is immune. Every single time you take a hard drug you risk addiction.

It's not a sin to drink if you don't get drunk.

There's a huge difference between asking "Is it a sin?" and "What will honor God?" What are your motives for drinking?

I will honor God with what I put in my body.
I will honor my body because
it is the temple of the Holy Spirit.
I will:

_____   _____

_____   _____

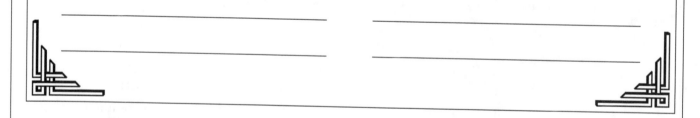

My **body** is God's temple.
I will honor God with what
I put in my body.

_____
Your Signature

1 Corinthians 6:19, 20
I will:

EXTRA ACTION

STEP 2

Put this list of "stimuli" on slips of white paper: back rub, headache, hug, drinking coffee, skydiving. Put this list of responses on slips of colored paper: relaxation, irritability, closeness, sleepiness, arousal, hyperactivity, exhilaration. Give each student one of slip of paper. (Discard what you don't need or duplicate some items on the list if you need more.) Tell students to find their match—the stimulus that produces the response on their card, or vice versa. Answers are somewhat subjective. Congratulate the winners—the two students who connected first. **Can a headache cause relaxation? Can skydiving make you feel sleepy (while you're diving, not after)? Of course not! Certain things you do to your body cause certain emotional and even spiritual responses. What kind of physical responses do drugs cause? But what about spiritual responses? When you take drugs, you take control of your body out of the hands of God and put it in the hands of a substance.**

STEP 5

Use Step 5 as directed. Then tell students to partner up. Have partners sit on the floor back to back. Partners should explain their commitments to each other. Then tell them to: cross their arms in front of their chest and push against each other to stand up. Once they have made it successfully (no using hands; no locking arms) they should remain standing and pray for each other's commitment. Use this activity as a final reminder that when students "take a stand" it is important to "lean on" each other.

SMALL GROUP

STEP 3

With a small group, you have a great opportunity to do location events. Not only are these location options visually effective, they also provide a sense of adventure and an element of excitement for your group. After you do the "human graffiti" project in Step 2, take your students on a walk to your sanctuary or worship center. When you arrive, discuss: **What is the purpose of this worship center? (It's a place to worship God, learn about God and His Word, be with other Christians, etc.) Why do you think so much time is spent keeping our worship center clean? Why do you think people try to behave better some-times when they come here? What would we communicate if we didn't keep this place clean or we didn't act respectfully in it?** Study the Scripture as directed in Step 3 that says our bodies are temples of the Holy Spirit. Help students see why they should take care of and respect their bodies. If possible, stay in the worship center to end your lesson.

STEP 5

In a small group, you can be creative with how you facilitate additional accountability. Use Step 5 as directed. Then have students help you design a large poster— this can be as simple as putting a title like "Taking a Stand," "Taking the Challenge" or "The Drug Free Challenge" on top of a large sheet of posterboard. Encourage students to tape or glue their commit-ment cards to the poster. Remind students that doing this means that many people (other students, pastor, parents) will know they have made this commitment.

LARGE GROUP

STEP 1

Say: **Your challenge is to think up more jingles or slogans from beer or alcohol commercials than the other team can.** Give teams 45 seconds to brainstorm, then start by asking the girls to sing a jingle or yell out a slogan. The guys must respond with a different jingle or slogan. No jingle may be repeated during the game. When one team fails to come up with a new song or slogan in 15 seconds, the other team wins. Use this activity to discuss the prevalence of alcohol in our culture. What does it say about our culture when we can remember so many alcohol ads? What does it say about how lightly our culture views alcohol?

STEP 3

The "Human Graffiti" idea may not get all your students involved. But this idea at least will give them something fun to watch and listen to. Choose one student or adult you know will have a good sense of humor and play along with the "human graffiti" activity—or, if you're really brave, play the following role yourself. When students volunteer to read from the "Drug Info Sheet" (Repro Resource 12), supply them with whip cream, shaving cream, silly string, or something else fun and messy and let them "graffiti" your human volunteer at an appropriate place on his or her body. The discussion questions at the end of Step 3 should take on new meaning after this activity.

STEP 4

Many kids who have grown up in the church feel that a life without drugs, drunkenness, and mayhem somehow disqualifies them from having an effective testimony. Here are two possible ways to deal with this distorted sense of inferiority. Arrange for and include one testimony from someone who has consistently resisted the temptation to become involved in this lifestyle and allow this person to speak from a positive perspective about God's grace and protection and the lack of regret they now enjoy. Another way to make the same point would be to take the role of "devil's advocate" and engage your guests in a dialogue where you talk about how much you wished that you had a story like theirs so that you could share a powerful testimony like the one just given. Your guests will undoubtedly make a strong case for purity which will speak loudly to kids.

STEP 5

Making a "Drug Free Commitment" is measurable and concrete. But remember that drug and alcohol use is often merely a symptom of deeper issues. Be wary of stressing the behavior of saying no to drugs and alcohol in this session—and this series—without addressing some deeper issues. Encourage students to include when they write out their commitments other, less measurable ways to honor God with their bodies and their lives: I will get to know God more deeply, I will make wise choices about friends, and so on. You might be surprised how many of them live with their own struggles on a daily basis.

STEP 3

Be prepared to answer students' questions about the use of wine in the Bible. Group members may point out that Jesus changed water into wine at a party (see John 2:1-11). The Bible condones the use of a *little* wine (1 Tim. 5:23) but doesn't condone drunkenness (Eph. 5:18). Emphasize that the Bible certainly commands us to obey the laws of the land—and your students break the law if they drink.

STEP 4

During the testimonials, one or both of your guests may refer to drug addiction or alcohol abuse as either a sin or a sickness. If substance abuse is a sickness, then it should be taken to a doctor to be cured. If substance abuse is a sin, then it should be taken to the Great Physician. Substance abuse is fundamentally a sin that can rapidly progress into a sickness. In addition to the physical and mental effects already discussed, drug abuse can also have a terrible and unexpected impact on the spirit, including guilt, despair, pain, and suffering.

STEP 2

Sometimes activity can be a great way to encourage fellowship among your students. Divide your group into teams of four or five. You will need one 2' x 2' wooden platform for each team (a sheet of 1/2" plywood stabilized on 2' x 4's works well; if all else fails, this activity will still work with pieces of flat cardboard). Place the platforms in a circle. Each team must squeeze and fit on the platform, then answer the first question together. Then two volunteers must leave and move counterclockwise to the next platform. Teams answer the next question while huddled tightly together, then two students who did not move the first time must rotate for the third question, and so on.

STEP 4

Ask several adults or students to share about their past or present struggles with drug or alcohol use. Ask them to outline their testimony in four parts: what they feel led them to experiment with drugs or alcohol in the first place; how it effected their life; what caused/enabled them to stop; and, what lessons they learned. After each section of the testimony, have the person sharing pause and lead your students in a short time of prayer, focusing on what was just shared.

Step 1

As the girls list various drugs, don't forget that diet drugs are also frequently misused by adolescent girls. Discuss: **Are diet pills drugs? What kind of side effects do they have? Should Christians use diet pills?**

Step 2

Bring in a couple of fashion magazines that your students are reading (*Vogue, Mademoiselle,* and so on.) Have students browse through and pull out pictures and articles that run contrary to the idea of our bodies being the temple of the Holy Spirit. There may be articles on unhealthy diet plans (for example, eat nothing but grapefruit seeds and cheese curds for a month), pictures of ultra-thin models, or advice columns on how to drink and not get sick. Then have them go through the same magazines looking for pictures/articles that run complimentary to the idea that we need to take care of our bodies. Discuss: **Which set of articles/photos is larger? Why is that? Is the trend toward one direction or the other? What are some of the short-term effects of abusing our bodies? What are some of the long-term effects?**

Step 2

Your guys want and need to know that being a temple of the Holy Spirit is more manly than using drugs. Use the directions for Step 2 with these variations. When you make the newsprint outline, make it large, manly, and muscular. Cut the heads of a few muscle men out of muscle magazines and let your guys pick one and glue it to the top of the body outline. (The head will be smaller than the body but that will make it funny.) Before using Repro Resource 13, discuss: **What does it mean to be manly?** Whatever words students come up with, write them on the body outline. **Why do some people think it's "manly" to use drugs?** When you use Repro Resource 13, ask students if destroying your body has anything to do with being courageous, strong, powerful, or anything else they used to describe manliness. Encourage them by helping them see that when they take care of and build their bodies they honor and glorify God.

Step 4

There are a number of things you can do to make the testimonies "guy friendly." First, choose male speakers. Also, prepare your speakers to talk about their experiences with wanting to fit in with other guys, needing to look cool and tough, the way that guys often enjoy and even crave physical "highs," and so on. In addition to the discussion questions listed in Step 4, ask your speakers: **Was taking drugs a way to impress your friends? Why do guys want so badly to impress other guys? What would you say to someone today who thinks using drugs or alcohol is part of "being a man?"**

Step 1

Drugs are fake fun. They give fake solutions, fake confidence, fake emotions, and fake wisdom. No one is really more fun, braver, cuter, or more brilliant because of drugs. Just the opposite is true. Drugs stunt the real growth and fun of a person. So to emphasize the point that Christians walking in the Holy Spirit have more fun than people who anesthetize their minds, how about blowing out of the classroom and having some real fun (or staying in the class and throwing a party). Go play a game in a park, chow down on ice cream, have a joke-telling session (come prepared with some great jokes). Do something you know your students will enjoy. When you are done, point out that the end result of drugs is the *dulling* of fun, diminishing of imagination, and dampening of personality.

Step 3

Put limburger cheese in a plastic, sealable bag. Seal it and bring it to class out of sight. When you begin to discuss the idea that Christians bodies should be treated with respect as temples where God dwells, quietly drag out the cheese and undo the seal on the bag. The aroma will no doubt have an instant effect. Say things like: "Hey, I don't mind . . . It's not hurting anyone . . . I don't do this very often . . ." and other things teens say to justify why they bring stuff that stinks (such as drugs) into God's temple (their bodies.).

STEP 2

Introduce the discussion by showing a number of clips of drug use. Ahead of time, prepare a two–five minute video including clips from TV shows and movies, and still-life shots from magazines of people discussing and using drugs.

STEP 4

A testimony on video can either compliment or replace your "live" testimonies. Two ideas: 1) Go to a drug rehab center and ask for permission to interview a recovering teenager. For added effect, include clips of the hospital entrance, walls, and waiting room. 2) Interview students' parents talking honestly about their stories of drug and alcohol use.

STEP 1

Begin brainstorming a list of all the kinds of drugs students can think of. Write a list on the a piece of newsprint. Use the discussion questions at the end of Step 1. Or, remember that if you're really pressed for time you can skip Step 1. If your group is conditioned to dive right into the meeting, you can usually start the session with Step 2 and not miss out on much "meat."

STEP 4

Prepare your speakers to give their testimonies in one minute or less. This way they can hit the high points and be available for questions afterward. If you don't have time to find speakers, give your own testimony, whether you used drugs in the past or didn't.

STEP 5

Briefly explain how students may use Repro Resource 13, then send it home with them. This will give them a chance to think about their commitments. Give students a chance to share next week.

STEP 1

Marijuana, particularly amongst the Rasta, hip hop, and punk youth cultures, is not considered a drug, but just a "stronger cigarette." Discuss: **Is marijuana a drug? Why or why not?** Since many church teens will give the answer they believe you want, split them into two groups and ask that each group create a defense as to "why" or "why it is not" a real (or hard) drug. Let the debate begin. After, to show the acceptance of marijuana in our culture as a friendly not harmful drug, ask them to list every nickname they can think of, for example: MJ, Bo, Mary Jane, Buddha, Indo, Budd, Refa, Blunt, and Weed.

STEP 3

A number of Pentecostal and Holiness churches use the phrase "Get high in the Spirit." Use Step 3 as written, then teach students that there are two kinds of getting high in the spiritual universe. 1) The Greek word "pharmakia" is sometimes translated as "witchcraft" and often refers to a destructive pseudo-spiritual high generated by Satan via physical drug use and abuse (Gal. 5:20; Deut. 18:10-12, 1 Sam. 15:23, Exod. 22:18). 2) The Greek word "paraclete" on the other hand is translated "Holy Spirit" which refers to a constructive spiritual high which gives comfort and power in a personal relationship with Jesus Christ (Acts 2:1-21; John 14:16,26; 15:26; 16:7). Teach students that the first-century church saw drug involvement as witchcraft which comes from the Greek root we use as pharmacy or pharmacist. To conclude, ask students to compare and discuss how inadequate a witchcraft high is compared to the Holy Spirit high, like the one received in the second chapter of Acts.

STEP 2

Read each of the following four statements one at a time: **All drugs should always be avoided; Alcohol is a drug; Tobacco is a drug; Drugs will never mess me up—I can handle it.** After each statement, ask your students to stand at the left side of your room if they agree with the statement or the right side of the room if they disagree. Ask some students to explain why they stood where they did.

STEP 4

Instead of interviewing the guest speakers yourself, ask students themselves to get up close and personal with the guests. This will both help students get more actively involved with the testimonies and help avoid either silence or potentially random questions from junior highers. Choose two students (one senior higher and one junior higher) ahead of time and ask them to come to your meeting 30 minutes early so they can meet with you and the two people giving the testimonials. Pair up one student with each guest speaker. Explain that the student will be interviewing the guest speaker. Help the student develop three–four questions that the student can ask during Step 4. Make sure that the students and guest speakers are clear on the questions before you begin the session.

STEP 3

Use Step 3 as directed. Then break into three groups and assign each one of the following passages: Judges 16; 2 Samuel 11; Acts 8:9-23; Acts 4:32—5:11. Instruct groups to report back to class on these questions: **What "one little hit" was your character(s) tempted to take? How did he (they) give in to the temptation? What was the result?** After the presentations, conclude by saying: **Temptation to do drugs is just another tool the enemy uses in his attempt to turn our hearts and minds away from Christ.**

STEP 4

If possible, make arrangements for your group to drive over to a local halfway house at the end of Step 3. Most halfway houses will allow visitors to come in and listen during group or Bible study time. Your students will see and hear first-hand the destructive end results that start with "just one little hit." If you can't go during the meeting, you might set up an alternate time. Once there, you may want to volunteer your time to help paint or complete some other project.

STEP 5

Consider these options as ways to honor your students' Drug Free Commitments.
• Hold a dinner banquet that honors students' commitments. Invite parents and friends. Let students take turns briefly explaining why they made commitments.
• Have your senior pastor sign the commitment sheets and/or recognize students at a Sunday morning service.
• Feature students in a church or youth group newsletter.

DATE USED:

Approx. Time

STEP 1: *Drug Runners* _____
❑ Large Group
❑ Mostly Girls
❑ Extra Fun
❑ Short Meeting Time
❑ Urban
Things needed:

STEP 2: *Human Graffiti* _____
❑ Extra Action
❑ Fellowship & Worship
❑ Mostly Girls
❑ Mostly Guys
❑ Media
❑ Combined Junior High/High School
Things needed:

STEP 3: *Who, Me a Temple?* _____
❑ Small Group
❑ Large Group
❑ Little Bible Background
❑ Extra Fun
❑ Urban
❑ Extra Challenge
Things needed:

STEP 4: *Testimonials* _____
❑ Heard It All Before
❑ Little Bible Background
❑ Fellowship & Worship
❑ Mostly Guys
❑ Media
❑ Short Meeting Time
❑ Combined Junior High/High School
❑ Extra Challenge
Things needed:

STEP 5: *The Drug Free Challenge* _____
❑ Extra Action
❑ Small Group
❑ Heard It All Before
❑ Short Meeting Time
❑ Extra Challenge
Things needed:

SESSION 5

Throwing the Life Preserver

YOUR GOALS FOR THIS SESSION:

Choose one or more

☐ To help students realize that they might be God's best tool to help their friends who struggle with drugs and alcohol.

☐ To help students understand basic intervention principles from the ministry of Jesus that will make a difference in the lives of their friends who struggle with drugs and alcohol.

☐ To provide students with practical strategies for helping their friends who abuse drugs and alcohol.

☐ Other:_____

Your Bible Base:

John 4:1-26, 39

STEP 1

Would You Rather . . .

(Needed: tape)

Place a long piece of tape down the middle of your room.

In today's youth culture, it's hard enough for teens to tell a friend his or her shoe is untied, much less confront a friend about drug and alcohol use. Relativity and tolerance are the highest values of the culture.

Explain to students that you will read two choices. They should decide which they'd rather do, then move to the appropriate side of the room. Read the choices below, one at a time. When you read the first of two choices, point to the left side of your room. When you read the second, point to the right side.

Would you rather tell your friend . . .
- **"Your clothes don't match" or, "You didn't make the team"?**
- **"You made me angry" or, "You made a mistake"?**
- **"You have a drug problem" or, "I have a problem with the way you talk to me"?**
- **"You didn't make the school play" or, "You've got toilet paper stuck to your shoe"?**
- **"Your crush asked someone else to homecoming" or, "What you said this morning made me mad"?**
- **"You drank too much last Friday and made a fool of yourself" or, "I'm really concerned about you. I think you need to get some help with your drinking"?**
- **"You're spending way too much time at the mall" or, "I've heard a rumor that you're doing drugs. Is it true?"**

Discuss: **Is confronting your friends hard or easy?**
Why is confrontation so hard?
What's the hardest thing to confront your friends on?

Advice Sharing

(Needed: index cards)

Make four or more sets of question cards by writing the questions listed below each on its own index card. Make sure to number each card. Divide into four or more groups (optimal size: three to six students). Give each group a second set of index cards numbered one through nine. Have students take turns choosing a numbered index card and then answering the question card with the corresponding number (for example, if they choose a "6," they answer Question Card #6).

Questions:

1. On a scale of 1 to 10, how hard is it to stay drug free?

2. Share about a friend or someone you know who has struggled with drug or alcohol use in the past. (No names please.)

3. Do you ever fear that you might become drug dependent or an alcoholic? Why or why not?

4. What percentage of people who start trying drugs do you think get addicted to drugs? Why do you think some people are able to use drugs for a long period of time and not get addicted while others get addicted right away?

5. Do you believe relying on God alone can be enough to resist the temptation to experiment with drugs and alcohol?

6. Do you think people who are addicted to drugs and alcohol can just stop if they put their minds to it? Why or why not? If not, what do they have to do to overcome their problem?

7. On a scale of 1 to 10, how hard do you think it is to stop using drugs or alcohol once you start using them? Why?

8. Share about a time you confronted someone you knew who had a drug or alcohol problem. If you have never confronted a person with a drug or alcohol problem, tell why not.

9. Flash forward five years into the future. You never thought it would happen to you, but you find yourself with a serious drug problem. You know you're out of control but you feel like you can't tell anyone. Would you want your friends to confront you or leave you alone? Why? How would you want your friends to confront you?

OPTIONS

EXTRA ACTION

FELLOWSHIP & WORSHIP

EXTRA FUN

MEDIA

SHORT MEETING TIME

URBAN

What Would Jesus Do?

(Needed: copies of Repro Resource 14, Bibles, pencils, chalkboard or whiteboard)

O P T I O N S

SMALL GROUP

LARGE GROUP

HEARD IT ALL BEFORE

LITTLE BIBLE BACKGROUND

MEDIA

SHORT MEETING TIME

URBAN

JR.HIGH HIGH SCHOOL COMBINED

EXTRA CHALLENGE

Pass out copies of "Insight Cards" (Repro Resource 14) and pencils. Break into three small groups. Write these questions on the board: **What was Jesus' attitude toward her? How did He approach her? How did Jesus confront her? How did He follow up the challenge?** In small groups, students should read John 4:1-26, then write down on their "insight cards" any insights they learn from Jesus about how to help others with their problems. Wherever possible, students should try to produce insights that answer the questions above. When you come back together to discuss each group's answers, be prepared with the following insights of your own. Intersperse these into the conversation as needed.

What attitude did Jesus take toward her? (verses 7-9) Jesus accepted her for who she was and treated her with dignity and respect. Most Jewish men considered themselves above both Samaritans (who were half-Jews) and women. But Jesus saw past the Samaritan woman's labels and treated her the way she deserved to be treated.

How did He approach her? (verse 10) He initiated contact. He put Himself out there and was willing to get involved personally.

How did Jesus confront her? (verses 16-19) He waited until she was asking questions of Him. He didn't water down the truth. He spoke clearly and boldly. He challenged her to think differently.

How did He follow up the challenge? (verses 25-26) He helped her get past her problem and helped her experience a relationship with God. Even though this is just one conversation, Jesus gives us a clear example of how we can and should confront people.

In closing, discuss: **How can these insights from Jesus' example help you help your friends with drug and alcohol problems?**

STEP 4

What Not To Do

(Needed: cassette tape, tape player, copies of Repro Resource 15, paper, pencils)

Ahead of time, recruit students to read the scenarios on "To Do Or Not To Do?" (Resource Resource 15) onto cassette tape. (If you can't find a tape recorder, you can always just role play the scenarios "live.")

Tell students to pair off. Pass out paper and pencils. You might introduce this activity by saying something like: **You are going to hear three scenarios played on tape that reveal what not to do in terms of helping your friends who have drug and alcohol problems.** Play the scenarios from the tape. Have pairs respond to these two questions on their paper: **First, what did the confronter do wrong? Secondly, how would you do it differently to do it right?** Discuss students' answers to each situation one at a time.

OPTIONS

SMALL GROUP

LARGE GROUP

FELLOWSHIP & WORSHIP

MOSTLY GUYS

SHORT MEETING TIME

STEP
5

A Friend In Need . . .

Challenge each student to pray for one friend who's struggling with drug abuse. You might say something like: **Close your eyes and think of a friend you may have who is struggling with drug or alcohol abuse. I believe God will bring someone to your mind. Pray for your friend right now. Ask God to help them.** Leave about a minute of silence, but then take your challenge to students one step further. Challenge them to commit to God to put a confronting strategy into action. While students' heads are still bowed, you might say something like: **Are you willing to confront your friend? You may be God's best tool to help them. If you're willing to confront them, make a commitment that's just between you and God. Pray that God will give you wisdom and the right words to say. Pray that your friend will get some help.** Leave a few more minutes for silent prayer, then dismiss.

OPTIONS

EXTRA
ACTION

HEARD IT ALL
BEFORE

MOSTLY
GIRLS

MOSTLY
GUYS

EXTRA
FUN

JR. HIGH
HIGH
SCHOOL
COMBINED

EXTRA
CHALLENGE

NOTES

Insight Cards

When I read about how
Jesus confronted someone
in trouble, I think:

When I read about how
Jesus confronted someone
in trouble, I think:

When I read about how
Jesus confronted someone
in trouble, I think:

When I read about how
Jesus confronted someone
in trouble, I think:

When I read about how
Jesus confronted someone
in trouble, I think:

When I read about how
Jesus confronted someone
in trouble, I think:

NOTES

To Do Or Not To Do?

Scenario #1

Don't reject the person, reject the practice.

FRIEND: You know you have a pretty bad drug problem, Bill.

BILL: Yeah, I know, I know.

FRIEND: You're hanging around a bunch of losers lately.

BILL: Hey! Maybe they have problems you just don't understand.

FRIEND: All I understand is that you're going to be a loser too, Bill.

BILL: Who made you judge and jury of my life? I thought you were supposed to be my friend.

FRIEND: Not anymore, Bill. I am a Christian, and Christians don't hang around losers!

Scenario #2

Don't be afraid to confront directly and assertively; you might be saving a friend's life (or, "Don't beat around the bush").

FRIEND: Hey Steve, what are you going to do tonight?

STEVE: Party and get drunk like I do every Saturday night. What else?

FRIEND: You don't want to do that!

STEVE: Why not?

FRIEND: It's just not good for you, that's all.

STEVE: Well neither are all those french fries you eat but I don't see you stopping that.

FRIEND: Oh, uhm, well, maybe next weekend you could come with me to a movie instead of a party.

STEVE: Well maybe, but I think there's a party that might be funner.

FRIEND: Uh . . . I don't think "funner" is a word.

STEVE: Hey why don't you come with me? It might loosen you up! You Christians are so uptight!

FRIEND: Well I don't think so. But try not to get drunk tonight, o.k.? Maybe next week we can do something together, okay?

STEVE: Sure. Maybe.

Scenario #3

Have practical advice for your friends when you talk to them about their drug/alcohol problem.

FRIEND: Sue, I'm your friend and I'm really concerned about the drugs you've been doing. You've changed.

SUE: I know, you may be right, but I just can't seem to stop.

FRIEND: But you have to stop. Just don't do it anymore.

SUE: But you don't know how hard it is.

FRIEND: Maybe I don't, but you just have to!

SUE: How? I've tried. It never works.

FRIEND: I don't know . . . maybe you should talk to someone.

SUE: Like who?

FRIEND: How should I know? What about your parents?

SUE: Yeah, right!

FRIEND: Well, I don't know. There must be someone or something you can do to get help. Just pray to God.

SUE: I do pray, but it doesn't seem to help. I wish I knew what to do.

FRIEND: So do I.

Mike and Ryan

❶

Michael and Ryan had grown up together. Preschool, elementary school, Boy Scouts, youth group.

They even went with each other on family vacations. And although their friendship had experienced ups and downs over the years, even as high school juniors they were still each other's best friends. Or, at least that's what they said.

But the truth was, ever since Michael made varsity football this year, he had begun to hang out more and more with the guys on the team. Michael was getting into a world that Ryan didn't want any part of: the party scene. It began with a party at the end of "hell week" last summer. Michael went and got drunk for the first time. Although he later repented at a youth group next weekend and decided to not do it again, little by little he was sucked back in. It began first with beer, then harder liquor, and then marijuana.

❷

For a long time, Ryan tried to talk to Michael about his partying. It was awkward for Ryan, especially because he was feeling abandoned by Michael and his new group of friends. But Ryan knew confronting his friend was the right thing to do.

"I know drinking isn't right," said Michael when Ryan first confronted him. But Michael continued to drink anyway. He justified his actions: "It's not like I'm an alcoholic," he said. "I've just always been such a straight kid. I'm just playing around a little. It's just for fun. Don't worry. I promise I'll stop as soon as football is over, OK?"

"Hey," Michael added as Ryan was walking out the door, "Thanks for checking up on me."

That last comment frustrated Ryan more than anything. He felt like Michael was patronizing him. What Ryan didn't realize was that Michael would remember Ryan's words. And just in time.

❸

Michael's team won the league championship that fall. Of course, the team held a huge party to celebrate. By 2 A.M., Michael was completely fried. He was wasted and half asleep. Michael's friend Brian offered to give Michael a ride home. "No, I'd better not go home like this," Michael said. Then he added, "See ya later."

But Michael never did see Brian later. Brian's car ran off the road. He was killed when his car hit the highway divider. He should have never been driving in his condition. Too much alcohol.

Michael was still hung over when he got the news that Brian was dead. Michael didn't even go home. He went straight to Ryan's. Ryan held his friend while Michael broke down and wept. He was broken thinking about Brian. He was broken thinking about his own life. How close he was to getting killed, also. How close he was to wasting his own life if he didn't do something about his problem. It was Ryan's words of confrontation that came back to him now. What he once patronized he now respected. Ryan had been the only one who cared enough to say something.

❹

Later that day, Ryan was right by Michael's side when he told his parents and their youth leader about his partying. He knew that Ryan didn't approve of his partying but he never doubted Ryan's commitment to him as a person. It was that support and accountability that gave Michael the strength to walk back to God.

STEP 2

Stand in a circle. Start by naming a "sticky situation"—one that requires students to decide whether or not to confront someone. Toss the ball to anyone in the circle. The student that catches the ball must share a response then toss the ball to a new person. Continue until every person gets an opportunity to answer. Examples of "sticky situations": your friend is struggling with drug abuse; your sister overslept her alarm and is about to be late; a senior at school is picking on a freshman.

STEP 5

This activity will work any time you want to encourage your students. Use it here to encourage students in their commitments to confront and help peers struggling with drug or alcohol abuse. As directed in Step 5, have students choose a person to pray for and decide on a way they might confront that person. Divide your group into two groups and form straight lines with each group facing the other. Have students in the first group reach out and grab the hands of the students across from them in the second group. Give any student who wants the opportunity to stand in front of the two lines and, detail his or her confrontation strategy (for example, he or she might say something like, "I will confront John at school by . . . "), and ask for accountability from the group. The student should then walk, jog, or run between the two lines. Students in the lines raise their arms just before the jogging student reaches them and lower their arms as soon as the jogging student has passed. Encourage all students to shout encouragement loudly as the student goes by.

STEP 3

Discuss one or more of these warm-up questions that will help you build deeper community with your group and prepare them to hear the Bible Story: **Name a time when a friend confronted you. What happened? How did you respond? Then what? Name a time when you had to confront someone else. What happened? How did he or she respond? Then what? Name a time when you should have confronted a friend but didn't. What happened? Why do you wish you would have confronted your friend?** Use the Bible study and discussion questions as found in Step 3. Before moving on, return to the discussions you started at the beginning of this step and ask students: **How do you think Jesus would have responded to the situations we discussed earlier?**

STEP 4

Set up a roleplay scenario where students will confront their best friend who is struggling with drug abuse. First, assign the role of the drug-abusing friend. Then give three students index cards on which you've written three different attitudes: "Angry and judgmental," "Overly understanding and sympathetic but not really confronting," and "Confronting with love but direct." Students who have the cards should take turns roleplaying a scene of confrontation while acting out the attitude their card describes. Keep this activity flowing rapidly but smoothly by stopping one roleplay before it gets old and starting a new one right after. Ask: **Which attitude of confrontation was most like Jesus' attitude when He confronted the woman at the well?**

STEP 3

For a more controlled and focused time of study, have students get in groups of three. If possible, match an upperclassman with two underclassmen. Give groups five to six minutes to list as many things as they can think of that Jesus did to help the Samaritan Woman, then give them another three to four minutes to share their answers with one other small group. If time allows, expand on the students' answers to emphasize the key points as directed in Step 3 in the main lesson. Then discuss: **How can these insights from Jesus' example help you confront your friends who struggle with drug and alcohol problems?**

STEP 4

This variation will help you engage more students by giving them a writing activity to do while listening to the scenarios. Pass out index cards. When students listen to the taped scenarios from Repro Resource 15 as directed in the main lesson, encourage them to write down a short note to the fictional character who was the confronter in the scenario. After each scenario, have students turn in the cards and read a handful of the responses.

HEARD IT ALL BEFORE

LITTLE BIBLE BACKGROUND

FELLOWSHIP & WORSHIP

STEP 3

The lesson behind Jesus' encounter with the Samaritan woman is a universal one. It is as relevant today as it was in Bible times. Before you go into the discussion questions listed in Step 3, move your students into groups of two or three and have them rewrite the story in a modern setting. Encourage them to follow the story line from the Bible but to change details to place the encounter in your town or in a nearby city last week. Instruct each group to read its story to one other small group, then choose one or two to be read out loud to everyone.

STEP 5

Some church kids (especially those who are home schooled or attend a Christian school) may genuinely not have any friends or acquaintances with a drug or alcohol problem. If an organization in your community deals with families or individuals who struggle in this area, involve your students in a service project which will allow them to get to know some of the young people involved. Those kids can then become the focus of your students' prayers. If an off-site visit is impractical, ask the organization for names of adolescents that the kids in your group could write to and encourage. Coach your students not to be condescending or "preachy." If local agencies are hesitant to provide names, have your students write generic letters of encouragement and send them to a juvenile hall or prison to be posted for those who are struggling alone.

STEP 1

Instead of playing "Would You Rather," play "Who Would You Rather Hang With." Ask questions like: **Would you rather hang out with the President of the United States or Tom Cruise?** Students stand on the left wall to vote for the first choice and on the right wall to vote for the second. Continue the game comparing names of people your students are familiar with. Also compare homeless people with rich people, people of low repute with people of high repute, and so on. At the end of the game, switch gears and ask a true/false question: **Did Jesus hang out with people who drank too much?** The answer is almost certainly yes—Jesus hung out with prostitutes, the outcasts, and all sorts of people labeled "sinners" (for example, Matt. 9:10-13). Why? Because He loved them and He came to help them. Today Christians carry God's love to the lost. While it is in no way proper to join in the sins of sinners, it is also improper to hide the light of the Gospel from those who need it.

STEP 3

Point out several steps the woman made in her understanding of who Jesus was. First, she recognized the He was a Jew (see John 4:9). This might be the same as a student's drug abusing friend saying, "You are a Christian." In verse 19, she came to see Jesus as a prophet. The student's friend might say, "You might be worth listening to." The woman eventually recognized Jesus as the Messiah (see verse 29). The student's friend might find the Savior just as the woman did. Encourage group members to see substance abuse as one indication that a person needs to be told about the love of God and the way to find peace in Jesus.

STEP 2.

Ask students to get into groups of three or four. Say: **Today we're going to talk about judging others. The person whose birthday is closest to today will go first. Share a time when you were judged or confronted (fairly or unfairly), or a time when you judged or confronted someone.** Tell students to relate their sharing to drugs and alcohol if possible. Encourage students to share as honestly.

STEP 4

Lead students in a guided meditation using John 21:15-17. Turn the lights down. Say: **Put yourself in the story. Imagine where Jesus and Peter are standing, what the scene looks like, smells like. How are Jesus and Peter feeling? Is anyone watching? What is the mood?** Read the story a second time and say: **Now pretend you are Peter in the story. How do you feel? Why are you responding the way you are?** Read the story a third time and say: **Now think about what it would be like to be Jesus. What kinds of things would be on your heart? What do you think of the way Jesus is expressing Himself?** When you've finished reading the passage through three times, challenge students to take a few minutes praying for a friend they feel they need to confront. Ask them to pray for opportunity, courage, and Christian love.

MOSTLY GIRLS

MOSTLY GUYS

EXTRA FUN

STEP 1

It's important to get a list of local material/resources available to teenagers to deal with the topic of how best to say no to drugs and alcohol. Youth Service Bureaus and Community Service Agencies are great resources. This kind of information is particularly helpful when you discuss drugs and alcohol with girls because many girls struggle with self-esteem issues. Information you gather can help you teach your girls how to stand up for themselves.

STEP 5

If you made PRAY bracelets in Step 4 at the end of Session 2, you can close this series by giving girls two new beads to add to their bracelets. Bring in beads of many colors. Girls should pick one color bead to remind them of their own commitment to be drug free, then pick a second color to remind them to pray for any friends they know who struggle with drug or alcohol abuse. If you didn't make PRAY bracelets in Session 2, you can have girls make bracelets now having them string beads through thin pieces of leather.

STEP 4

Because of the "coolness factor," many guys become silent about their friends' drinking or drug problems Add this scenario to those listed on Repro Resource 15:

Kevin: Tonight's the night. My mom and dad are outta town. It's party time!

Rob:　Oh . . . What are you going to do?

Kevin: We got a couple of college guys to buy a keg for us. We're going to get trashed.

Rob:　Yeah . . . I guess I'm just going to go over to Jen's house and watch a movie.

Kevin: Hey dude . . . Why don't you come over? It'll be totally cool. You never know, you may even get a buzz!

Rob:　No, we're supposed to watch some movie. You know, crying, love, sensitivity, and all that.

Kevin: Whatever. All I know is I'm going to party tonight!

Rob:　Yeah. OK. See ya Monday.

STEP 5

Have students get with one or two other guys they know pretty well. Have the teams huddle together and think of two guys who struggle with drugs and alcohol. If possible, teams should try to think of guys whom all team members know. Challenge teams to come up with a strategy to confront in love the two guys they prayed for. Help teams set specific, measurable goals; for example: Two weeks from now I will have let Mark know that I care about him and I don't want to see him destroy his life on drugs. Finally, have the teams commit to praying for their guys once every day alone and once every other day (on the phone if they have to) as a team.

STEP 2

Start a roleplay by assigning one student to play the role of Teen 1: he is struggling with the fact that he likes the buzz he gets from alcohol; he is wondering if he wouldn't get a better buzz from trying a harder drug. Next assign the role of Teen 2, a long-time friend of Teen 1. Teen 2 is active in her youth ministry, committed to God, and sometimes labeled a "goodie-goodie." Give the first pair a few minutes to get the discussion going, then assign Teen 1 to a new student—instead of starting the roleplay over, have him jump right in and take over. Encourage the new student to take the conversation in a slightly new direction as he deems appropriate. After a few more minutes, replace Teen 2 as well. Continue to substitute like this as time permits. What you end up with is a roleplay that allows almost all the teens to participate and voice what they would do in a particular situation. Discuss: **What do you wish had been said but wasn't? What would you say differently next time? How hard is it to talk about God and His role in a struggle with drugs and alcohol? As "Teen 2" was it hard not to be "preachy"? What did you learn about how to (and how not to) talk to friends about drugs and alcohol?**

STEP 5

Close your series on drugs and alcohol by taking a few minutes to plan a special night of fun when you can honor and celebrate students' "drug free" commitments. You might throw a party or take your students to a special dinner at the end of the school year. Students will be motivated by having something fun to which they can look forward.

MEDIA

SHORT MEETING TIME

URBAN

STEP 2

The Repro Resource 16, "Mike and Ryan," is a story that can be read in four parts. You can break after each part to discuss what the characters should do next and what the difference is between confronting in love and confronting with judging. Add a visual component to this story by getting two talented actors to act it out on video for you ahead of time. Pause the video after each section of the story and discuss: **Should Ryan confront Michael? Why or why not? How should he confront Michael? Is Ryan judging Michael if he confronts him? Why or why not? How can Ryan confront Michael without judging him?**

STEP 3

To engage teens in the Bible study, have groups of four to six students read and act out John 4:1-26 without using words. Actors will have to think of creative hand signs and other ways to communicate the events of the story. Film these "silent movies." When you play them back, ask students to fill out the "Insight Cards" as directed in Step 3. Continue with the discussion as directed in the main lesson.

STEP 2

The Repro Resource 16, "Mike and Ryan" is a story that can be read in four parts. You can break after each part to discuss what the characters should do next and what the difference is between confronting in love and confronting with judging. Pause the reading of the story after each section and discuss: **Should Ryan confront Michael? Why or why not? How should he confront Michael? Is Ryan judging Michael if he confronts him? Why or why not? How can Ryan confront Michael without judging him?**

STEP 3

If you don't have time to discuss what students wrote on their "Insight Cards" in depth, have students to turn to one or two other people next to them and share their insights. But be sure to review for the students the specific insights outlined in the main text.

STEP 4

If you don't have time to discuss all the roleplay situations listed on Resource 15, tape and discuss only the first scenario. Follow the rest of the directions in Step 4, but add this question: **What are some other examples of things you should *not* do when you confront others?**

STEP 2

Many city teens often feel like God overlooks their problems. They feel hopeless. To help teens see God hasn't given up on them, be as practical as you can about how God communicates to Christians. If your students will relate to the analogy, explain that making Jesus Lord is like owning a top-rated computer with the fastest baud speed—God is always sending us "e-mail" from His Spirit to us. The Spirit e-mail we get is usually in one of these "E" categories:
1) Endorsing Spirit E-mail —Asks the believer to do something; called a prompting.
2) Encouraging Spirit E-mail —Empowers the believer to continue growing in an area desired.
3) Enforcing Spirit E-mail—Convicts the believer he or she should *not* do something.
4) Encrypted Spirit E-mail—A private message concerning God's will and plan for the believer's life.
5) Emergency Spirit-E-mail —Asks for the believer's practical and immediate action or reaction to a situation at hand.
Discuss: **Do you know any friends with a drug or alcohol problem? Is God sending you any "e-mails" about that? What is He saying?**

STEP 3

In addition to or instead of reading the story of the woman at the well, study the story of the ten lepers (Luke 17:12-21). Analyze the passage with the same questions given in the main lesson concerning how Jesus treated the woman at the well. City teens can relate to the rejection associated with leprosy. They will learn that even though they are sometimes treated like "lepers" by society, Jesus doesn't look down on them.

STEP 3.

This idea is a little more active and will help engage students in the Bible study. Ask for three volunteers to read John 4:1-26—one student should read the part of the narrator, another all the lines Jesus has to say, and a third all the woman's lines. After reading up to verse 15, "press the pause button." Discuss: **We'll soon find out the woman had some "secret sins." What would Jesus say to the woman if He wanted to both judge her and confront her? What would Jesus say to the woman if He wanted to confront her with love and not judgement?** Have the three volunteers continue reading John 4:16-26 according to their parts. You can then either complete Resource 14 in small groups or prepare two students to give two-minute summaries of their "insights"—but have them present the information in a casual and conversational manner.

STEP 5

To make the concluding step more concrete, ask students to tangibly offer a friend to God. After students pray for their friends as directed in the main lesson, ask them to write their friend's first initial on an index card. Have them fold the index card in half so that no one else can see the letter that they have written. Pass around offering baskets and ask students to place their index cards in the baskets as an offering to God and a symbol of their commitment to pray, confront, and love the person represented by the index card. Make it clear that no one will ever see the index cards, and that you personally will throw them in the trash after the session ends.

STEP 3

In addition to or instead of the Bible study in Step 3 in the main lesson, read Philippians 2:1-11. Based on these verses make a "To Do" list and a "To Don't" list that can work as guidelines for godly confrontation. For example, list "Have a servant's heart" on the "do" side and "Be condescending" on the "don't" side. Tell students to bow their heads and reflect on the following questions as you read them slowly:

STEP 5

Make "Inward Decision Journals" by folding card stock paper in half down the middle. On top of the left-hand side write "Other" and on top of the right-hand side write "Self." Challenge students to record times they remember to make others-centered decisions in the coming week and write a brief description down in the appropriate column. Most will discover that when they think about being others-centered they tend to put it into practice more as well.

DATE USED:

Approx. Time

STEP 1: *Would You Rather . . .* _____
❑ Little Bible Background
❑ Mostly Girls
Things needed:

STEP 2: *Advice Sharing* _____
❑ Extra Action
❑ Fellowship & Worship
❑ Extra Fun
❑ Media
❑ Short Meeting Time
❑ Urban
Things needed:

STEP 3: *What Would Jesus Do?* _____
❑ Small Group
❑ Large Group
❑ Heard It All Before
❑ Little Bible Background
❑ Media
❑ Short Time
❑ Urban
❑ Combined Junior High/High School
❑ Extra Challenge
Things needed:

STEP 4: *What Not To Do* _____
❑ Small Group
❑ Large Group
❑ Fellowship & Worship
❑ Mostly Guys
❑ Short Meeting Time
Things needed:

STEP 5: *A Friend In Need . . .* _____
❑ Extra Action
❑ Heard It All Before
❑ Mostly Girls
❑ Mostly Guys
❑ Extra Fun
❑ Combined Junior High/High School
❑ Extra Challenge
Things needed:

Unit Three: The Whole Story

Why Kids Are So Easily Fooled

by Duffy Robbins

I was only an eighth grader, so when my friend's mother started sobbing in front of me, I was embarrassed, scared, and confused. We had just returned to my friend's house from the mall, where we had been to a little gift and novelty shop. My friend had found what he thought would be the perfect Mother's Day gift. His mom was really into "country stuff," and this little box of rustic soaps had "country chic" written all over it. Using the cute name, "Road Apples," on the box just made it all the better.

It wasn't until my friend's dad got home later that night that we realized our mistake. It turned out that this novelty gift was more novelty than gift. And what my friend had so proudly presented to his mom that afternoon was an elegantly packaged box of cow dung. I guess that's why she started crying when he handed it to her with the words, "Mom, here's a little token of my affection...."

Today's teenager is growing up in a world that can be very confusing. Hardly a day goes by without someone making what sounds like a very special offer—something novel, nicely packaged, presented with a smile. It's hard to tell sometimes what you've actually been given.

As people who care about teenagers, an important part of our task is helping them to learn discernment. Some of the garbage out there can look pretty elegant. One man's soap is another man's cow dung. Woe to the person who rubs it in without checking it out!

Giving Kids the Whole Story

As a Sunday school teacher, Bible study leader, or maybe simply a Christian adult who cares, you have the opportunity with this curriculum to help kids learn how to sort out the gifts from the cow dung.

The problem, of course, in giving kids "the whole story" is that they so readily accept half of the story. They are no different from the rest of us. For example, let's consider that elegant little myth "A picture is worth a thousand words."

The truth, as author Neil Postman reminds us in his book *Amusing Ourselves to Death,* is that pictures tell us very little about reality. A picture tells us is what reality was in one little space for about one four-hundredth of a second. It doesn't tell us anything about reality outside of the framed image, out of camera range. It doesn't even tell us anything about what happened in the next four-hundredth of a second.

What did we really see? Who can tell without wading through all those thousand words that tell us the whole story? The writer of Proverbs reminds us of the fatal flaw in our sin-corroded reason: "There is a way that seems right to a man, but in the end it leads to death" (14:12). Our problem is that we buy into the story that seems right, without following the story to the very end.

Pretty Lies

The first bad decision in history was made by someone who thought that her eyes were giving her the whole story. "When the woman saw that the fruit of the tree was good for food and pleasing to the eye . . . she took some and ate it" (Gen. 3:6).

Little has changed since that first sad chapter. Today's teenagers are growing up in a culture that readily and intentionally encourages all of us to make decisions based on the way something looks.

We can help to counteract the pretty lies so elegantly packaged for kids by challenging them to look beyond the images they see. Encourage your students to watch commercials, movies, or TV shows asking, "What are we not seeing? What is not being shown?" Invite them to match real-life images with the words that they see and hear in the media. For example, under a newspaper story on the death of a drunk driver, a student might write "Here's to good friends whose night was kind of special." Under a story of a shooting outside a bar, a student might write "Another Coors Silver Bullet night."

Blurry Eyes

One of the reasons young people are so easily duped by the propaganda they hear from their teachers, friends, and/or the media is that they lack any clear sense of moral focus. When one is looking through a faulty moral lens, right and wrong, truth and untruth, are easily blurred.

An important part of helping kids refocus their moral lens is helping them understand the difference between what Chuck Swindoll describes as the "precepts" of Scripture and the "principles" of Scripture.

Driving on a highway, we see a sign stating a clear precept of law: "55 mph." It is clear from this precept that there is a set limit for movement on this highway. That is the law. Precepts are those signposts God puts in His word that tell us what we are and are not to do. "Do not lie. Do not steal. Do not commit adultery."

But what about the questions that fall between the cracks? Sure the Bible says not to have sex before marriage, but what about all of the other sexual intimacy that is not excluded by that specific precept? That's where we are guided by principles.

If a specific speed is not posted, we may see a sign that says simply "Drive Carefully." That's a principle. It doesn't give us a specific law, but it gives us a guideline. In Scripture, God often makes His will known not only by a specific law, but also by the guidelines of a principle.

As you work through these studies with your students, it will be important to keep bringing them back to a central question: What does God say about this matter in His Word?

One of the big mistakes that we make in youth ministry is that we become timid at this point. We won't always know "the will of God" in a situation. We won't always have the right answer to some question that a student confronts at school. That's fine. We need to be humble and honest enough to admit that. But when students come to us to work through an issue about which God has clearly spoken, it is blatant negligence not to tell them what God has spoken.

Worldly Wise

Abraham Maslow used the term "unconscious incompetent" to describe someone who is so ignorant that he or she does not even know how much he or she doesn't know. As you work through this curriculum, you will probably encounter a great deal of unconscious incompetence. Usually, it's manifest as arrogance. When you don't know how much you don't know, you tend to think you know it all! A lot of teens think they have all the answers because they haven't lived long enough to learn half of the questions.

However, it may be even more important to note that this condition is not solely the possession of adolescence. There are thousands of teachers, professors, counselors, and textbook writers who speak with absolute certainty and confidence about issues like the existence of God, the possibility of creation, the necessity of abortion and condom education, and the trustworthiness of the Bible. Sometimes they speak with such confidence that the average high school or college student is intimidated into believing every word he or she hears from these "experts." That's why it is important to nurture your students in healthy constructive evaluation.

If someone thinks he or she has all the answers, one of the best ways to help that person is to give him or her new questions. That may be why Jesus, the Master Teacher, often taught by telling parables and asking questions. The Pharisees and teachers of His day thought they had all the answers. Jesus had to confront them with some new questions. Don't be afraid to teach your students with questions—and to teach them to question.

The Key Ingredient

The greatest pitfall in teaching a series like this is to think that we aren't doing enough for the kids because we don't know all the answers, or we're not well read, or we're not theologically trained. Remember, though, that one of the key issues in this series is trust. A big part of helping kids get the whole story is helping them to understand that we are people they can trust.

That means being honest when we don't know something, and being honest when we do. The old adage is true: God does not need lawyers who will plead His case. He needs witnesses who will bear truthful testimony.

The main reason that your students will trust you will ultimately have little to do with their assessment of your academic brilliance or theological expertise. It will have much to do with whether they believe you truly love and care for them as people.

Duffy Robbins is chairman of the Department of Youth Ministry at Eastern College in St. Davids, Pennsylvania. He is also a well-known conference speaker, seminar leader, and author.

Are You Learning the Whole Truth at School?

The images on these two pages are designed to help you promote this course within your church and community. Feel free to photocopy anything here and adapt it to fit your publicity needs. The stuff on this page could be used as a flier that you send or hand out to kids—or as a bulletin insert. The stuff on the next page could be used to add visual interest to newsletters, calendars, bulletin boards, or other promotions. Be creative and have fun!

For the next few weeks we'll be looking at *The Whole Story*—things you might not be hearing in school about sex, science, history, and more! Come and learn the rest of the story.

Who:

When:

Where:

Questions? Call:

Unit Three: The Whole Story

SOCIAL SCIENCE 101

Right   Wrong

GENESIS CHAPTER 1

What does the Bible say?

Who will win?

Is there more to sex than this?

(Write your own message on the screen.)

Who Can You Trust?

YOUR GOALS FOR THIS SESSION:
Choose one or more

☐ To help kids realize that their (public) schools may not be teaching them "the whole story" in certain subjects.

☐ To help kids understand the relationship between church and state, especially in the public schools.

☐ To help kids decide to supplement what they learn in school by seeking out Christian truths, when necessary.

☐ Other:_____
_____

Your Bible Base:

Matthew 5:13-16
Philippians 2:14-5; 4:8
1 Peter 3:8-9, 13-17

STEP 1

You Don't Say

(Needed: Cards with the following "words to guess" and "words not to use" written on them, stopwatch)

Open the session with a game similar to "Taboo." Select three "clue givers" from the group. Give each one a card. On each card is a word the clue giver must try to get the group to guess; however, also on the card is a list of words the clue giver may not use in giving clues to the group. The object of the game is to get the group to guess the word in 30 seconds.

OPTIONS

EXTRA ACTION

HEARD IT ALL BEFORE

LITTLE BIBLE BACKGROUND

FELLOWSHIP & WORSHIP

MOSTLY GUYS

EXTRA FUN

MEDIA

SHORT MEETING TIME

Card #1
Word to guess: Birthday
Words not to use: Candles
　　　　　　　　Born
　　　　　　　　Happy
　　　　　　　　The name of any month
　　　　　　　　Cake

Card #2
Word to guess: Israel
Words not to use: Middle East
　　　　　　　　Country
　　　　　　　　Jews
　　　　　　　　Jerusalem
　　　　　　　　Bible

Card #3
Word to guess: Christian
Words not to use: Jesus Christ
　　　　　　　　God
　　　　　　　　Church
　　　　　　　　Religion
　　　　　　　　Faith

You'll also need to appoint a timekeeper and a judge to make sure the specified words are not used. If you want to play additional rounds, make up some of your own cards. But make sure you save Card #3 for last.

Afterward, discuss the game, using the following questions:

How hard was this game?

What was the challenge of it? (Finding new ways to talk about things.)

Remind group members of the last word guessed, *Christian*.

Ask: **Do you think it's possible to explain what it is to be a Christian without talking about God, Jesus, church, or faith? If so, how would we do that? Would we ever need to?** If no one mentions it, point out that these terms, while important to us as Christians, may turn some people off. Therefore, it might be a good idea to find ways to *show* our Christianity to people first, without beating them over the head with its content. (But eventually, of course, they will have to deal with Jesus Christ. After all, He is what Christianity is all about.)

As a follow-up question, ask: **Can you talk about your faith at school? How do you feel about that? Do you get the impression that it's frowned upon by teachers or fellow students? Is it hard to identify yourself as a Christian?** Listen carefully to group members' responses. This can set the tone for your approach to this session—as well as your approach to the whole unit.

STEP 2

What If?

Set up the following scenario (you may even want to act it out): **Let's say I'm your homeroom teacher and you're in class. I come into the room and say, "We have a new policy. We're going to start the day with prayer."**

How do you feel about that? Get a few responses.

"Yes, I'll pass out prayer rugs for all of you, and I want you to kneel down facing east as you pray."

How do you feel now? Get a few more responses.

"Raise your hands over your heads and bow down. I will now teach you the prayer of Allah, the one great God."

How do you feel now? What would you do? Would you go along with it? Would you say the words but really be thinking of the true God? Get a few more responses.

"Yes, ladies and gentlemen, we have a new policy. This school will be Muslim. We will be observing the fast of Ramadan in our cafeteria next month and we will collect

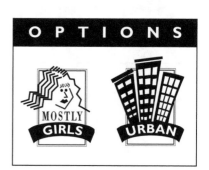

OPTIONS

MOSTLY GIRLS

URBAN

money each day. Part of this will go to the poor and the rest will fund our class trip to Mecca next summer. You will be required to attend."

How do you feel now? Get a few more responses.

Do you think something like this could ever happen at your school? Why or why not? (Probably not. The United States has built into its constitution the freedom of religion. We will never be required to worship a God we don't believe in.)

What if the teacher came in and said, "We're going to start the day with the Lord's Prayer"? How would you feel then? (Some might feel pretty good about that.)

How do you think Jewish students would feel about that? (Actually some might accept it as a generic prayer to God; but it's still a quote from Jesus, whom they do not worship.)

How do you think Muslims or Hindus or Buddhists would feel about that? (Most probably would not appreciate having to participate in a Christian prayer—even though they might be able to think of their gods while praying to the Christian God.)

How do you think atheist students would feel? (Out of it.)

Do you think this would ever happen? (Not now. But 30-40 years ago it *was* happening.)

One more question: **What if the teacher came in and said, "The school has decided that there is no God. We will not accept the mention of God in any class in this school. You are not allowed to pray or to meet with other believers. And I will now teach you the Humanist Creed, which we will recite every morning"? How would you feel about that?** (Offended, abused.)

Do you think this would ever happen? (Some might say that this is happening—maybe not to that extent—but faith is discouraged and humanism is assumed in many schools.)

Explain: **This freedom of religion is a tricky thing. It was quite a novel idea when it was put into the Constitution, and we're still getting the bugs out. How can you run a government without favoring one religion over another? It's not easy, especially when the overwhelming majority claims to belong to one religion, Christianity. It may be that, in the effort to make things fair, the government has leaned away from the majority, so now it's unfair to Christians.**

This gets really interesting when you start dealing with the public schools. How can you teach the essential knowledge of life without favoring one religion over another? One answer was to take religion out entirely—but that hasn't seemed to work. You wind up with a new God-free religion, which some are calling "secular humanism."

Reports from the Front

(Needed: Copies of Repro Resource 1)

Hand out copies of "Voices" (Repro Resource 1). Introduce it like this: **Let's take a closer look at some of the people involved in this issue. These are fictional character sketches, but you may know people who have similar views.**

Ask someone to read aloud the first character sketch. Then ask: **Is Beverly right? Do you think Christianity is against knowledge and education?** (Historically, the answer is yes and no. There have been times when certain Christian groups have opposed new knowledge that seemed to conflict with church teaching. Sometimes it's a matter of being careful about some new theory to make sure it doesn't lead people away from the basics of our faith. Some would say the opposition to evolution is an example of that. But Christians have also been leaders in education. Most of our great colleges today were founded as religious schools. Christians have also made a priority of offering education to poor people both at home and abroad.)

What sort of Christians do you think Beverly is referring to? What sort of Christians do you think she should talk to? (She's probably referring to the outspoken Christians who oppose what she teaches. To her, these people seem ignorant. She needs to hear from intelligent Christians who will discuss their views with her, while showing her love and respect.)

Do you know teachers like this? What could you do to change their minds? (Probably a loving spirit and an inquiring mind would get through to such a person better than anything else.)

Have someone read aloud the second character sketch. Then ask: **What does Rob really want to happen?** (Specifically, to be excused from singing Christian songs. Generally, he wants respect for his religious beliefs. He wants people to realize that their views may not be his.)

Does Rob have a point? Do you think Christian songs should be banned from public school Christmas concerts? Why or why not?

How would you explain your views to Rob?

Have someone read aloud the third character sketch. Then ask: **Do you agree with Kristina's argument? Why or why not?**

O P T I O N S

EXTRA ACTION

LARGE GROUP

MOSTLY GIRLS

MEDIA

JR. HIGH
HIGH SCHOOL
COMBINED

How could Kristina and other Christians at her school demonstrate their faith, aside from the pregame basketball prayer? (The overriding point is that we can't depend on institutional customs to show our faith. Our Christianity is shown in our personal behavior, our love, our joy, our peace, our patience, etc.)

Have someone read aloud the fourth character sketch. Then ask:

Do you think the angry mother was right in protesting the book? Why or why not?

Do you think the principal did the right thing? Why or why not? If no one mentions it, point out that the principal is working within the system, while still trying to shine for Christ. There is a lot that can be done to create an atmosphere of love and acceptance even when an outspoken witness for Christ might not be possible.

STEP
4

The World and the Word

(Needed: Chalkboard and chalk or newsprint and marker)

OPTIONS

SMALL GROUP

LITTLE BIBLE BACKGROUND

SHORT MEETING TIME

JR. HIGH / HIGH SCHOOL COMBINED

EXTRA CHALLENGE

Divide into four teams and assign each team one of the following Scripture passages:
- Matthew 5:13-16
- Philippians 2:14-15
- Philippians 4:8
- I Peter 3:8-9, 13-17

Instruct the teams to look up their assigned passages and, based on those passages, answer these four questions (write them on the board):

1. What kind of treatment should we expect from the world?
2. What should our attitude be?
3. How should we behave?
4. What effect can we have?

Leave plenty of space next to each question to write down the teams' responses. Point out that not all of the passages will answer all four questions.

Give the teams a few minutes to read and discuss their passages. Then have each team read its passage aloud and share its answers.

Use the following information to supplement the teams' responses.

Team #1—Matthew 5:13-16
- *What kind of treatment should we expect from the world?* (Nothing specifically mentioned in this passage.)

- *What should our attitude be?* ("Saltiness"; maybe "purposefulness"; we should shine like a light.)
- *How should we behave?* (We should do good deeds.)
- *What effect can we have?* (We can cause people to praise God. As "salt," we can have a preserving, enhancing effect.)

Team #2—Philippians 2:14-15
- *What kind of treatment should we expect from the world?* (It's a "crooked and depraved" world, so we should expect to be treated as though we don't belong.)
- *What should our attitude be?* (Not complaining or arguing.)
- *How should we behave?* (Blameless, pure, shining like stars.)
- *What effect can we have?* (As "shining stars," we can light the way for others trapped in darkness.)

Team #3—Philippians 4:8
- *What kind of treatment should we expect from the world?* (Nothing specifically mentioned in this passage.)
- *What should our attitude be?* (Seeking out true, noble, right, pure, lovely, admirable, excellent, and praiseworthy things to think about.)
- *How should we behave?* (Our actions should reflect the things we are thinking about, and should be true, noble, right, pure, lovely, admirable, excellent, and praiseworthy.)
- *What effect can we have?* (Nothing specifically mentioned in this passage.)

Team #4—I Peter 3:8-9, 13-17
- *What kind of treatment should we expect from the world?* (To be insulted, to be caused to suffer for doing right, to be asked about our hope, to be spoken of maliciously.)
- *What should our attitude be?* (Sympathetic, loving, compassionate, humble, prepared to answer people's questions, gentle, respectful.)
- *How should we behave?* (We should live in harmony with one another. We should resist repaying evil for evil and insult for insult. We should be eager to do good.)
- *What effect can we have?* (Those who oppose us will be put to shame by our gentle spirit.)

[NOTE: Peter was writing to people who were being seriously persecuted for their faith. We're not in that situation yet; but even if our society heads in that direction, we are called to be loving, gentle, respectful, and not frightened.]

Salt Talk

(Needed: Copies of Repro Resource 1 that you handed out earlier, pencils)

Sum up the Scripture study by saying: **As Christians, what treatment should we expect from the world? Mistreatment, sometimes. Perhaps misunderstanding. John 3:20 says that those who do evil hate the light. If we are shining like lights, this "crooked, depraved" generation will not like us. So we shouldn't be surprised if some people at school dislike our Christianity.**

What attitude should we have? Gentle, loving, positive. We shouldn't fight fire with fire. We fight hate with love, violence with forgiveness. That's Christ's way. And while we don't need to be naive, we should focus on the good things in our society, those "excellent and praiseworthy" things that please God. What should our behavior be? Good, righteous, exemplary. And what effect will we have? Maybe none. But maybe we can show someone the value of a relationship with God. Maybe we can be "salt" in our schools, making them kinder and gentler places.

Ask: **What one attitude might you need to change, as you deal with your school life? Is it fear? Vengeance? Anger? Anxiety? Complaining? Choose one area you want to work on and write it down on the back of your resource sheet.** Give group members time to do this.

Then ask: **What one area of behavior might you need to change? Are you feeling pressure to act in un-Christian ways? Are you acting in hateful ways toward people who aren't Christians? How can you "shine like a light" in your school? See if you can come up with one target area to change, and write that down also.**

Let's pray about these areas now and in the coming week. Close in prayer, asking God for wisdom and strength for your group members in these matters.

OPTIONS

SMALL GROUP

LARGE GROUP

HEARD IT ALL BEFORE

FELLOWSHIP & WORSHIP

MOSTLY GUYS

EXTRA FUN

URBAN

EXTRA CHALLENGE

VOICES

Beverly

Since the time of Galileo, Christianity has stood in the way of knowledge and education. As a teacher, I have to recognize this. I will not put up with Christian prejudice in my classroom.

Look at the whole evolution debate. The church set us back 50 years. Think of where we'd be now if we had been able to teach the theory of evolution when it was first developed. And now in the areas of genetic engineering and psychoanalysis and anthropology—wherever you look—Christians oppose the advancement of knowledge. Whenever you hear Christians speak up, they're being closed-minded and bigoted. We don't need that.

If in my classroom I can free a student from the prison of Christian teaching, I will gladly do so.

Rob

I'm a junior in high school and I think everyone should have the right to express his or her religious views—as long as those views don't offend others. But sometimes I do get offended. You see, I'm Jewish. And most of my friends at school go to Christian churches.

I think Christmas is the worst. It's fine to get the week off—I don't mind that—but there's all this stuff that goes with it. Like, I'm in the school choir. And we sing this Christmas concert with all sorts of Christian songs. I mean, why should I have to sing songs praising this baby in a manger when I don't even believe in him? I think of all the things that have been done by Christians against my people, and I have a hard time singing those songs.

I'll survive. We Jews always do. But it just doesn't seem fair.

Kristina

I can't believe they're trying to stop our basketball team from praying before games. The team's always done it, and no one's had a problem with it—except maybe some Jews or atheists in the stands. The guys on the team like it. Some of the best players are real Christians and they say it pumps them up for the game. And we made it to the state finals last year, so it must work.

Everywhere you turn, they're trying to take religion out of the schools. I think it's awful. I mean, if you don't depend on God, who can you depend on? This school would be a lot better place if there were more Christians around. Why can't everyone see that?

Sylvia

I'm a high school principal and, let me tell you, it isn't easy—especially these days. I got a call from an angry mother of one of our students. "That English teacher gave my daughter an obscene, pornographic book to read!" the mother said. "As a Christian, I will not let that filth into my house."

I met with the teacher, and then called the mother back and finally figured out what the problem was: There were a few minor "swear words" in the book, that's all. I'm not defending that language, but it's nothing these kids don't hear on TV.

We ended up allowing the girl to read a different book, which was fine with everybody. But as she left, the teacher said, "It's a shame she'll never get to read that other book. It had a lot of good characters." I had to agree.

The ironic thing is, I'm a Christian too. But I guess I try to show my faith by caring for people and doing a good job, and not by protesting bad words. I sympathize with the mother. She feels the whole culture spinning out of control and she wants to protect her daughter. But I don't think the answer is to curl up in a corner and close our eyes. I think we have to put on our hip boots, wade in, and try to make things better.

EXTRA ACTION

STEP 1

Instead of "Taboo," play "Freshman Disorientation." Before the session, come up with the times and classes for a hypothetical class schedule (for example, 8:00—U.S. History; 9:00—Earth Science; 10:00—P.E.; etc.). Write each time/class on a 3" × 15" strip of poster board. Make two sets of these strips. To start the meeting, have two teams compete to see which one can rearrange its set most quickly following your instructions. Start with the strips in chronological order, top to bottom, for the first round. Say: **Rearrange the classes in alphabetical order.** For the second round, say: **Rearrange the classes by the number of letters in each class title, most to least.** For the third round, say: **Rearrange the classes by time of day.** For the fourth round, say: **Rearrange the classes from most favorite to least favorite, in the opinion of the oldest person on your team.** After declaring a winner, note that keeping track of classes is just one of the many stresses kids face at school. Another can be living as a Christian among non-Christians.

STEP 3

This activity can either supplement or replace the case studies. Form groups of three. Two people in each group will be players; the third will be a referee. Have the two players play any game that can be refereed (bean bag toss, tiddledywinks, etc.) About a minute into the game, announce that referees are now on the side of one player or the other, as well as being refs. After another two minutes of play, stop the game. See whether the referees' judgment was affected by taking sides. Ask: **What might happen if church and state were "on the same side"—with each using its influence to keep the other in power? What happens when the state sees itself as being on the opposite "team"?**

SMALL GROUP

STEP 4

If you can't manage four study teams, skip the Philippians 4:8 passage and read the remaining three passages together as a group. Before reading, assign each group member to listen for one of the following categories and to halt the reading by standing up when he or she hears something that falls into that category. The categories are as follows: (1) what the world may do; (2) what we should do. Anyone who stands up should repeat the phrase that fell into his or her category.

STEP 5

If it seems awkward to deliver a mini-lecture to a small group, try the following instead. Ask kids what disclaimers (usually "fine print" warnings) they've seen on TV shows, medicine bottles, or elsewhere. Write suggestions on the board. (Examples may include the following: "This program contains material which may be offensive to some viewers"; "Your mileage may vary"; "Not to be taken internally"; "Consult physician before use"; etc.) Then ask which of these statements might apply to the things kids are taught at school. If time allows, have kids come up with their own disclaimers for what they hear at school, and brainstorm places where they can get "the rest of the story" (Bible, church, parents, books, etc.)

LARGE GROUP

STEP 3

Have volunteers play the parts of Beverly, Rob, Kristina, and Sylvia. The rest of the group will be the school board. (Arrange your seating to accommodate this if possible.) Explain that half of the members of the school board are Christians; the others are not. Each volunteer will make a presentation to the board. Beverly is a candidate for superintendent of the school district. Rob wants the board to ban Christmas songs from the winter concert. Kristina is protesting the board's decision not to allow prayers before games. Sylvia has been accused by two Christian parents of allowing "dirty books" in school. The "board" will discuss and vote on what to do about each issue.

STEP 5

Ask kids whether they think they're strong enough to hold up a pop can. Most will say yes. Have each person put his or her arms straight out, shoulder height, palms up and together. Lay a full pop can across each pair of palms. Tell kids to stay like that while you deliver the mini-lecture. (Skip the writing exercise.) Kids' arms should get tired pretty quickly. After a few kids' arms droop, have other kids prop them up. Point out that even strong Christians can find it tough to go it alone in a public school; we need to "hold each other up" on campus as well as in the group. Close by drinking the pop together.

STEP 1

Some kids shrug off repeated exhortations to stand out at school; they'd rather blend in, and go along with the crowd. Try inserting the following object lesson toward the end of Step 1. Bring a head-shaped Styrofoam wig stand (available at beauty supply stores, wig shops, and some secondhand stores) and a can of petroleum-based spray enamel. Provide plenty of ventilation. As you talk about some of the flak Christians can get at school, spray the paint on the head. Instead of just being colored by the paint, the Styrofoam will be eaten away. (NOTE: Test the paint on the underside of the head before the session to make sure you have the right kind.) Use this to illustrate the fact that we can be worn down by something we thought would never get "beneath the surface."

STEP 5

Chances are kids have heard the "Be salt and light" message before. To get them to see it in a new way, draw a generic map of a school (classrooms, gym, hallway, parking lot, etc.) Have kids brainstorm what might go on in each area if there were *no* Christian influence there for the next 25 years. Then say: **Let's say you do nothing to change that— and then your kids have to go to this school. How would you explain to them what you did— or didn't do?**

STEP 1

The follow-up question at the end of the step assumes all group members are Christians. If you think some of your kids aren't, use these questions instead: **Have you ever seen another person talk about his or her faith at school? If so, what happened? Do you think it would be easier to talk about your beliefs in front of a class or just to a friend outside of class? Have you ever wanted to talk about your beliefs in school? If you did, what happened? If you didn't, what stopped you?**

STEP 4

You may want to explain the following words from the passages. (1) *World* in Matthew 5:14 and Philippians 4:8 is translated from a Greek word that means "orderly arrangement"; it refers not just to the planet but to the way things are in the world, the present world system and people who are part of it. (2) In Bible times *salt* was used to preserve food as well as to season it. The idea here is that salt is supposed to enhance whatever it touches—not be changed by it. (3) *Depraved* (Phil. 2:15) means evil, perverted, corrupt (ruined by sin). (4) *Blessing* (I Pet. 3:9) is translated from a Greek word meaning "fine speaking"; it refers to speaking well of someone, praising him or her, wishing the person the best.

STEP 1

Announce that for the next few minutes kids can do only things they could do in public school. Ask a couple of kids to pray—which they'll probably say they can't do. Ask what choruses group members would like to sing; they'll probably say they can't do that, either. Ask for testimonies of what God is doing in their lives; kids will probably decline to answer. Encourage kids to worship mentally— which they can do, as long as it doesn't interfere with learning. After briefly discussing the differences between school and church, thank God for freedom of worship. Then sing a few of the praise songs kids can't sing in school.

STEP 5

For a fellowship-oriented response, have group members form pairs. Have partners write down their class schedules for each other and draw stars next to the ones during which they need prayer the most. (One star means everything's fine; four stars means either a lot of anxiety or conflict, or a big opportunity to talk about faith.) Instruct partners to keep each other's schedules as prayer reminders this week. Have them pray for each other at this point in the session if there's time, and if kids are comfortable doing that.

MOSTLY GIRLS

MOSTLY GUYS

EXTRA FUN

STEP 2

To help group members become more involved in the issues, create three teams and have each team present a skit debating one of the following scenarios mentioned in the session: a school policy requiring kids to pray to Allah, a school policy requiring recitation of the Lord's Prayer, and a school policy requiring recitation of the Humanist Creed. Give each team some notes from Step 2 about its scenario. After a few minutes, have each team present its debate for the rest of the group.

STEP 3

Use the character sketches in "Voices" (Repro Resource 1) as written, but change Rob's name to Rebecca. As you discuss each sketch, talk about whether that issue is currently a part of your group members' lives and what their responsibilities are concerning that issue.

STEP 1

For a more hands-on, less verbal opener, play "Metal Detector." Bring something that makes an electronic sound (an alarm, a hand-held video game, etc.). Have group members stand as if they're lining up to go through a metal detector. One group member will stand on the side with the noisemaker. He will beep the noisemaker once, and the first person in line must remove a metal object (coin, key ring, etc.) from his pockets. The beeper will then beep again and the person must remove another object. The goal is to beep exactly the right number of times; if the beeper stops beeping before all the objects are removed, he loses. If the beeper beeps one too many times (after all the metal objects are removed), he loses. After winning or losing, the beeper goes to the end of the line and the person just beeped becomes the beeper for the next person. Tie this into the fact that some schools use metal detectors to keep out weapons, and we sometimes feel we have to leave our faith at the door too.

STEP 5

Being gentle and loving may not appeal to some guys, who would prefer to restart the Crusades when they feel persecuted. Try this object lesson to remind guys that muscle power doesn't always get the job done. Bring a Chinese finger trap—one of those woven tubes into whose ends you stick your fingers, getting stuck when you pull. (Look for the trap at a store that stocks novelties.) Have a few guys try to escape the trap by pulling with all of their might. The secret, of course, is to gently push your fingers toward each other, then remove them from the expanded tube. Point out that sometimes brute force only increases our own frustration, and patient sensitivity can help us achieve our goals.

STEP 1

Form two teams—with one being twice as big as the other. Play three five-minute games: (1) either touch football or volleyball, (2) a spelling bee, and (3) a simple relay race in which all members of a team must run, one at a time. Afterward, discuss whether being "in the minority" was a disadvantage or an advantage. (In Game 1, it was a disadvantage; in Game 2, it may have been neither; in Game 3, it was an advantage.) Then talk about the fact that many Christian kids feel outnumbered in public school. Ask: **What are the disadvantages of being on a much smaller "team"? Might there be some advantages too?**

STEP 5

You'll need tennis balls, a wall, a laundry basket, and a pillow. Place the basket on the floor about eight feet from the wall. Have teams compete to see which one can bounce the most tennis balls off the wall and into the basket. After determining a winner, try again—this time holding a pillow on the wall and having kids try to bounce the ball off it and into the basket. Chances are that it won't work. Use this as an illustration of how a "soft" answer can stop an argument (Prov. 15:1, KJV)—a good way to keep a hostile non-Christian's taunts from turning into a fight.

STEP 1

Bring a few copies of a daily newspaper that includes a "religion page" or religion section (which is often in the Saturday edition). Form as many small groups as you have copies. Groups should analyze the religious content and be prepared to answer these questions: **(1) What impression of Christianity do you think non-Christians get from this page or section? (2) Do you think there should be a separate religious section, or should the religious news be mixed in with the rest of the paper? Why? (3) How is the treatment of religious news in this paper like the way religion is treated in your school? How is it different?**

STEP 3

Before the session, interview (or have a couple of group members interview) one of the following on video or audiotape: a school administrator, a teacher, or a school board member. The interviewee need not be a Christian. Be sure to explain how the interview will be used—to add another perspective to a discussion on how issues of church and state affect kids in public schools. Here are some questions you might ask: **(1) What role do you think religion should play in a public school? (2) What do you wish Christians would do to keep church-state problems from getting out of hand in our district? (3) What's your advice for a Christian student who wants to share his or her faith with school friends and teachers?** Play and discuss the interview rather than using the cases on the Repro Resource.

STEP 1

Instead of playing "Taboo," give kids two minutes to rearrange your meeting place to look as much like school as possible. Leave it that way for the rest of the session. Ask: **Do you think church should be more like school, or should school be more like church? Why?** Then use the follow-up questions at the end of the step. Condense the mini-lecture at the end of Step 2 to **Freedom of religion is a tricky thing.** To save time in Step 3, use only the Rob and Kristina cases.

STEP 4

Use just the Matthew (Team 1) and 1 Peter (Team 4) passages. In Step 5, skip the mini-lecture. Replace the writing exercise with the following: **Think of one non-Christian at school—a teacher, student, or administrator—who treats you badly, irritates you, or to whom you feel inferior. Now think of one positive, helpful thing you could do for that person this week.** Have kids share their ideas if they're willing.

STEP 2

If you're in an urban community that has a larger Jehovah's Witness presence than Islamic, include the following observations in your explanation:

• **Armageddon will happen soon; tell everyone of this prophecy.**

• **Everyone must use the name Jehovah—and not Jesus—when praying, because Jesus is not all-God. He is simply the best and first of Jehovah's perfected beings.**

• **Everyone must study the New World Translation Bible, which makes changes to and omissions from the Christian Bible.**

• **Everyone will sell copies of Watchtower magazine and record his or her sales to gain favor with Jehovah.**

STEP 5

Take the salt image a step further. Ask: **Why is salt needed in society?** Some will say that it's needed in cooking—for potato chips, for instance. Read aloud Mark 9:50 ("Have salt in yourselves"). Point out that this is a Christian challenge. Salt preserves and purifies. Likewise, the Gospel preserves a Christian's inner integrity so that his or her real and pure flavor (godly personality) can come out.

STEP 3

Younger kids may find it hard to relate to the characters on the Repro Resource. Try presenting similar issues in a form kids will understand: **(1) Your science teacher believes that Christians never think for themselves, that they're prejudiced against anything new. She believes the best thing she can do for Christian kids like you is to get you to reject what you've been taught in church. (2) Rob is a Jewish guy in your school choir. It really bothers him that in the winter concert he has to sing Christmas songs about Jesus. Rob is a nice guy, and like you, he wants to be true to his faith. He asks you to go with him to the music teacher and request different songs for the concert. (3) Until last week, your basketball team always prayed before games. But now the school board says you can't. (4) Your English teacher wants you to read a novel that has a few swear words in it. You think it's a pretty good book, but when your mom saw it she called the principal to complain.** In each case, kids should tell what they would *feel* like doing and what they think they might actually *do*.

STEP 4

Skip Philippians 4:8 and use three teams. Before kids read, put these objects on a table: saltshaker, flashlight, bent spoon, star-shaped stickers, hymnbook, and toy handcuffs. Give teams five minutes to read their passages and to correctly distribute the objects that go with each passage before you discuss. (Matthew—salt and flashlight; Philippians—spoon [reference to crookedness] and stars; I Peter—hymnbook [harmony] and handcuffs [persecution].)

STEP 4

Add Romans 13:1-7 to the list of passages to be studied. Discuss it, using questions like these: **Based on this passage, how do you think God sees public schools? Christian schools? Home schooling? If you go to public school, what should you do about a rule you think discriminates against you, such as banning Bible studies on school grounds?** (We should submit to authorities; yet the democratic system does allow for legal change.) **How could God use a teacher who gives Christian kids a hard time? Do Christian students owe respect and honor** (vs. 7) **to non-Christian teachers and administrators?**

STEP 5

Ask: **How are you handling the challenges of living with kids and teachers at school who disagree with you? You have three choices: fight, flight, or bring light.** Pass out index cards and pens. Have kids write down their current classes in a column on the left. Then have them write three column headings (Fight, Flight, Bring Light) at the top of the card on the right. For each class, kids should put a check mark under one of the three columns to grade themselves on how they're dealing with non-Christians in that class. As you discuss results, read the following verses to shed light on the desirability of each of the three responses: James 1:19-20 (fight); 2 Timothy 1:7-8 (flight); Matthew 5:14-16 (bring light).

DATE USED:

Approx. Time

STEP 1: *You Don't Say* _____
❑ Extra Action
❑ Heard It All Before
❑ Little Bible Background
❑ Fellowship & Worship
❑ Mostly Guys
❑ Extra Fun
❑ Media
❑ Short Meeting Time
Things needed:

STEP 2: *What If?* _____
❑ Mostly Girls
❑ Urban
Things needed:

STEP 3: *Reports from the Front* _____
❑ Extra Action
❑ Large Group
❑ Mostly Girls
❑ Media
❑ Combined Junior High/High School
Things needed:

STEP 4: *The World and the Word* _____
❑ Small Group
❑ Little Bible Background
❑ Short Meeting Time
❑ Combined Junior High/High School
❑ Extra Challenge
Things needed:

STEP 5: *Salt Talk* _____
❑ Small Group
❑ Large Group
❑ Heard It All Before
❑ Fellowship & Worship
❑ Mostly Guys
❑ Extra Fun
❑ Urban
❑ Extra Challenge
Things needed:

Starting Line

YOUR GOALS FOR THIS SESSION:
Choose one or more

☐ To help kids learn the biblical account of creation, and how it is a reasonable explanation of the universe's beginning.

☐ To help kids understand the conflicts between a biblical view of creation and the theories of evolution they are probably learning in science class—and to see ways these views might work together.

☐ To help kids plan their approach to science class.

☐ Other:_____
_____

Your Bible Base:

Genesis 1; 2:7
Job 38:2-7
Psalm 33:6-8
Isaiah 45:11-12

STEP 1

Creative Enterprise

(Needed: Paper, pencils)

O P T I O N S

SMALL GROUP

FELLOWSHIP & WORSHIP

MOSTLY GUYS

EXTRA FUN

SHORT MEETING TIME

URBAN

Open the session with a creative project. Explain to your group members that they will be given a choice between two team assignments. One team will be writing a poem or song. The other team will be planning a group activity for some evening later in the year. Give kids a minute to choose which team they want to join. Put the teams on opposite sides of the room and give them 10 minutes to work.

You might suggest that the "poem/song" team write its masterpiece line by line. That is, one person composes the first line, another adds a second, and so on. Possible subjects might include: "How I felt when I woke up this morning"; "Science Class Blues"; "Your favorite (or least favorite) food."

The "activity" team might plan one of the following: a game night in which the object is to lose, a badminton marathon, a scavenger hunt in a mall, or any one of a number of other options.

After 10 minutes or so, have each team present its idea to the whole group. Then talk a little about how the ideas came to be.

In the case of the poem or song, did it start out to be about one thing and then change to another theme? How did each person on the team contribute to or change the concept? With the activity, how did the details come about? Did one person have the germ of the idea, and another person develop it?

Summarize: **You have just been involved in creation. That's right. Whenever we do something creative, we are using God-given abilities—and in a way we're mirroring what He did when He created the world.**

And yet you were also just involved in evolution. Your ideas evolved. One person said this, then another said that, and soon the idea was changing into something better. Even when people write songs and poems by themselves, this happens. The ideas *evolve* in their minds.

Today we're going to be talking about something you've probably discussed in science class at school: the beginning of the universe. You know of the debate between creation and evolution. But let's start our discussion by considering this: The process of creation can involve the process of evolution. Maybe we can find a good way to understand both points of view.

Middle Ground?

(Needed: Copies of Repro Resource 2, three actors who are prepared to perform the skit)

If possible, distribute copies of "Point/Counterpoint" (Repro Resource 2) to three group members before the session. Assign roles, and have the actors read through the skit a couple of times to familiarize themselves with it. [NOTE: The skit is written for two girls and one guy. However, if necessary, you can change the names of the characters to accommodate the sexes of your actors.]

At this point in the session, introduce the actors and have them perform the skit. Afterward, lead the rest of the group in a round of applause. Then discuss the skit.

You don't want to get into the specifics of the debate at this point in the session; that will come later. But do raise the following questions.

Why aren't these two debaters agreeing on anything? (Each has already decided that the other is totally wrong. They are convinced that there is no middle ground in their debate.)

Late in the sketch, one character mentioned "faith in the basic principles of Darwinism." Do you think that belief in evolution is a "faith" or "religion"? Why or why not? (It could be thought of that way. It is "science" as long as it investigates evidence and presents hypotheses. But when it starts trying to explain the beginnings of the universe or of humanity, it is on religious turf. And certainly when scientists use their findings to deny the existence of God, that is a religious assumption.)

If we could be sure that scientists were looking at the evidence honestly (and not trying to disprove God), should we as Christians be afraid of what they find? (No. "All truth is God's truth." As Christians we can be eager to find out the truth about this world that God has made.)

When scientific findings seem to disagree with the Bible, what gives? How do we solve this problem? (If we accept the Bible as God's revealed truth, we have two options: [1] The scientific findings are wrong. Remember that science is built on guesswork—*educated* guesswork, but still guesswork. We need to examine the scientific process to make sure all the conclusions are valid. [2] Our *interpretation* of the Bible is wrong. We may be assuming some things that aren't necessarily biblical.)

In the Beginning...

(Needed: Chalkboard and chalk or newsprint and marker)

OPTIONS

Let's take a look at what the Bible says about creation. Then we'll discuss how the biblical account might fit with scientific theories.

Have the group turn to Genesis 1. Ask someone to read the first two verses aloud. Ask group members to describe their mental pictures of the events in these verses. You might jot down key words on the board: heavens, earth, formless, empty, darkness, Spirit, waters. Point out that it's almost as if a canvas is being spread out, on which God will paint the world He's about to make.

Explain that the next six days of creation are described next. Write the numbers 1-6 on the board, and quickly assign the following passages to six group members.

- Day 1: Genesis 1:3-5
- Day 2: Genesis 1:6-8
- Day 3: Genesis 1:9-13
- Day 4: Genesis 1:14-19
- Day 5: Genesis 1:20-23
- Day 6: Genesis 1:24-31

Ask each person to look up his or her assigned verses and tell the group what was created on that day. Write the answers on the board as they are named. It might look like this:

1. Light/darkness
2. Water/sky
3. Land/sea; vegetation
4. Sun, moon
5. Fish, birds
6. Animals, humans

Have someone read aloud Genesis 2:7. Ask: **What is significant about this verse?** (God created humans in a special way. He did not merely "wind up the creation machine" and let it go. He *personally* breathed life into humans.)

Point out that whatever else we may accept from evolutionary theory, we cannot buy the concept that humans are merely advanced animals, the latest in a chain of evolution. We are specially created by God.

Yet it is also interesting to note that humanity was created "from the dust of the ground." That is, God used something He had made, and remade it into something else. We find a similar statement about beasts and birds in Genesis 2:19. Some "theistic evolutionists" (people who believe that God created the world using evolution) would claim that these verses allow for a process of evolution that begins with dust, from which God formed new creatures in many stages. Certainly this is not conclusive, but it is a possibility.

Explain: **It's only natural that we should be curious about where we—and the world we live in—came from. And because the Bible doesn't explain exactly how and when God created us, there's room for us to speculate. However, not everything is open to speculation.**

Form three groups, and assign one the following passages to each group: Isaiah 45:11-12; Psalm 33:6-8; and Job 38:2-7. Instruct the groups to read through the passages and find statements regarding "non-negotiables"—those things that aren't open to speculation—in the creation debate.

Use the following information to supplement the groups' responses.

Isaiah 45:11-12—God made the earth and created mankind. He says so Himself. He also makes it clear that He is in charge of everything. As we debate the specifics of creation, we should do so with an attitude of acceptance of these facts and obedience to the One has the power to marshal the "starry hosts."

Psalm 33:6-8—God is so powerful that He was able to speak the world into existence. As we debate the specifics of creation, we should maintain an attitude of reverence and make sure we do not limit God's power in our theories (by saying things like, "God *couldn't* have created the world that way, because…").

Job 38:2-7—To those who are convinced they have the answers concerning the hows and whens of creation, God says, "What do *you* know? Were you there when I created the earth?" As we debate the specifics of creation, we should maintain an attitude of humility. Regardless of what scientific evidence and logic seem to indicate, there is no way that we can say with any kind of confidence that we have all the answers concerning creation.

Point out that these verses don't give us many specifics of the creation process, but they let us know clearly that we must be humble and reverent in dealing with our Creator. Sometimes evolutionists can become proud, focusing on humans as the pinnacle of an evolutionary process. But we must always see ourselves as the creatures of God, and duly submissive to Him. A proper attitude will help us put some of the specifics into place.

Making Sense

(Needed: Chalkboard and chalk or newsprint and marker, copies of Repro Resource 3)

OPTIONS

Write the following three words on the board: microevolution, macroevolution, and evolutionism. Explain: **I'm not going to try to teach science to you. You can get that at school. But as you sit there in class, look for these three terms, and try to distinguish one from the other.**

What is microevolution? Probably very few, if any, of your group members will know the answer to this. That's OK. You might even want to encourage some humorous guesses ("the gradual development of the microphone," "the evolution of people named Mike," etc.).

Explain that microevolution is the process of development that involves relatively small, subtle, gradual changes within a species. For instance, human beings tend to be taller now than they were 500 years ago. There is significant scientific evidence to support this. All creatures evolve in some way through the generations. As Christians, we don't need to have any problem with this. Peter was probably taller than Abraham (who lived thousands of years before Peter). The horse Paul rode to Damascus was probably genetically evolved from the horses Pharaoh's army used to chase the Israelites centuries earlier.

What is macroevolution? Again, if no one knows the answer, encourage some humorous guesses ("the evolution of the Big Mac," "the gradual development of macaroni," etc.).

Explain that macroevolution is the assumption that all life evolved from inorganic matter. It involves radical changes from one species to another (e.g., the evolution from monkey to human). While many scientists swear by this theory, there are significant gaps in the evidence, and many assumptions are made. But even this doesn't have to threaten our faith, according to some Christian scholars. (They point out that the Bible says humans *and* animals were made "from the dust of the ground.") Those who hold this view assert that God still controlled the whole process.

What is evolutionism? (The "-ism" indicates it's a belief, almost a religion. Evolution*ists* talk in near-religious terms about the evolutionary process. Most of them have ruled out God as any important force—although some will speak of the "wisdom" of evolution or the "will" of chance. This, of course, we must disagree with.)

Hand out copies of "Four Views" (Repro Resource 3). Introduce it by saying: **Let's look at a few different ways that Christians try to put the evidences and facts of creation together.**

Have someone read aloud the first section, "The Seven-Day Literal Theory."

Then ask: **What do you think of this theory? Do you believe it?**

Do you think it's possible that the scientific establishment—and all the evidence it claims proves the world to be millions of years old—could be that wrong?

Do you think this view interprets Scripture correctly?

Have someone read aloud the second section, "The Gap Theory."

Ask: **Do you think creation could have happened like this?**

If so, why doesn't the Bible tell us more about the "old world"?

Do you think this view interprets Scripture correctly?

Have someone read aloud the third section, "The Indefinite Age Theory."

Ask: **Do you accept the definition of "day" as an indefinite period of time?**

Does the "day-age theory" help at all? What about the point concerning the sun's creation on the fifth day?

Do you think this view interprets Scripture correctly?

Have someone read aloud the fourth section, "The Poetry Theory."

Ask: **Does this theory do justice to Scripture?**

Isn't it dangerous to suggest that the Bible is presenting something in a nonfactual way? Wouldn't that affect the way we view other passages—especially things like miracles and supernatural occurrences?

What's the Difference?

(Needed: Chalkboard and chalk or newsprint and marker)

Some might say that all this creation-evolution stuff doesn't matter. "Do your nice religion thing," they might say, "but don't let it keep you from doing your homework. If it makes you happy to believe in God, fine, but that has nothing to do with scientific truth." So they might say. But

O P T I O N S

LARGE GROUP

HEARD IT ALL BEFORE

FELLOWSHIP & WORSHIP

MOSTLY GIRLS

EXTRA FUN

JR. HIGH HIGH SCHOOL COMBINED

EXTRA CHALLENGE

they're wrong. **Believing that God is our Creator has important consequences in our lives.**

Call two group members forward to serve as object lessons. Say: **Let's say this person [A] is created by God, while this person [B] is a product of evolution, the forces of chance.**

As you go through the following "interviews," invite the whole group to supply answers for your questions.

Ask Person A: **How do you feel about being created? How do you feel about your Creator?** (Grateful, excited to be able to have a relationship with Him.)

Ask Person B: **How do you feel about the forces of chance?** (Fortunate to have turned out so well; insignificant, recognizing that there was no design involved in his or her makeup.)

Ask Person A: **How does it make you feel to know that you were personally created by the Ruler of the universe?** (Significant, important, special.)

Ask Person B: **How does it make you feel to know that you just sort of happened, that you are at the end of a long line of creatures whose ancestors included slime, slugs, and monkeys?** (Insignificant; unimportant; perhaps sometimes he or she still feels like slime; maybe glad to be developing.)

Ask Person A: **Does it ever occur to you that God made you for a reason? Does that give you a sense of purpose in your life?** (It should. We should glorify God and seek to please Him, using the unique gifts He has given us.)

Ask Person B: **What about you? Do you have any sense of purpose, knowing that you are the result of chance?** (Probably not. Maybe to make the world a bit better for the next species in the evolutionary chain.)

Conclude: **How we view this matter of our origin makes a great deal of difference in our attitude. Believing in a Creator gives us a sense of specialness and purpose. No matter what position you take in trying to deal with scientific evidence, you need to make sure that God is in the picture.**

Read aloud Ecclesiastes 12:1a: "Remember your Creator in the days of your youth."

Ask group members to bow their heads. Then ask them to visualize their science class, or wherever they might be forced to deal with this question of creation and evolution.

Ask: **How will you deal with it? What attitude do you need? Patience? Love? Gentleness? Boldness? Do you need to cut through what you're being taught, chewing the meat and spitting out the bones? Ask God to give you strength to respond correctly in those moments.**

Then close the session in prayer, asking God for that strength for your group members.

Point | Counterpoint

MODERATOR: Good evening and welcome to Point/Counterpoint, the weekly debate program that focuses on the issues. I'm your host, Lucille De Monterey. Our topic today: creation versus evolution. On the creation side, our guest is Dr. Tyler Firmament, professor of Bible and religious doctrine at Mid-Atlantic Bible College. On the evolution side, we have Dr. Sandra Primate, professor of natural sciences at the Eastern Montana Institute of Technology. (*FIRMAMENT and PRIMATE nod.*) In Round One, we ask each debater to present his or her basic argument. Dr. Firmament has won the toss and chooses to begin. Sir.

FIRMAMENT: The Bible says that God created the heavens and the earth in six days. God said it; I believe it; that settles it. If one totals the years in the Bible's genealogies, one can date the creation to 4004 B.C. Even allowing for some missing generations, the earth cannot be more than 10,000 years old, biblically speaking.

MODERATOR: Dr. Primate now responds.

PRIMATE: That's ridiculous. Carbon dating and other proven scientific methods show that the earth is millions, if not billions of years old. It is the product of a primieval explosion. Life evolved from primitive forms, as proven in the fossil record. We have volumes of evidence of the evolution of the species, as Darwin originally theorized and as others have developed.

MODERATOR: And now it is my opportunity to try to find some points of agreement. Dr. Firmament, is there anything in Dr. Primate's position that you can agree with?

FIRMAMENT: Absolutely not. Dr. Primate is obviously a godless scientist bent on destroying the moral fabric of our society. If we are merely animals, then we have no souls. I can't accept that.

MODERATOR: Dr. Primate, any points of agreement?

PRIMATE: No way. Dr. Firmament—if he really is a doctor—is just trying to blind everyone to simple scientific truths. I don't see how anyone who knows anything about science can still believe in this childish concept of "God."

MODERATOR: But in your own view, Dr. Primate, you mention a "primieval explosion"—a "big bang," if you will. Can you say what caused that big bang? Couldn't that have been the work of God? Couldn't that have been His way of creating the universe?

PRIMATE: Ridiculous. That's just an attempt to enslave science to religious blindness.

MODERATOR: And Dr. Firmament, wouldn't it be possible to see those six "days" of creation as periods of time—each one maybe millions of years long—in which God oversaw the evolution of various species.

FIRMAMENT: The Bible says nothing about evolution. It is a godless idea.

MODERATOR: But couldn't God have used evolution as a tool in His creating—in the same way that He used, say, an earthquake to free Paul and Silas from jail?

FIRMAMENT: That's not the same thing at all.

PRIMATE: But why do you insist on putting a "God" in there at all? That's a primitive notion. Can't you accept the fact that it just happened?

MODERATOR: But isn't it true, Dr. Primate, that the fossil record does not show an even development from species to species, but has numerous gaps that are hard to explain—unless you allow for a God who specially molds the next species.

PRIMATE: It's not hard to explain at all—if you keep your faith in the basic principles of Darwinism.

FIRMAMENT: So it's a faith now? I thought you didn't have any faith!

PRIMATE: Certainly not an ignorant faith like yours!

MODERATOR: I see we're already moving into our second round of competition. As you know, our debate format has not been a very popular one, so we've created—

PRIMATE: Watch your language!

MODERATOR: So we've *developed* a new format that may get better ratings. We hope it will still help us reach a resolution.

FIRMAMENT: Hey!

PRIMATE: She said "resolution," you imbecile, not "evolution."

MODERATOR: So let me introduce our Point/Counterpoint "Challenge Match." In this corner, fighting for creation, we have Tyler "Mad Dog" Firmament!

FIRMAMENT: I won't let Darwin make a monkey out of me!

MODERATOR: And in this corner, the Primate Princess!

PRIMATE: Wait till I get my paws on you, Bible-brain!

MODERATOR: We'll be back with the action after this word from our sponsor.

NOTES

FOUR VIEWS

The Seven-Day Literal Theory

The Bible means exactly what it says. There is no good reason to think otherwise. At the beginning of time, God created the world in six 24-hour days. This all happened maybe 10,000 years ago, not the millions of years that evolutionists claim. They will talk about the fossil record—but those fossils were made by the flood of Noah's time. The scientific belief in evolution is a house of cards, assumptions built on assumptions built on other assumptions. Our theory of scientific creationism is an even better way to explain the actual evidence.

The Gap Theory

There is a world of difference between Genesis 1:1 and 1:2. "God created" in verse 1, but the earth is empty and dark in verse 2. Something had to have happened in between. That something was the fall of Satan. Satan was cast out of heaven, to the earth, where he wreaked havoc (Isaiah 14:12-15; Ezekiel 28:14-17). As a result of Satan's havoc, God had to remake the world (described in Genesis 1:3 and following). This re-creation could have occurred in seven 24-hour days, and about 10,000 years ago. The fossil record, then, dates from the old world, the original creation, which was much older.

The Indefinite Age Theory

The word for "day" can mean any period of time. "Evening and morning" are just metaphors for the beginning and end of God's work in that time period. And since the sun wasn't created until the fifth day, it's kind of hard to think about a 24-hour period. So it's fine to date certain aspects of creation back millions of years. Those "days" may have been millions of years long, as God tended the evolutionary process.

This view is closely related to the "day-age" view, which says that each "day" of creation was a 24-hour day, but then many years passed before the next day of creation. Either way, it's an old earth, and there's time for the evolutionary development of the species that God created.

The Poetry Theory

Genesis 1 is poetic language for a process of creation we could never fully understand. We shouldn't puzzle over the details. We should merely accept the fact that God created all that is, and we can accept the testimony of science about *how* He did so. The Bible was never intended as a science textbook. It just tells us the important truths about God.

NOTES

STEP 3

Get several boxes of animal-shaped cookies, crackers, and candy (animal crackers, gummy worms, goldfish crackers, etc.) and 14 paper plates. Number six plates from 1-6; do the same with six others. On the other two plates pile the animals—an equal number of pieces on each plate. Put the numbered plates on a table at the front of the room. Form two teams and have them stand at the back of the room. Put an animal-laden plate in front of each team. At your signal, each team will read Genesis 1:3-31. Then one person on each team will take an animal from its plate, go to the front of the room, and put the animal on the plate whose number corresponds to the biblical day on which that animal was created. When that person returns to the team, the next person will repeat the process. The catch: Each person must move like the animal he or she picked. (You can require kids to moo, oink, quack, etc., if you think they'll go along with it.) The first team to put all of its animals on the correct plates wins.

STEP 4

Illustrate microevolution by having kids stand in a line, side by side. The person on one end will strike a pose, put on a facial expression, and then freeze. The next person will then freeze with slightly different pose and expression. Continue the process down the line; then compare the first and last poses and expressions. To illustrate macroevolution, have teams create six step-by-step drawings that show how one writing tool—a pencil—might evolve into another writing tool—a computer. Point out that most of the intermediate "tools" wouldn't work—just as most "in-between" species wouldn't survive. Then, while Repro Resource 3 is read, have each person mold and remold a lump of clay to represent a key word in each view.

STEP 1

If your group is very small, you may not be able to show how ideas evolve through team-member interaction. Instead, pass out paper and pens. Have each person draw a picture one line at a time. Before any lines are drawn, announce that kids will be drawing a barn. Let them draw a line. Then say: **I've changed my mind. Let's draw a rocket ship. Use the line you've drawn and add one more.** Continue this process, changing the subject of the drawing after each line. Other subjects might include a house, a coat hanger, a cat, a car, and a TV set. After a few minutes, have kids put down their pens. The person who's done the best job of drawing (with the fewest extraneous lines) your most recently announced subject wins. Use this as an example of how something can evolve during the process of being created.

STEP 3

How can a few kids cover Genesis 1? Instead of having six readers split up the chapter, have individuals take turns reading just the following verses as you call out the references: Genesis 1:1, 3, 6, 9, 11, 14, 20, 24, 26. Then read the list in the basic session plan to summarize what was created on each day.

STEP 3

The bigger your group, the more fun this activity will be. Have your whole group act out the six days of creation. Start each section of Genesis 1 (see the basic session plan for the six sections) with everyone lying on the floor. As you or a volunteer reads Genesis 1, have kids separate from each other like the light from the darkness (vs. 4), sprout from the ground like vegetation (vs. 11), orbit like the moon (vs. 16), crawl and leap like animals (vs. 24), etc. If you have enough kids, have them act in teams, competing to win a team prize for Best Performance in an Original Creation.

STEP 5

Make the same point as the Person A/Person B activity, but involve everyone with the following activity. Give each person a fortune cookie (available by the box in supermarkets as well as in Chinese restaurants). Have kids mill around with their eyes closed. Each person must give a fortune cookie to the first person he or she bumps against. Kids should read their fortunes and discuss with their partners whether the fortunes seem to apply. Then have partners give individualized compliments or advice to each other. Finally, ask how kids felt about both experiences. Point out that just as getting personal advice or compliments means a lot more than getting a generic "fortune" by chance, believing that you were created by a personal God gives life much more meaning than believing you're an accident.

STEP 3

The sheer familiarity of the creation story may cause some kids to tune it out. To get their attention, start with a made-up "tribal" creation myth like the following: **In the beginning, there were no cattle, no people. The jupjup bird did not sing his sweet song. The Great Kangaroo Woman in the sky was sad; she cried a tear that turned into a diamond. When the Evil Lizard Warrior struck the diamond with his sword, the jewel shattered and became the stars in the sky. Each star gave birth to a jupjup bird, and the birds wove a nest that became the earth. The Great Kangaroo Woman was so happy that her tears of joy touched the stones of the earth, which became the plants and animals. And every jupjup bird with a feathered plume became a man or woman—which is why the jupjup bird has no plume today.** Have kids compare and contrast this myth against Genesis 1. Ask: **Which is more believable? Why?**

STEP 5

The meaningless existence of Person B may seem exaggerated to kids, especially if they have friends who believe in evolution and who seem to lead satisfying, moral lives. Emphasize the issue of truth rather than feelings. Have group members form pairs. Explain that one person in each pair believes in creation, the other in chance. Raise a few moral questions for the pairs to debate for one minute each. For example: **(1) Should terminally ill people be allowed to commit suicide? If so, why? (2) If you could steal 10 million dollars and get away with it, would you? Why or why not?** Point out that chance believers may have systems of morality, but human systems have no ultimate authority; one is as good as another. The Bible, on the other hand, claims to reveal objective truth from the Creator.

STEP 3

Kids may wonder where the biblical account of creation came from. After all, there weren't any people around to see it happen. Explain that it's reasonable to assume that Adam and Eve passed the story on to their children, and they passed it on to theirs, and it became an oral tradition—a history that isn't written down. The story, along with others like the Flood, could have been written down and preserved in Egypt by Joseph and others. Moses, guided by God's Spirit, may have taken all these materials and compiled them into the first five books of the Bible. God's involvement (see 2 Tim. 3:16) would be necessary to fill in the prehuman gaps in the story, and to make sure the whole account was accurate.

STEP 4

If kids wonder how so many views can spring from the same Bible, explain that each view starts with different assumptions. For example, the Seven-Day Literal Theory assumes that the word translated *day* means a 24-hour period, that the age of the earth can be estimated by adding up the ages of people listed in Old Testament genealogies, and that current methods of dating fossils are unreliable. The Gap Theory assumes that *day* might or might not mean 24 hours, that the earth could be as old as most scientists say it is, and that the Isaiah and Ezekiel passages refer to Satan (others disagree). Note that these are all *interpretations* of the same Bible, just as four people might interpret the meaning of a painting differently. That doesn't mean there's something wrong with the painting—or the Bible. To demonstrate this, you might have each group member draw a picture of the same thing. Afterward, note the differences in their "interpretations."

STEP 1

Let kids enjoy fellowship over refreshments they create themselves. Depending on whether you meet in the evening or morning, supply either (1) all sorts of ingredients for sandwiches or (2) toaster waffles and a lot of toppings. Award a prize for the most original (yet edible) creation. As kids eat, encourage them to talk about the most creative meal they ever saw or ate. Use this to either replace or lead into the team project activity in the basic session plan.

STEP 5

Supply magnifying glasses and objects from nature that display patterns—leaves, flowers, rock crystals, wood with a distinctive grain, etc. Have kids examine these patterns, and discuss how they give evidence that a Designer is behind them. Then spend some time "magnifying" the Creator by singing (or just reading aloud) creation-oriented songs like "Joyful, Joyful, We Adore Thee," "All Creatures of Our God and King," and "How Great Thou Art."

MOSTLY GIRLS

MOSTLY GUYS

EXTRA FUN

STEP 3

After the groups have read their assigned passages and identified the "non-negotiables," ask: **Since God doesn't provide us with clear information about everything He does, how difficult is it for you to accept not knowing? Is it wrong to ask questions when the answers may not be clear-cut? If we knew everything there was to know about God, His character and His behavior, do you think we would have the same relationship with Him? Why or why not?**

STEP 5

Instead of doing the "interviews" with individuals, divide the group in half. Have half of the group respond to the questions for Person A, and the other half respond to the questions for Person B. Then have everyone write on the back of Repro Resource 3 at least three reactions or feelings she has about the fact that her Creator planned that she be born.

STEP 1

Many guys won't be attracted by the prospect of writing a poem or song. They'll want a traditionally "male" project. So give them the following choices. Teams must come up with either (1) a new game that uses a baseball, a hockey mask, a golf club, *and* a volleyball net; or (2) a design for a car that has two wheels and goes underwater.

STEP 2

The skit on the Repro Resource may be too cerebral for some guys. For something more down-to-earth, stage a disaster simulation. Warn kids to wear grubbies. Bring several rolls of toilet paper and several bottles of ketchup. Have group members form at least three teams. All but one of the teams must create a disaster scene (car accident, bomb-blast aftermath, plane crash) using all team members. Toilet paper should be used as bandages; ketchup should be used for blood. Teams must not reveal the cause (train collision, hurricane, etc.) of their disasters. After three minutes, the remaining team will examine the scenes and come up with possible explanations of what happened. If you like, let the investigators award a prize for the most creative scene. Use this as an illustration of how evolutionists and creationists, after viewing the results of creation, disagree in their explanations of the cause.

STEP 1

Set up two typewriters with paper in place. Have a stack of paper next to each typewriter, in case you need more. Have group members form two equal teams. Explain that the first person on each team will be blindfolded, and will type with one finger for 15 seconds. Then the next person in line will do the same thing. The process will continue until all members on both teams have had a chance to type blindfolded. Then you'll take a look at each team's papers. The team with the most actual words of three letters or more will win a prize. After playing the game and awarding a prize, ask: **Was this a game of skill or a game of chance?** (Chance, unless kids cheated.) **It's pretty hard to put letters in the right order when you leave it to chance. Do you think the world and all the living things in it could have evolved by chance? Why or why not?**

STEP 5

Throw a "Dinosaur Party" to wrap up your meeting. Before the session, invite kids to wear clothes that have dinosaur designs (give a prize for the most dinosaurs on one person if you like). Serve appropriate refreshments (Dinosaur Grrrhams, Gummy Dinosaurs, dinosaur eggs [anything round or oval-shaped], Prehistoric Punch [any beverage you want to serve], etc.). You may want to note that "scientific creationists" believe that dinosaurs and people walked the earth at the same time; others believe the creatures were extinct by the time man appeared. Either way, dinosaurs were just as much a part of God's creation as other animals were.

STEP 2

Instead of performing the skit, rent the video of the movie *Inherit the Wind*—a fictionalized version of Tennessee's famed Scopes "monkey trial." In the film, a sympathetic lawyer (based on real-life attorney Clarence Darrow) defends a teacher's right to teach the theory of evolution in public school. Testifying for the creationist side is a character based on orator William Jennings Bryan—who comes off as an ignorant, emotionally unstable buffoon. During the session, play the climactic courtroom scene toward the end of the movie in which the Darrow character makes a fool of the Bryan character on the witness stand. Then ask: **How did it feel to watch this scene? Are people still arguing like this about creation and evolution today? Why do you think the play *Inherit the Wind* is still studied and performed in high schools today? Do you think it should be?**

STEP 3

Before the session, rent the video of *Genesis,* the first film in the New Media Bible (also known as The Genesis Project). This video is available through Christian film distributors and some Christian bookstores. To introduce the Genesis 1 study, play just the opening sequence—the six days of creation. Ask: **How is this like the way you picture God's creation of the world? How is it different?**

STEP 1

To save time, combine Steps 1 and 2 into a single activity. Have a "creationist" team come up with an anti-evolution bumper sticker, and an "evolutionist" team come up with an anti-creationism bumper sticker. The results should allow you to discuss both the creation/evolution process of coming up with ideas, and the battle between the two sides. To save even more time, skip Steps 1 and 2 entirely. Just ask: **How do you feel when the subject of evolution comes up in school? Have you or Christians you know gotten into arguments or had problems with a science teacher over the subject? If so, what happened?**

STEP 3

To shorten the Genesis 1 study, see the "Small Group" option. Of the Isaiah, Psalms, and Job passages, use only one or two. In Step 4, after defining micro-evolution and macroevolution, simply acknowledge that Christians interpret the Genesis account differently; if you don't have time to summarize the four views, hand out Repro Resource 3 for kids to take home and read later.

STEP 1

You may want to consider using dance instead of a poem or song in the opening activity. First, challenge a young person who thinks he or she can dance well to come to the front of the room and do a simple (but clean) dance move for 10 seconds. Then challenge another person to "improve" the first person's move by adapting it into another move (in 10 seconds). Continue this process with successive challengers. Afterward, you can use the "evolution" of the dance moves as a lead-in to a discussion on creation and evolution.

STEP 3

Many teenagers believe that science and Scripture have very little to do with each other. Explain that since God created the universe, accurate scientific laws will not contradict God's Word, but will testify to its truthfulness. Write on the board the following "simple versions" of Isaac Newton's three laws of motion:

1. Nothing moves or happens unless something else causes it to.

2. If something moves, it goes in the direction it was pushed.

3. Every action has an opposite reaction.

Then have group members compare Newton's laws with Genesis 1:1-5, and try to find some "common ground" between the two sources. For example, Genesis 1:2 says the earth was "formless and empty" (nothing was moving or happening—see Newton's first law) until God began creation. Verse 4 says God separated darkness from light (two opposites—see Newton's third law).

STEP 2

Younger kids may not understand parts of the skit on Repro Resource 2. So instead of using the skit, introduce the concept of miscommunication by having the group play bilingual charades. The game is played like regular charades, but with a twist. The words to be guessed are in Spanish (or another language if most of your group members speak Spanish) and the clues are in English. For example, a player trying to communicate the word *gato* (cat) might act out the word got and point to his or her toe. Other words to guess: *perro* (dog); *barba* (beard); *tio* (uncle); *biblioteca* (library); *iglesia* (church). After playing a couple of difficult rounds, paraphrase from the Repro Resource a few issues on which creationists and evolutionists "don't speak the same language."

STEP 5

Junior highers may be uncomfortable with the open-ended "you decide what you believe" approach. They may want the debate settled before they leave the room. For their benefit, emphasize that there is an answer to every question that can be asked about creation and evolution; some are known and some aren't. The most important thing to remember is the one we can be surest of: that God is the Creator of everything. To help kids find more answers than you can give in this session, you might want to recommend books like *It Couldn't Just Happen* by Larry Richards and *Don't Check Your Brains at the Door* by Josh McDowell (Word).

STEP 3

Form small groups; give each a good Bible dictionary and a commentary. Have group members look up the meanings of the words *create* and *day* as used in Genesis 1. Ask: **Could the Hebrew word for create mean "make from something" as well as "make from nothing"? Could the word for *day* mean a long period of time as well as 24 hours? How does the translation of these words affect our view of how God made the world?**

STEP 5

Write on the board (or just read) and discuss the following quote from Bryan Appleyard's secular book, *Understanding the Present: Science and the Soul of Modern Man* (Doubleday, 1993): "Science is not a neutral or innocent commodity. . . . Rather it is spiritually corrosive, burning away ancient authorities and traditions. It cannot really coexist with anything. Scientists inevitably take on the mantle of the wizards, sorcerers, and witch doctors. Their miracle cures become our spells, their experiments our rituals." Ask: **What is Appleyard saying?** (That science tends to become its own religion.) **Do you think he's right? Why or why not? How might this relate to the controversy over evolution? Should Christians be anti-science? Why or why not?** (Instead of opposing science, we can keep it in perspective.)

DATE USED:

Approx. Time

STEP 1: *Creative Enterprise* _____
- ❏ Small Group
- ❏ Fellowship & Worship
- ❏ Mostly Guys
- ❏ Extra Fun
- ❏ Short Meeting Time
- ❏ Urban

Things needed:

STEP 2: *Middle Ground?* _____
- ❏ Mostly Guys
- ❏ Media
- ❏ Combined Junior High/High School

Things needed:

STEP 3: *In the Beginning . . .* _____
- ❏ Extra Action
- ❏ Small Group
- ❏ Large Group
- ❏ Heard It All Before
- ❏ Little Bible Background
- ❏ Mostly Girls
- ❏ Media
- ❏ Short Meeting Time
- ❏ Urban
- ❏ Extra Challenge

Things needed:

STEP 4: *Making Sense* _____
- ❏ Extra Action
- ❏ Little Bible Background

Things needed:

STEP 5: *What's the Difference?* _____
- ❏ Large Group
- ❏ Heard It All Before
- ❏ Fellowship & Worship
- ❏ Mostly Girls
- ❏ Extra Fun
- ❏ Combined Junior High/High School
- ❏ Extra Challenge

Things needed:

More Than Machines

YOUR GOALS FOR THIS SESSION:

Choose one or more

☐ To help kids learn what the Bible says about sexuality.

☐ To help kids understand how modern views of sexuality regularly conflict with biblical teaching.

☐ To help kids decide to uphold personal sexual morality, in spite of what school or society may be teaching.

☐ Other:_____

_____

Your Bible Base:

Song of Songs 1:2-4
1 Corinthians 6:12-20
Colossians 3:1-8

Fun Factory

(Paper and pencils [optional])

Have everyone stand up. Explain that you're going to build a "human machine." One person will start with a repetitive motion, and others will connect with that person's motion, until the whole group is buzzing and whirring like a giant machine.

Beginning this activity can be difficult, due to kids' reluctance. You may want to start the first motion yourself or get the biggest "ham" in the group to do it. If some members refuse to participate, don't force them.

If your group members enjoy the activity, try it again, maybe adding sound, slow motion, and/or fast motion.

This can be a lot of fun if kids get into it. Or it may fall flat if they don't. If you think your group members would absolutely hate this activity, try another plan. Divide them into two or three teams. Distribute paper and pencils to each team. Assign each team the task of designing a machine. Think of some crazy tasks for these machines to do—walking the dog, doing your homework, turning school lunches into tactical weapons, etc. After a few minutes, have each team share its ideas with the rest of the group.

When the machine activity is finished, introduce the session. **We're going to talk about sex today. Specifically, we're going to talk about the sex education you get in school—and what's missing. The machine activity was silly, but it had a point. Often sex education courses treat our bodies like machines. They make sure we know all the mechanics of our sexuality, but they don't tell us much about why we are sexual or what the purpose of our sexuality is.**

And of course we don't get any better information from TV, movies, or music either. These media treat us like lust machines—always wanting and needing more, more, more sex. That's a dangerous approach to sex education, one that can really mess up our views.

How can we sort it all out? How can we be more than mere machines? That's what we'll be finding out today.

STEP 2

Attitudes

(Needed: Copies of Repro Resource 4, pencils)

Hand out copies of "Attitude Check" (Repro Resource 4) and pencils. Go over the directions. There are three columns next to each statement. Group members need to consider whether their school friends, parents, and school sex-education class would agree (Y) or disagree (N) with each statement. (They may also write "M" for "maybe" if they're not sure.)

Give group members a few minutes to fill out their sheets. Then ask volunteers to share their responses. Of course, the answers will vary. Some kids have more conservative friends than other kids do. Some parents are strict and others are permissive. Sex-education classes vary. No matter what their responses are, make sure group members are thinking about these various influences—and what effect these influences have on them.

STEP 3

Turn on the Light

Ask a mature group member to read aloud Song of Songs 1:2-4 (or read it yourself). Then ask: **Does it surprise you that there are verses like this in the Bible?** (It might. Some people think that the Bible is silent concerning sex, that sex exists in some "unspiritual" realm.) Point out that in Song of Songs (also called Song of Solomon), we have a whole book of love poetry. Sex *is* a beautiful thing, given to us by God, as an expression of committed love.

Have the group turn to Colossians 3:1-8. Ask someone to read aloud the first four verses. Then ask: **What's Paul saying here?** (We should set our minds on heavenly things, and not be filled with earthly thoughts that displease the Lord. We have a new life with the risen Lord. We should not dally in the old ways of sin.)

OPTIONS

EXTRA ACTION

HEARD IT ALL BEFORE

LITTLE BIBLE BACKGROUND

SHORT MEETING TIME

JR. HIGH HIGH SCHOOL COMBINED

Have someone read aloud verses 5-8. Ask: **What does Paul want us to do?** ("Put to death" the sins of our old nature, including various sexual sins.)

How do we put these things to death? (Stop doing them. That's part of the old life. Christians now have a new life in Christ.)

Point out that our non-Christian friends will not understand this. They will still be dwelling on their sexual thoughts and actions. But we are different. We are "raised with Christ" to a new life.

Have group members turn to I Corinthians 6:12-20. Ask someone to read aloud verses 12 and 13. Then explain: **In this passage, Paul is quoting some of the Corinthians' own sayings and responding to them. Some Corinthians were saying, "Because our sins are forgiven, we can do anything. Everything is permissible." Paul replies that everything may be permissible, but not everything is helpful. Some activities lead us into bondage.**

We know that's true with some addictive behaviors, like taking drugs. It's also true of sex. You probably know people who are so into sex, they're almost consumed by it. That's all they think about. Paul says, "I will not be mastered by anything."

In verse 13, the Corinthians are saying that food exists for the purpose of being eaten, and our stomachs exist to be filled with food. How does that reasoning relate to the area of sex? (The Corinthians probably were arguing that sex was meant to be enjoyed, and our sexual appetites are meant to be satisfied—so we should live it up!)

Does that reasoning make sense to you? Why or why not?

How does Paul respond? (He says our earthly bodies are temporary. But while we have them, the purpose of our bodies is not to satisfy our sexual appetites, but to glorify God.)

Ask someone to read aloud verse 14. Ask: **What does this verse mean when it says God will "raise" us?** (He gives us a new kind of life with Christ, new priorities, and new purposes. So there is much more to our lives than just indulging our lusts. Because we will have bodies in God's eternal future, it's important how we value them now. They were created for immortality, not immorality!) If no one mentions it, point out that God does not just tell us what not to do; He also gives us power—the power of His resurrection—to say no to sexual appetites.

Have someone read aloud verses 15-17. Ask: **What does this say about our bodies?** (They belong to Christ. In fact, they are part of Christ's body.)

Why isn't it right to have sexual relations with prostitutes? (We would be defiling our bodies, which belong to Christ.)

Do you think this applies to all sexual relations outside of marriage? (Probably. The point is that sexual relations are not just for one person's pleasure. Sex creates a physical unity between two people. In a marriage, this is good and beautiful—the two "become one flesh."

But outside of marriage, it becomes a mockery. Outside of marriage, sex is just a physical thing, denying the spiritual element of marital love, and defiling our bodies.)

Have someone read aloud verses 18-20. Ask: **Why should we "honor God" with our bodies?** (Because we do not belong to ourselves; we belong to Him. Also, we are temples of the Holy Spirit, God's dwelling place.)

What "price" were we bought with? (The sacrifice of Christ on the cross.)

How can we honor God with our bodies? (By maintaining sexual purity. Also, by obeying and serving Him.)

STEP
4

Voices in the Dark

(Needed: Copies of Repro Resource 5)

We've looked at Scripture passages that say we should remain pure, but how easy is it to obey those passages in real life?

Distribute copies of "Profiles in Confusion" (Repro Resource 5). Explain: **The people on this sheet may be like some people you know. If these were your friends talking to you, how would you respond?**

Give group members a minute to read the first section. Then ask: **How would you respond to Jack if he were a friend of yours?** (He is cheapening himself and his sexual partners. Sex was intended to be a beautiful sharing of committed love within a marriage. He is engaging in "counterfeit sex." He may believe he's not hurting anyone now, but he's crippling his future relationships and those of his partners.)

Give group members a minute to read the second section. Then ask: **Do you think Julie is right? Is it OK to have sex if you love the person?** (Love is not a feeling; it's a commitment. One may feel a great deal of love toward someone, but that doesn't justify sex. Sex is reserved for the most intimate relationship—the wife and husband who promise to forsake all others. Julie may believe that she and her boyfriend will get married someday; but getting sexually involved with him before marriage is like running up charges on a credit card in the hopes that she'll get a well-paying job someday. She may think the future marriage will justify the present sex. But it doesn't work that way. Sex

O P T I O N S

EXTRA
ACTION

LARGE
GROUP

LITTLE
BIBLE
BACKGROUND

MOSTLY
GIRLS

MEDIA

URBAN

is intended for those in a current marriage commitment. It is an expression of their *present* unity.)

Give group members a minute to read the third section. Then ask: **Have you ever felt this way? How would you respond to Rachel?** (There are people who treat others as human beings and not as sex objects. And if those people get together and encourage each other, they can withstand the media hype and keep their priorities straight.)

Give group members a minute to read the fourth section. Then ask: Do you agree with Terry? Do you think the Bible is too harsh? How would you respond to Terry? (The Bible is clear that the practice of homosexuality is sinful, something God does not like. A debate rages over whether people are born with a tendency toward homosexuality, but it really doesn't matter. Even if someone "is" gay, that person is commanded not to indulge his or her homosexual desires. These may not be evil people, but they—like everyone—are responsible for their actions. God knows what's best for us, and He has determined that homosexual relationships are not healthy, not whole, and not pleasing to Him. We must accept His Word, even if we'd rather not.)

Give group members a minute to read the fifth section. Then ask: **How would you respond to Charity?** (God forgives our sin. He picks us up, cleans us up, and lets us start over. Let the past be past and start fresh with a desire to please God. If our only motivation for right living is a desire to protect our personal purity, we lose that motivation when we stumble. But our best motivation is the desire to please God each new day.)

STEP 5

Cleaning Up

Ask: **So what about you? What's your life like? What temptations do you face? Where have you stumbled?**

Refer back to Repro Resource 5. Say: **Take a look at the opinions of your friends, your school, even your parents. How do they compare with what the Bible says? How do your own views compare with Scripture?**

This is a time to think about cleaning up your own act. How can you become more obedient to God in the area of sexuality? I want you to choose one point of action, something you can begin to do this week. And I want you to write

this down on the back of your resource sheet. You may want to use a code word or something, just in case someone sees this paper, but I want you to write something down with the intention of doing it this week.

Maybe you are involved in a sexual relationship that you need to stop.

Or maybe your nonsexual relationship is getting too hot, and you need to cool it for a while.

Maybe you're indulging in sexual fantasies, pornography, or masturbation, and you need to regain control of your life.

Maybe you're beginning a dating relationship and need to establish good habits at the start.

Maybe you need to revise your attitudes about some of the things listed on this sheet.

Maybe you need to reach out in friendship to someone who needs God's forgiveness.

Maybe you need to stop participating in the sexual joking among your school friends.

Whatever it is, write it down and ask God to help you with it this week.

Close in prayer, asking for God's strength for your group members as they attempt to put aside sinful desires and live lives that are "raised with Christ."

Attitude Check ✓

For each statement, consider what your friends at school, your parents, and your school sex-ed class (or teacher) would think about it. In the appropriate column, put a "Y" for Yes if they would agree with it, an "N" for no if they would disagree, or a question mark if you're not sure how they would respond.

	School Friends	Parents	School Sex Ed
1. It's OK to have sex with someone if you really love that person.			
2. It's natural to think about sex much of the time.			
3. AIDS is God's judgment on sexually promiscuous people.			
4. You should not have a sexual relationship with someone outside of marriage.			
5. If you're still a virgin, you're weird.			
6. As long as you use "safe sex," you can do whatever you want sexually.			
7. If a guy gets a girl pregnant, he should marry her.			
8. If a girl gets pregnant, she should be ashamed of herself.			
9. It's OK to be involved with someone sexually, as long as you don't go all the way.			
10. Sex is a beautiful thing.			
11. Homosexuality is something God hates.			
12. In order to be considered attractive, you have to act sexy.			
13. Some people are just born gay. They have no choice in the matter.			
14. Every person should make his or her own decisions about sex. There's no right or wrong.	Y		

PROFILES IN CONFUSION

JACK

I like sex, OK? That's not a crime, is it? I see a beautiful girl and I want her. I'm not hurting anyone. Both of us get pleasure from it. And yes, we use "protection." You'd have to be crazy not to, these days. So I don't see what the problem is. It feels good; I do it. So what?

JULIE

Brent and I have been dating for over a year. I really love him, and he loves me. We'll probably get married sometime in the future, after high school or college. But in the meantime, we're just totally wrapped up in each other. We've also been sleeping together whenever we can. I know my parents wouldn't approve, but they don't understand how much we love each other. I know it's not the "Christian" thing to do, but I don't see what's wrong with it. Why should we have to wait if we love each other now?

RACHEL

Sex is disgusting. Every guy I know has just one thing on his mind—and it's not football. And girls are just as bad these days. Every day in the locker room it seems like girls are comparing notes on whom they've slept with and how good it was. It's so demeaning. Why can't people see each other as human beings and not just as bodies to conquer? I don't think I'll ever be able to find a real relationship. I'm giving up hope.

TERRY

Have you ever disagreed with something the Bible said? That's how I feel about homosexuality. I'm not gay, but I have some friends who are. I don't really understand them, but I like them. They're cool people. And yet I read in the Bible how homosexuality is this major sin, an abomination to God and all that. How can that be? I mean, these guys are just being what they are. Can that really be wrong?

CHARITY

I messed up. I was saving myself for marriage. I was going to be a pure bride for my husband, whenever God would give me one. But then I met this guy, and fell in love. Like, crazy in love. Like, I-can't-see-straight in love. And I just knew that this relationship would last forever. He was my knight in shining armor. And, well, we had sex. A lot. And then we broke up. He was gone, and what was left for me? I had nothing more to "save for marriage." So when I started dating another guy, it was hard to say no to him. And then the next guy, and the next. I don't like myself very much now, but I don't know how to get back to what I was.

STEP 3

Give each group member a marker and a cardboard box—any size, any shape. Explain that just as a box has several sides, sexuality does too—the physical side, the emotional side, etc. Have kids label four sides of their boxes "Emotional," "Mental," "Physical," and "Spiritual." As you study the Bible passages, kids should keep track (by making check marks on the appropriate sides of their boxes) of how many times they hear a reference to each "side" of sex. After discussing the passages, have kids compare the number of check marks in each category. Ask: **What sides of sexuality do these passages seem to emphasize? How does that compare with the emphasis in sex education classes? Which sides do you think kids need to learn the most about? Why?**

STEP 4

Have group members form teams. Give each team at least seven sheets of construction paper and some markers. Each team should make the following traffic signs: "Stop," "Yield," "Slow," "Danger," "Maintain Speed," "No Parking," and "Keep Right." When the signs are done, read aloud the profiles on Repro Resource 5. After you read each profile, each team should discuss it for 30 seconds and decide which sign or signs to hold up as a response to the person in the profile. For example, kids might think Julie should "Stop" what she's doing, indulge in "No Parking" with Brent, and stay out of "Danger." Let each team explain its reasons for choosing the signs. Allow group members to suggest other signs that might also be appropriate.

STEP 1

You may find it hard to build much of a "machine" with just a few "parts." Try the following activity instead. During the week before the session, ask kids to bring items they value—due to sentimental, monetary, or practical worth. To start the session, let kids show these items and tell why they're so valuable. After everyone has had a chance to do this, take out a handful of coins. Offer to buy the items for a penny apiece. Then offer a nickel, then a dime. Act offended that kids won't take you up on your offer, and ask what the problem is. When they explain that the items are worth far more, point out that a lot of people don't seem to feel the same way about sexuality. They're willing to give away their virginity for practically nothing, and encourage others to do the same.

STEP 5

If the "written confession" would be awkward for your small group, try the following activity instead. Have each group member find on Repro Resource 4 one area in which he or she disagrees with the prevailing attitude in sex-education class. Then have each person come up with at least three reasons for holding his or her opinion—reasons that could be shared in sex-ed class. If kids find no areas in which they disagree with teachers or textbooks, they should do the exercise using the "School Friends" answers on the sheet.

STEP 2

Filling out and sharing responses to Repro Resource 4 might take too long in a large group. Here's an alternative. Get three volunteers. Dress one to represent School Friends (using a letter jacket if possible); dress another to stand for Parents (using dowdy clothes and padding); and dress the third as "School Sex Ed" (using a lab coat or graduation gown). Tape three sheets of paper along the wall—one marked with a Y, one with an N, and one with a question mark. Read the first statement from Repro Resource 4 aloud. Have one group member come up and move the three costumed people around until they're standing under the symbols (Y, N, or ?) that reflect that group member's answer. Do the same with the other statements on the sheet, letting a different group member respond each time.

STEP 4

Allow more individual participation by holding a "press conference." Choose a person to play the role of each character on Repro Resource 5. Each character will make his or her statement (reading the appropriate part of the sheet) and then be questioned by reporters (the rest of the group). Divide the reporters into three groups: those from the sensationalist tabloid *National Defiler*, those from the Christian youth magazine *Off-Campus Life*, and those from a public high school newspaper. The tabloid reporters should seek sleazy details; the Christian reporters should challenge the positions taken by the characters; the school paper reporters should ask questions that reflect a lack of absolute values. [NOTE: So that characters are prepared to answer questions, let them know during the week before the session what they'll be doing.]

STEP 1

The negative statements about sex education and the media at the end of Step 1 may lead kids to tune out—if they think you're going to spend the session griping about "the modern world." Use the machine activity to illustrate the importance of having a purpose (unlike the machine), and the fact that sex education needs to include the *why* of our sexuality. Have group members brainstorm the top ten things they think kids need to know about sex. Then discuss which of those things are missing from their own health classes.

STEP 3

The idea of setting our hearts and minds on things above (Col. 3:1-2) may have become a meaningless, wimpy-sounding cliché to kids. As you read those phrases, get kids' attention by pausing to set a radio on a particular station. Explain that setting our hearts and minds on something is like tuning into it, locking it in, concentrating. You might ask kids to recommend radio stations that don't feature songs or talk condemned in Colossians 3:5, 8. When you read I Corinthians 6:19, give kids a new perspective on "your body is a temple of the Holy Spirit" by smashing a miniature house (the type sold in toy stores for model railroad layouts) with a hammer. Ask kids how *they* would like to live in a house that had been trashed. How do they think the Holy Spirit feels about it?

STEP 3

Explain the following biblical terms as needed. *Raised with Christ*—Because Christ has set us free from being slaves to sin, it's as if we ended our old lives and started new ones. *Things above*—God's kingdom, His priorities, Himself (including Christ, who has a special place of honor, which is what "the right hand" stands for). *Earthly things*—Not just anything physical, but the wrong attitudes and actions that someone with an "earthly nature" (a mind and heart not yet changed by Christ) tends to be preoccupied with. *Your life is now hidden with Christ in God*—We belong to Him, are connected to and protected by Him; it's as if we're already in heaven with Him. *Members of Christ*—Our bodies, not just our spirits, are part of Him. *One flesh*—A reference to the physical union in sexual intercourse, first mentioned when God made Adam and Eve. *The Holy Spirit . . . is in you*—Each person who receives God's Son as Savior receives His Spirit too who guides and comforts us. *Bought at a price*—Jesus paid with His life on the cross so that we could live forever, belonging to Him.

STEP 4

Kids may not be clear on the Bible's view of the issues raised in the profiles on the sheet. These passages may help: Matthew 5:27-28 (Jack); I Corinthians 7:8-9 (Julie); Matthew 6:33-34 (Rachel); Romans 1:21-27 (Terry); I John 1:9 (Charity).

STEP 1

Bring one or more boxes of assorted (varied shapes and sizes) plastic bandages. Give each person a bandage as he or she enters. Have kids put their bandages on the palms of their hands. When everyone has arrived, tell kids to hold up their hands and walk around the room, looking at each other's palms. Kids should find those with the same size and shape of bandage and form small groups accordingly. After small groups are formed, have them discuss this question: **What scars have been left by romantic relationships in your life or in the lives of people you know?** Then point out that romantic and sexual relationships leave scars because we're emotional as well as physical beings—and that sex education needs to help us deal with emotions as well as "plumbing."

STEP 5

Before the session, draw a giant open Bible on a sheet of poster board. Don't write anything on the two pages that show. Each page should be of equal size. At this point in the meeting, note that God could have left the subject of sex out of His Word, just as we sometimes tend not to talk about it in church. But then we wouldn't know how sex was really meant to work. Have group members form two teams. Give each team Bibles and a concordance. Each person will need a marker or pen. Have the teams compete to see which one can first fill one of the poster board Bible pages with written-out verses about sex. (Height of the letters must be no more than half an inch.) After declaring a winner, spend some time thanking God that His Word provides "the rest of the story" about sex.

STEP 4

Distribute copies of "Profiles in Confusion" (Repro Resource 5) and discuss each section. However, as you discuss the sections, ask for two different responses. First, ask each group member to respond from her own perspective; discuss these responses. Then ask group members to respond according to how they think their guy friends would respond. If there are differences in these perspectives, discuss reasons for those differences.

STEP 5

As group members refer back to "Attitude Check" (Repro Resource 4), have them mark the statements to indicate their personal attitudes. Have them identify the items they feel very strongly about as well as the items that they're not very sure of. Encourage group members to spend some time in prayer, asking God to guide their thoughts as they take a stand for what He says is right.

STEP 1

If your guys aren't keen on pantomime, play "Big Talkers." At your signal, the first guy will start telling a tall tale about how cool or smart he is. When you say **Stop!** (which you could do at any time), the next guy will start a tall tale about *himself.* The catch is that each tale must start with the last word spoken by the previous person. (You be the judge of what that word was.) Anyone who takes longer than five seconds to start his story is out. After the game, discuss the tendency of guys to "talk big" about their sexual exploits. Ask: **Is listening to "big talkers" a good way to get educated about sex? Why or why not?**

STEP 5

Many guys crave sexual information—to be stimulated if not educated. Try this object lesson on where to get information on sex. Bring three pairs of eyeglasses—one normal, one with a lens covered by paper, and one whose lenses are smeared with petroleum jelly. Explain that we get a clear view of sex from the Bible (hold up the normal glasses); we get a partial (strictly physical) view from most sex-education classes (hold up the "one-sided" glasses); and we get a distorted view of sex from pornography (pass around the smeared glasses). Ask: **What might happen to you if you wore the one-sided glasses all the time?** (You'd see things in only two dimensions; one eye might get weaker than the other, affecting the way you see everything.) **What if you wore the smeared glasses all the time?** (You couldn't find your way around; you'd get stuck in a fantasy world.) Note that getting sexual information from these sources has a similar effect. Encourage guys to supplement health classes with the Bible's view of sex, and to steer clear of pornography.

STEP 1

Have group members form two teams. Put two pets (frogs, hamsters, mice, cats, dogs, etc.) on leashes or strings, and give one leash or string to the first person in line on each team. Kids will be running a relay race—led by the pets. Teams can try anything (yelling, waving their arms, offering food, etc.) to get the pets to go, as long as they don't touch or hurt the animals. After the game, discuss the frustrations of letting the animals lead. Then discuss the problems that result when we allow ourselves to be led around by our hormones.

STEP 5

Bring two boxes of facial tissue. The boxes should be the inexpensive, cardboard-only kind in which the tissues lie flat—not the type with plastic in the opening which holds up one tissue at a time for easy plucking. Put the boxes on opposite sides of a table. Have group members form two teams. Line each team up single file so that its members can reach a box as they run past the table. Each person's task is to run past the table and pluck exactly one tissue from his or her team's box. Anyone who doesn't run fast enough (you be the judge) is out. Anyone who gets more than one tissue at a time is out. Appoint a monitor for each team to count tissues after each round. The team that has the most remaining players when its box is empty is the winner. Use this game as a reminder that even though our society says it's OK to have more than one sexual partner, the Bible prescribes exactly one—your spouse.

STEP 1

Tell kids in advance that they're going to see a video about "the birds and the bees." Put up posters and make announcements to that effect. Then, to start your meeting, show a minute or so from any children's video or nature documentary that shows birds, bees, or both. Then ask: **What does the phrase "the birds and the bees" make you think of? Why do you think that phrase is used to describe sex education? If you've seen any real videos or films in school that were about sex, what did you think of them?**

STEP 4

Replace or supplement the written profiles with a song to discuss—one that describes the physical side of a sexual relationship but ignores the moral issues. Use a current song, or one of these older ones: "I'm So Excited" (The Pointer Sisters); "Give in to Me" (Michael Jackson); or "Burnin' Love" (Elvis Presley). Ask questions like these: **What do you like about this song? What don't you like? How is this song's view of sex similar to the Bible's view? How is it different? Based on what we read in Colossians and I Corinthians, what might bother the apostle Paul most about this song?**

STEP 1

Here's a shorter opener. Bring an action figure or doll that does just one thing (throws a knife, wets a diaper, grows hair, etc.). Have kids guess what it does and how it works. Then explain that some people think sex is just as mechanical and one-dimensional—an impression kids might get from some sex-education classes. To save time in Step 2, don't pass out the Repro Resource; read the statements and have kids report only the attitudes shown in their sex-education classes (not those of friends or parents). Kids should indicate their answers by nodding or shaking their heads.

STEP 3

After reading the Song of Songs passage, skip the Colossians passage and go directly to I Corinthians. In Step 4, use only the cases of Jack, Julie, and Terry—which reflect attitudes kids are most likely to encounter in sex-education classes.

STEP 1

Try the following variation of the opening activity. Set up enough tables and chairs for all of your group members to be able to sit side by side. Explain to your group members that they are part of a "conveyor belt" that, once turned on, must continue until you turn it off. Turn the "machine" on by giving the first person an object (perhaps a canned good). That person will pass the object to the next person, who will pass it to the next person, and so on until it reaches the end. Then the last person in line will bring the object back to you for another round. The activity sounds simple enough—until you start placing many objects on the "conveyor belt" at the same time. Remind group members that their machine cannot stop until you say so.

STEP 4

Because many urban teens have experienced sex, defining *purity* may be necessary. Some young people assume they can never approach God in purity because they are not sexually pure. So, before you begin this activity, explain to your group members that purity can begin when you ask the Lord for forgiveness. Point out that purity results from an inner decision to live for Christ.

STEP 2

Junior highers may not know what others think about the issues on Repro Resource 4. Use the following activity instead. Bring LifeSavers candies, thread, tape, and two blindfolds. Hang the LifeSavers from the ceiling around the room so that they dangle at kids' eye level. Form two teams; then have each team choose a representative. Blindfold the reps, spin them around, and have them try to find and eat the LifeSavers without using their hands. Each team should shout directions to its rep (and misleading directions to the other team's rep). The rep that eats the most candies in two minutes wins a prize for his or her team. Use this activity to illustrate the problem of deciding whose advice to follow when you don't know where you're going. Ask: **Where do you think kids should get information about sex? How about advice? What should you do when you get conflicting advice from TV, friends, parents, school, and church?**

STEP 3

Read I Corinthians 6:18-20. Ask: **If Paul taught your health class, how might he answer a kid who says, "Sex is fine as long as you don't hurt anybody"?** (Sexual sin hurts you, and hurts the Holy Spirit if you're a Christian.) **Why don't many health teachers say, "When it comes to sex, honor God with your body"?** (They can't talk about religion; they don't believe it; etc.) Read I Corinthians 6:9-11. Ask: **How are these verses different from what you're likely to hear in public school?** (Many teachers avoid saying that certain behaviors are wrong—like sex outside of marriage and homosexuality). Read I Corinthians 5:9-13. Ask: **How should we treat non-Christian teachers and classmates who don't believe what the Bible says about sex?** (We shouldn't judge them. We should be concerned about what we and other Christians believe and do.)

STEP 1

If your kids would find the human machine activity "beneath" them, try the following activity. You'll need a recorded song and sheet music for the same song. Form two groups and put them in separate rooms for three minutes. One group will learn all it can about the song from the sheet music; the other will learn all it can from listening to the song. Regather the whole group and ask each group: **How would you describe the "feel" of the song? Can you quote any lyrics from memory? How much of the melody can you sing?** Point out that the group with the sheet music may have learned more about the structure and lyrics of the song, but the listening group probably learned more about the emotional and aesthetic side. Use this to illustrate the difference between learning about the physical side of sex and the moral and emotional aspects.

STEP 5

Have kids brainstorm how to turn the following facts into questions they could ask in health class to spur discussion of values: **(1) Condoms fail to prevent pregnancy about 10 percent of the time. The AIDS virus, being much smaller than a sperm cell, has a greater chance of getting through a condom. (2) As the influence of religion has decreased in Western culture, the number of unwanted pregnancies has increased. (3) Teenagers are often encouraged to wait for sex until they're "ready." Yet they're faced with specific age limits for voting, driving, working, and drinking alcohol.** (Sample question: "Why do people say using condoms is 'safe sex' when condoms fail and the AIDS virus is small enough to get through them?")

DATE USED:

Approx. Time

STEP 1: *Fun Factory* _____
- ❏ Small Group
- ❏ Heard It All Before
- ❏ Fellowship & Worship
- ❏ Mostly Guys
- ❏ Extra Fun
- ❏ Media
- ❏ Short Meeting Time
- ❏ Urban
- ❏ Extra Challenge
Things needed:

STEP 2: *Attitudes* _____
- ❏ Large Group
- ❏ Combined Junior High/High School
Things needed:

STEP 3: *Turn on the Light* _____
- ❏ Extra Action
- ❏ Heard It All Before
- ❏ Little Bible Background
- ❏ Short Meeting Time
- ❏ Combined Junior High/High School
Things needed:

STEP 4: *Voices in the Dark* _____
- ❏ Extra Action
- ❏ Large Group
- ❏ Little Bible Background
- ❏ Mostly Girls
- ❏ Media
- ❏ Urban
Things needed:

STEP 5: *Cleaning Up* _____
- ❏ Small Group
- ❏ Fellowship & Worship
- ❏ Mostly Girls
- ❏ Mostly Guys
- ❏ Extra Fun
- ❏ Extra Challenge
Things needed:

The Rest Is History

☐ To help kids learn how important religion—specifically Christianity—has been in world history.

☐ To help kids understand how their school history courses may underplay the importance of religion.

☐ To help kids develop an appreciation for their Christian heritage.

☐ Other:_____

_____

Your Bible Base:

Genesis 45:4-8; 50:20
Proverbs 21:1
Isaiah 7:18-20; 45:1-5

Twenty Questions

(Needed: Index cards, pencils)

Hand out index cards and pencils. Instruct group members to write their names on the cards. Then have them write down something they did in the past year—along with the reason for doing it. For instance, someone might write, "I went to the mall last week." And the reason might be: "I needed a new pair of basketball shoes." Explain that you will be reading some of the responses aloud, so group members shouldn't write anything too personal. After a minute or so, collect the cards. Then go through them to find a few good ones.

Explain that you're going to play "Twenty Questions." You will select a card, call forward the person who wrote it, and read to the group what the person did. Then the group has to guess the reason for doing it, by asking the person "yes-no" questions. The person may answer only "yes" or "no" (or "sort of" or "not really") to each question that is asked. See if the group can guess the motive using 20 questions or less. Play two or three rounds.

When the game is finished, explain: **We're going to talk about history today. You may not know it, but religion—specifically Christianity—has played a huge role in most major historical events. Sometimes public schools don't know how to teach that. They will teach you what happened, but not necessarily why it happened. But as we've just seen in this game, the why helps us understand a great deal.**

An Extracurricular History Quiz

(Needed: Copies of Repro Resource 6, pencils, prizes)

OPTIONS

LARGE GROUP

MOSTLY GIRLS

MEDIA

URBAN

JR.HIGH HIGH SCHOOL COMBINED

Announce that you're going to give a pop quiz, and the subject is history. After a few groans from your group members, explain that there will be prizes (perhaps candy bars) for everyone who participates— and extra prizes for the three people who score highest on the quiz.

Hand out copies of "The Other Side of History" (Repro Resource 6). Give group members about five minutes to complete the quiz. Then go through the answers as a group.

Use the following information to supplement discussion of the quiz.

(1) In the 900's B.C., Israel became a major power in the Mideast. They did it not through military battles, but through shrewd trading and alliance making. Who was the king at this time? (b—Solomon.) Egypt and later Assyria were major powers in the area, but for about half a century, Israel dominated.

(2) For two and a half centuries (A.D. 64-311), the Roman Empire carried on a war against a segment of its own people. Though these people were unarmed and nonthreatening, they eventually "defeated" the Empire. Who were these people? (b—The Christians.) The Roman persecution against Christians was not constant; it came in cycles over about a 250-year period, and was often vicious. But ultimately Christianity outlasted the Empire, and even became the official religion of Rome.

(3) Early in the second century, Governor Pliny wrote to Emperor Trajan with a problem. What was this problem? (b—He had interrogated two Christian women and found that they were harmless. Therefore, he didn't understand why should he keep arresting Christians.) Trajan responded that Pliny shouldn't go hunting for Christians, but if they were being nuisances, he should arrest them.

(4) This Christian leader, before he became a Christian, was a speech writer for the Roman Emperor, and was a potential candidate for emperor himself. Who was he? (a—Augustine.) Augustine was a favorite of the leading senator of his day, and seemed to have a fine political future. But after his conversion, he devoted his life to Christian service.

(5) In 732, Charles "The Hammer" Martel won the Battle of Tours, stopping the spread of a mighty force that had been sweeping through the Mediterranean world for the previous century. What was that force? (b—The Muslims.) If it weren't for Martel, we might be speaking Arabic

today. After their defeat, the Muslims stayed in North Africa and the Mideast and, in Europe, progressed no farther than Spain.

(6) The Crusades were: (d—All of the above.) They were wars between Muslims and Christians over the Holy Land. Their purpose was to convert Jews and Muslims to Christianity by force. (Coincidentally they're also what Billy Graham calls his events.) Fought in several stages in the Middle Ages, the Crusades were zealous but largely misguided attempts at Christian outreach and land acquisition.

(7) In 1492, Columbus sailed the ocean blue. Why? (d—All of the above.) Columbus wanted to make money, spread Christianity, and find a new route to the east. He was a devout Christian, though he had a few odd ideas about the faith. For him and many who followed him, the exploration of the New World was an attempt to spread Christianity. Sometimes they tried to do this with military power, unfortunately; but there were also many peaceful missionaries who sought to share Christ with the Native Americans.

(8) In 1517, Martin Luther tacked a notice on the church door at Wittenberg, and the world was changed forever. What did the notice say? (c—It listed 95 critical questions about the way the Catholic church was doing things.) Luther was especially bothered about the fraudulent fund-raising for a new cathedral in Rome. This act sparked the Protestant Reformation, which was both a theological revolt against the Catholic church and a political revolt against Roman power.

(9) In 1620, the Pilgrims set up their colony in Massachusetts. What was their stated purpose? (b—The glory of God and the advancement of Christianity.) The Mayflower Compact spelled it out clearly. This was a Christian community that landed at Plymouth Rock.

(10) In the 1600's, Protestants and Catholics fought the Thirty Years War for control of Europe. How long did this war last? (b—Thirty years.) Duh—and guess who's buried in Grant's Tomb? Protestant-Catholic fighting raged for several centuries in Europe. (In fact, we still see it today in Ireland.) The fighting may have started with some theological disagreement, but it quickly became a question of political power.

(11) This man, along with his hymn-writing brother, led a religious movement that swept England and America in the late 1700's, especially among the poor. Some think that England was spared a bloody revolution, like the one France had in 1789, because this man gave the poor people hope. Who was he? (b—John Wesley.) Wesley is considered the founder of the Methodist Church, one of the great popular movements of history.

(12) Which document contains these words: "all . . . are endowed by their Creator with certain unalienable rights"? (a—The Declaration of Independence.) Some of our "founding fathers" were genuine Christians. Others were deists, who held a vague belief in God. Whatever their beliefs, they united on this assertion that God was the author of human rights.

(13) In the late 1700's, Robert Raikes, a devout Christian, started a bold new program that began to improve the educational prospects of

poor children in England and eventually worldwide. What was this program?
(d—Sunday school.) Previously, poor children had no time for schooling, since they had to work in the factories six days a week. But Sunday
was their day off. Raikes began teaching them the Bible, as well as
reading, writing, and arithmetic. For many kids, it was a step toward
a better life.

*(14) This Virginian was a solid Christian who helped write the U.S.
Constitution. Later he became the fourth president of the United States.
Who was he?* (b—James Madison.)

*(15) The abolitionist movement was a major social and political force
in the early 1800's in England and the U.S. What was its purpose?*
(a—To stop the slave trade and to free slaves.) The movement was
primarily made up of Christians. Some would say they forced the
U.S. Civil War by pressing the slave issue.

(16) Which of these schools was established as a Christian college?
(d—All of the above.) Churches were at the forefront of education
in the 1700's and 1800's. Most of our oldest colleges and universities
have Christian roots.

*(17) William Jennings Bryan was a major figure in U.S. politics and
religion around the turn of the century. What was he known for?* (d—All
of the above.) Bryan ran for president three times—as a Democrat in
1896, 1900, and 1908. He prosecuted Scopes (for teaching evolution in
public schools) in the famous "Monkey Trial." And he was Secretary of
State under Woodrow Wilson prior to World War I, before he resigned
in protest of growing American militancy.

*(18) John F. Kennedy was the first man of his religion to be elected
U.S. President, and he faced some opposition for it. What was his religion?*
(c—Roman Catholic.) Some people feared that, as president, he would
be a puppet of the Pope.

*(19) This twentieth-century president openly claimed to be "born again"
and even taught Sunday school at a Baptist church in Washington D.C. Who
was he?* (c—Jimmy Carter.)

*(20) In the 1980's, the Catholic church was a significant force support-
ing the resistance movement led by Lech Walesa against the Communist
government in what country?* (b—Poland.)

After you've gone through the answers on the quiz, have group
members tally up their scores. Award prizes to the top three scorers.

STEP 3

What's Missing?

(Needed: Three copies of Repro Resource 7)

Ask: **How many of you knew the answers to every question on this quiz, and didn't have to guess at all?** Probably very few, if any, group members knew all the answers.

But you have history classes at school. Why didn't you learn this information there? (Some kids may have heard some of this information at school, and just forgotten it. Others may have had only *American* history classes, and may not be familiar with world events. Still others may not be taught anything in history class that has to do with religion.)

How often does your history teacher talk about religions—especially Christianity—and how religious beliefs have affected history? Get a few responses.

We talked earlier about how important it is to know not only *what* happened in history, but also *why* it happened. But often the whys have to do with religious beliefs, and teachers are reluctant to talk about them. Let's get some humorous insight into this problem.

Ask for three volunteers (preferably a guy and two girls) to perform a skit. Give them copies of "The Committee" (Repro Resource 7). Have them read through it once, and then perform. Afterward, lead the group in a round of applause.

Afterward, ask: **Do you think there are any dangers or problems with emphasizing the role religion—particularly Christianity—has played in history?** (There is a tendency to "gloss over" or "explain away" bad things done in the name of Christianity. The Crusades, for example, were the result of a noble ideal to spread Christianity throughout the world. However, the violent methods used by the Crusaders to spread the faith must be condemned.)

Why do you suppose non-Christian textbook writers leave out some Christian material in their history texts?

Use the following answers to supplement group members' responses:

• Perhaps they don't understand the importance of religion. They may not see it as a compelling force in people's lives.

• Some may be afraid to get involved in religious controversy. For instance, was it good or bad that Charles Martel stopped the Muslims at Tours? It depends on whether you're Christian or Muslim.

• Some may be convinced that Christianity has hurt society. For instance, European attempts to "Christianize" Native Americans resulted in massacres and the dismantling of a culture.

Point out that *Christians* may be able to distinguish between personal Christianity and the institutional Christianity that has caused so many problems throughout history—but outside the church, it all looks the same.

He's Got the Whole World . . .

Have group members turn to Genesis 45. Take a moment to set up the story. **Joseph was sold into slavery by his brothers, and he wound up in Egypt. There, after several other adventures, he became second in command of the whole country. He helped Egypt prepare for a famine by storing grain. When the famine struck, who should show up begging for grain? His brothers. In this scene, Joseph reveals his identity to his brothers.**

Have someone read aloud Genesis 45:4-8. Ask: **According to Joseph, who was really responsible for getting him to Egypt?** (God.) You might want to underscore the point by reading aloud Genesis 50:20, where Joseph says, "You intended to harm me, but God intended it for good."

Ask: **How do you think a secular historian would see this event?** (Through wise planning, Egypt averts a disaster and survives a famine.)

But we have a behind-the-scenes view. What is the biblical explanation? (God intended for Joseph to save Egypt from famine—and to give the Israelites a place to stay during some tough times.)

Have someone read aloud Isaiah 7:18-20. Explain that Israel is being warned (in poetic language) about an imminent downfall. Ask: **Who is the "razor" in verse 20?** (The king of Assyria.)

Why do you think he is called that? How will he "shave" the nation of Judah? (We know from history that the Assyrian army invaded Israel and Judah and actually captured most of the territory around Jerusalem. In that way, the Assyrians "shaved off" all of Jerusalem's provinces.)

O P T I O N S

EXTRA ACTION

HEARD IT ALL BEFORE

LITTLE BIBLE BACKGROUND

SHORT MEETING TIME

EXTRA CHALLENGE

Verse 18 says that God will call "flies" from Egypt and "bees" from Assyria. What are these? (Armies that will invade the land of Judah.)

Explain: **The history books, if they covered this event, might say, "The mighty nation of Assyria swept through the Mideast with its technologically superior army." But we know that God was behind it, allowing Assyria to invade, "using" Assyria as a barber would use a razor.**

Have group members turn to Isaiah 45:1-5. Ask someone to read aloud verse 1. Explain that Cyrus was a Persian king. The Jews had been defeated by the Babylonians, who took them captive for 70 years. Then the Persians defeated the Babylonians, so Cyrus was in charge of the fate of the captive Jews. Cyrus was a kind, gentle king, and he allowed the Jews to return to Jerusalem.

Ask: **What does the Lord call Cyrus in this verse?** (His anointed.)

What does it mean to be anointed? (Chosen by God to do special things for Him.)

Why did God call Cyrus "anointed"? (God would use Cyrus to do good things for His people, the Israelites.)

Have someone read aloud verses 2-5. Then ask: **Was Cyrus a believer? Did he trust God?** (No. In verse 5, God says, "you have not acknowledged me.")

How could God "anoint" Cyrus and use him when Cyrus didn't even acknowledge God? (God can use anyone He wants.)

Explain: **The history books might say, "Cyrus developed his kinder, gentler policies and—in a new era of international goodwill—allowed the Jews and others to return to their homelands." But we know there's more to the story. God empowered Cyrus, and He used Cyrus to get His people back home.**

Have someone read aloud Proverbs 21:1. Ask: **What does this verse tell us?** (God is ultimately in control of what kings decide to do. That does not mean that they will choose to trust Him. They may, in fact, be intending to do evil—as the king of Assyria was. But God uses all their intentions to work *His* will.)

Summarize: **When an historical event rapidly unfolds— the fall of Communism in some parts of the world, for instance—many people choose to look at it on a purely human level. Analysts determine various political and social reasons for it. But we know there's more. The prayers of millions of Christians, in the Communist world and outside of it, helped to destroy Communism in Eastern Europe and the former Soviet Union.**

We will not always understand why God does what He does, but we can be confident that He is ultimately in control. We have no business saying that "God calmed

the waters so Washington could cross the Delaware." But we may say that God has used Washington's victories to accomplish some good things.

Most history classes will teach historical events on a human level. That's fine. They have to. It would be nice if they did a little more to recognize the importance of religion in human decisions, but you can't expect that of them. But we should approach history from another level. We must remember that God is working behind the scenes in all of history, accomplishing His will. We can trust Him for that.

Thanksgiving

(Needed: Copies of Repro Resource 7 that you handed out earlier)

In closing, ask group members to think about what God has done—and is doing—in history. Point out that not only is God involved in human events, we can also talk with Him about those events.

Ask group members to write a short prayer on the back of Repro Resource 7 that includes one or more of the following:

(a) thanking God for some historical event (like the founding of the U.S., or the dismantling of the Berlin Wall) that has positively impacted the world today;

(b) questioning God about why He allowed some historical event (like the Vietnam War or the Nazi holocaust) to occur;

(c) asking for God's help in some current event (like an environmental danger or an imminent war).

Give group members a few minutes to write their prayers. Then invite volunteers to read their prayers aloud. Encourage group members to continue praying regularly about their concerns.

NOTES

THE OTHER SIDE OF HISTORY

1 In the 900's B.C., Israel became a major power in the Mideast. They did it not through military battles, but through shrewd trading and alliance-making. Who was the king at this time?

(a) David   (c) Hezekiah

(b) Solomon   (d) Elvis

2. For two-and-a-half centuries (A.D. 64-311), the Roman Empire carried on a war against a segment of its own people. Though these people were unarmed and non-threatening, they eventually "defeated" the Empire. Who were these people?

(a) The Jews   (c) The Muslims

(b) The Christians   (d) Da Bears

3. Early in the second century, Governor Pliny wrote to Emperor Trajan with a problem. What was this problem?

(a) The Christians were taking over his province.

(b) He had interrogated two Christian women and found that they were harmless. Therefore, he didn't understand why he should keep arresting Christians.

(c) He was converting to Christianity.

(d) He could not get to the next level on his Nintendo game.

4. This Christian leader, before he became a Christian, was a speechwriter for the Roman Emperor, and was a potential candidate for emperor himself. Who was he?

(a) Augustine   (c) Aquinas

(b) Constantine   (d) Pat Buchanan

5. In 732, Charles "The Hammer" Martel won the Battle of Tours, stopping the spread of a mighty force that had been sweeping through the Mediterranean world for the previous century. What was that force?

(a) The Protestants   (c) The Mongols of Genghis Khan

(b) The Muslims   (d) Invaders from the planet Nectron

6. The Crusades were:

(a) Wars between Muslims and Christians over the Holy Land   (c) Billy Graham meetings

(b) An effort to convert Jews and Muslims to Christianity by force   (d) All of the above

7. In 1492, Columbus sailed the ocean blue. Why?

(a) To make money   (c) To find a new route to the East

(b) To spread Christianity   (d) All of the above

8. In 1517, Martin Luther tacked a notice on the church door at Wittenberg, and the world was changed forever. What did the notice say?

(a) "Free food!"

(b) Ichabod—"The Glory Has Departed"

(c) It listed 95 critical questions about the way the Catholic church was doing things.

(d) It invited everyone to come to a Bible study at the monastery.

9. In 1620, the Pilgrims set up their colony in Massachusetts. What was their stated purpose?

(a) A new realm of brotherhood for all people

(b) The glory of God and the advancement of Christianity

(c) A colony that could supply England with needed grain

(d) Chowing down with the Indians

10. In the 1600's, Protestants and Catholics fought the Thirty Years War for control of Europe. How long did this war last?

(a) Six days
(b) Thirty years
(c) One hundred years
(d) All of the above

11. This man, along with his hymn-writing brother, led a religious movement that swept England and America in the late 1700's, especially among the poor. Some think that England was spared a bloody revolution, like the one France had in 1789, because this man gave the poor people hope. Who was he?

(a) Oliver Cromwell
(b) John Wesley
(c) John Adams
(d) John Lennon

12. Which document contains these words: "all ... are endowed by their Creator with certain unalienable rights"?

(a) The Declaration of Independence
(b) The U.S. Constitution
(c) The Gettysburg Address
(d) The script for *Star Trek VI: The Final Frontier*

13. In the late 1700's, Robert Raikes, a devout Christian, started a bold new program that began to improve the educational prospects of poor children in England and eventually worldwide. What was this program?

(a) Head Start
(b) Tutoring
(c) IQ tests
(d) Sunday school

14. This Virginian was a solid Christian who helped write the U.S. Constitution. Later he became the fourth president of the United States. Who was he?

(a) George Washington
(b) James Madison
(c) James Monroe
(d) James Earl Jones

15. The abolitionist movement was a major social and political force in the early 1800's in England and the U.S. What was its purpose?

(a) To stop the slave trade and to free slaves
(b) To halt the sale and consumption of alcohol
(c) To elect Christians to public office
(d) All of the above

16. Which of these schools was established as a Christian college?

(a) Harvard University
(b) Oberlin College
(c) Moody Bible Institute
(d) All of the above

17. William Jennings Bryan was a major figure in U.S. politics and religion around the turn of the century. What was he known for?

(a) He ran for president three times.
(b) He prosecuted Scopes in the famous "Monkey Trial."
(c) He was Secretary of State prior to World War I.
(d) All of the above

18. John F. Kennedy was the first man of his religion to be elected U.S. President, and he faced some opposition for it. What was his religion?

(a) Baptist
(b) Mormon
(c) Roman Catholic
(d) Voodoo

19. This twentieth-century president openly claimed to be "born again" and even taught Sunday school at a Baptist church in Washington D.C. Who was he?

(a) Ronald Reagan
(b) Harry Truman
(c) Jimmy Carter
(d) Boris Yeltsin

20. In the 1980's, the Catholic church was a significant force supporting the resistance movement led by Lech Walesa against the Communist government in what country?

(a) Czechoslovakia
(b) Poland
(c) Cuba
(d) Santa Monica

T H E
COMMITTEE

DEBBIE: I'd like to call to order the meeting of the school board subcommittee for textbook selection. Now, each of you was given several textbooks to consider for the history classes. Do you have any to recommend?

FLORA: Well, yes I do. It wasn't on the list, but I found this at the Solid Word Bookstore: *Man Proposes, God Disposes.* It goes through history and shows how God made all the good things happen, and how He judged all the bad things.

HANK: Oh, that's real objective. What about the Crusades? Was that a good thing or a bad thing?

FLORA: I don't know. Let me check. (*She burrows into the book.*)

HANK: *Man Proposes, God Disposes,* huh? I think I know where to dispose of that.

DEBBIE: Have you come up with anything better, Hank?

HANK: Well, yes, I have. *Human Progress Through the Ages.* Right here on the cover it says: "Easily rejects the religious myths surrounding human history and focuses on the triumph of the species." Obviously, this is what we need. With a text book like this, we won't have any trouble with the Supreme Court, if you know what I mean. (*He hands the book to Debbie.*)

FLORA: (*Still reading her own book*) Good!

DEBBIE: Good?

FLORA: And bad. The Crusades were both good and bad, the book says. It was a good idea, but the Crusaders massacred too many people, so they were punished with a few more centuries of darkness until the Reformation.

HANK: What about the Renaissance?

FLORA: (*Reading*) I don't see anything on that.

HANK: The Enlightenment? Anything on that?

FLORA: No. Let me see. Oh, here are the founding fathers, those dear old Christian men. George Washington, Benjamin Franklin, Thomas Jefferson.

HANK: Christian men? That's ridiculous! Ben Franklin wasn't exactly what you'd call a model Christian! Does your book tell you about that?

FLORA: (*Scanning the book*) No. "God blessed him by sending the lightning upon his kite."

HANK: I don't believe it. How could a history book leave out all that stuff.

DEBBIE: But from what I can see, Hank, your book doesn't say anything about the religious motives of, say, Emperor Constantine with the conversion of the Roman Empire—

HANK: It was all politics.

DEBBIE: Or St. Augustine—

HANK: An opportunist.

DEBBIE: Or the church of the Middle Ages—

HANK: Gypsies, tramps, and thieves.

DEBBIE: Or the Reformation—

HANK: A class struggle.

DEBBIE: Or the Great Awakening in America—

HANK: Media hype, that's all it was.

DEBBIE: Or the abolition movement.

HANK: Pompous do-gooders.

FLORA: (*Still reading her book*) "And God calmed the waters so George Washington could cross the Delaware."

DEBBIE: We're past that now, Flora. Try to keep up.

HANK: But don't you see? We can't trust Christians with history. They turn it all around.

DEBBIE: But does it help to ignore the religious commitment of the major figures of history? That's just as twisted, too. Can't we be honest about what happened and why?

HANK: No, I don't think so.

FLORA: (*Looking up*) What happened? Why?

DEBBIE: Never mind.

EXTRA ACTION

STEP 1

For more action, try the following opener. Before the session, write each of the following situations on a separate index card: "It's Thanksgiving and the turkey burned up"; "You're trying to set the world record for the tallest sandwich"; "You haven't eaten in three weeks"; and "You've got nothing else to do." To start the session, give each card to a volunteer. Each volunteer will then pantomime making a peanut butter sandwich as someone in that situation might do it. Teams will try to guess what the situation is. The team that guesses the most situations wins. Tie this activity into the importance of knowing *why* things happen. To make Step 2 more active, give each person at least one question and one answer that you've cut from Repro Resource 6 (making sure you've mixed the questions and answers thoroughly, and that all questions and answers are passed out). Let kids mingle for five to ten minutes, trying to match questions with answers. In Step 3, skip the skit and have kids act out exaggerated "Christian versions" of Washington crossing the Delaware or cutting down the cherry tree. (For example, in crossing the Delaware, Washington might pose with a Bible raised aloft while his men sing "Shall We Gather at the River?")

STEP 4

Have group members form three teams. Each team will study one of the Bible stories in the session. To explain its passage to the rest of the group, each team must form a human pyramid. The person at the top will tell what the "tip of the iceberg"—the visible, human part of the story—is. Those on the bottom will tell what God was doing behind the scenes.

SMALL GROUP

STEP 1

"Twenty Questions" could become tedious with a very small group. If you need an alternative, try this. Before the session, place a variety of small items (thimble, salad croutons, paragraph torn from a newspaper, toy soldier, linked paper clips, photo, etc.) on a large serving tray. Pack as many items on the tray as you can; then cover them with a cloth. At the start of the session, remove the cloth and tell kids to examine the items for 30 seconds. Then give the group a written quiz, asking only about items that were *not* on the tray—without mentioning that they weren't there, of course. (Example: If you included no postage stamps, you might ask: **What color was on the background of the Elvis stamp?** If you included no dice, ask: **How many dots were on the top of the dice?**) Group members must stay silent during the quiz. Afterward, see how kids did. Tie this activity into the fact that certain crucial items—like the role of religion—are often left out of history classes.

STEP 5

Take advantage of your group's size by having a more personal discussion of history and school. Ask questions like these: **What events from history make you feel good about being a Christian? Which ones make you feel bad? If Jesus has been mentioned in your history classes, how was He described? How did you feel about that? What grade would you give your history teachers when it comes to treating Christians fairly? If your school has weeks or months emphasizing the history of certain ethnic groups, do you think it should have one about Christians? Why or why not? If there were a "Christian History Week" at your school, what would you want to see included?**

LARGE GROUP

STEP 2

A large group may get restless while you're answering the quiz. Instead of using the quiz, have two teams act out the following "history" as you read it. Appoint a director of each team who will guide his or her actors. Each event you describe will feature two "sides"; Team A will take the first side you mention, and Team B will take the second. Encourage kids to clash dramatically but not violently. Say: **And now, a brief history of the modern world. (1) Between A.D. 64 and 311, the Roman Empire carried on a war of persecution against a segment of its own people—Christians. (2) In 732, Charles Martel and his army won the Battle of Tours, stopping the spread of Islam before it could sweep over Europe. (3) During the Middle Ages, the Crusades took place—with misguided Christians trying to convert Jews and Muslims by force. (4) In the 1500s, Martin Luther and others took on the Catholic church. (5) In the 1600s, Protestants and Catholics fought the Thirty Years War for control of Europe. (6) In the 1800s, the abolitionists—many of them Christians—opposed slaveholders, leading to the Civil War. (7) In the late twentieth century, the church in Eastern Europe and the Soviet Union helped bring about the fall of Communism.** As time allows, mention nonconfrontational events from the quiz.

STEP 3

Since the skit will involve just a few kids, try another activity instead. Have two teams debate the following statement for three minutes: **Christian missionaries have had a negative effect on the rest of the world.** Help teams prepare by listing good and bad effects that "missionary" work (from the Crusades to current Bible translation and medical help) has had on the people involved. Use the rest of the step as written.

STEP 3

Kids may have heard the U.S. called a "Christian nation" and all its founding fathers dubbed Christians. They may think you're going to repeat all that, and tune you out. Derail their assumptions by sharing facts like the following:
(1) Thomas Jefferson believed the miracles in the Bible didn't happen.
(2) Ben Franklin didn't believe that Jesus was God.
(3) George Washington wrote that America was not a Christian nation.
(4) Slavery was an institution in "Christian" America for nearly a hundred years. Note that being honest about the role of Christianity in history means just that—being honest.

STEP 4

Teenagers may have heard repeatedly that God is in control—but don't see how that's possible. Is He behind every event? What about terrible things like the Holocaust? Explain that people have puzzled over questions like these for thousands of years. God is ultimately in charge of the universe and has the power to intervene as He wishes (Ps. 2). The Bible describes many examples of how He's done so. But Jesus suggested that our explanations of why things happen (for example, that God is punishing someone by letting a tragedy occur) can be dead wrong (John 9:1-3; Luke 13:1-5). We won't know many "whys" of history until we get to heaven. Until then, we should tell God honestly how we feel about things that happen and how we want them to turn out (Ps. 77:7-12).

STEP 3

As they hear about some of the more embarrassing moments in church history, kids may wonder: Does God want Christians to conduct "holy wars" like the Crusades? Explain that Christians disagree over whether there's such a thing as a "just war" in which evildoers must be stopped. God commanded ancient Israel to fight other nations, but few if any world leaders today could truthfully say that God told them to launch a war on His behalf. Efforts to convert people by force (as in the Crusades and the Inquisition) don't reflect the way God deals with people; He allows them to freely choose whether to accept His Son. He wants a loving relationship with people, not a forced one. These passages may be helpful: James 1:20; Matthew 5:43-48; 23:37.

STEP 4

The Isaiah 7 passage may raise questions in kids' minds. For example, why would God let the Assyrians do this if He loved Israel so much? (To discipline them, to bring them back to keeping their covenant with Him. They had wandered away from God, and it was in their best interest to have a good relationship with Him.) Why did Isaiah talk about flies and razors instead of coming right out and saying what he meant? (Symbols are used frequently in the Bible, especially in predictions about the future. Sometimes the symbols hid the meaning from those who weren't supposed to understand. Sometimes the prophecies came to the prophets in visions, and symbols were all they could use to describe the sights they saw.)

STEP 1

Use the following activity to introduce the history theme and reinforce group identity at the same time. Challenge group members to create an "instant youth group museum" immortalizing your group for posterity. Kids have 10 minutes to do the job, and can use only items and people now in your meeting place. (Examples: A kid who always gets to the refreshment table first could freeze as a statue in an eating position; "relics" like a volleyball or a group member's shoes could be displayed.) Provide index cards and pens so that "museum displays" can be labeled. Let kids elect a tour guide to take you through the museum when it's done.

Or you could create an "instant scrapbook," using an instant camera to capture re-enacted events in the life of your group.

STEP 5

Close with worship that focuses on how God will wrap up human history His way. Read aloud Revelation 21:1-7. Ask: **Before this happens, what's one way in which you might influence history as an expression of worship to God?**
To get kids thinking, you might remind them how other believers have influenced history—running for government office; joining a movement, such as the abolitionists or prohibitionists, that they believed was doing God's work; inventing a way to help people through rescue missions, medicine, Sunday schools, etc.; working for God in other countries as missionaries, teachers, etc. Some songs you might want to sing: "King of Kings and Lord of Lords," "Majesty," "Crown Him with Many Crowns," "Our God Is an Awesome God," and "He Is Lord."

MOSTLY GIRLS

STEP 1

Instead of having group members write on index cards something they did in the past year, expand the time frame to include things they've done at any time in their lives. Ask them to write something that others may not know about them. Play "Twenty Questions" as described, but in addition to guessing the reason for the action, group members must guess who wrote it. You may want to add an additional challenge by giving each person the choice of writing something that is not true. Then, as you play the game, group members have to decide not only who wrote the clues, but also whether the events really happened.

STEP 2

After group members have individually completed "The Other Side of History" (Repro Resource 6), have them form four teams. Assign each team five different questions from Repro Resource 6. Each team will answer its assigned questions for the rest of the group and, if possible, give some background information regarding the answers. (You may want to provide the teams with background information from the session.)

MOSTLY GUYS

STEP 3

The skit may be too subtle for some guys. If you need something more obvious, try the following activity. Before the session, videotape a football, basketball, hockey, or baseball telecast. Cue it up to an eventful section. At this point in the session, choose two volunteer sportscasters. The first will be a die-hard fan of one team, the other an eternally loyal follower of the other team. Play the video segment with the sound off. As it plays, your sportscasters will do play-by-play commentary that reflects their loyalties, hamming it up as much as possible—praising their own teams to the skies and cutting down the opposition. After a few minutes, turn off the tape and let the "audience" rate the sportscasters. Use their performance to illustrate the danger of distorting history by reporting it from one viewpoint or another. That's one reason schools avoid discussing the role of religion in history.

STEP 5

Have group members form teams. See which team can list in three minutes the greatest number of positive, male, Christian role models from history (other than Jesus Himself). (Examples might include Moses, Peter, David, Paul, Joseph, Daniel, John the Baptist, John and Charles Wesley, former President Jimmy Carter, inventor George Washington Carver, martyred missionary Chet Bitterman, scientist Isaac Newton, and baseball player Orel Hershiser.) After declaring a winner, ask: **What is one quality in each of these men that you think is worth having? Which person on this list do you identify with most? Why?**

EXTRA FUN

STEP 1

Bring a large mirror, a roll of aluminum foil, a sheet of poster board, a supply of eyebrow pencils, and makeup remover. Have group members form three teams. Each team member must use an eyebrow pencil to make himself or herself up as a cat. The team whose members do the best job (in your judgment) wins. The catch is that Team A gets to use the mirror. Team B gets the foil instead. And Team C gets the poster board. Emphasize that no one may help anyone else. After judging the results, ask: **Why was it so much easier for Team A to get the job done?** (It had a mirror, which gives a much more accurate reflection than foil or poster board.) Point out that history that ignores Christian contributions doesn't give an accurate reflection of reality. That can affect the way we see ourselves; if we think Christians have done nothing but start "holy wars" and write hymns, we won't be too eager to identify ourselves as Christians.

STEP 5

Have group members sit in a circle. Each person should write the first sentence of a humorous prophecy about the person to his or her left: "How (name of person) Will Change History." After one sentence, everyone passes his or her paper to the right and a sentence is added. Continue the process until the papers almost reach the people they're written about. Then have those who wrote the first sentences read the prophecies aloud. [NOTE: Caution kids not to write anything derogatory about each other. Those who read the prophecies aloud should skip any nasty comments. If you think you can't trust kids to do this, do the reading yourself and edit as you go.]

STEP 2

You'll need access to a variety of recorded music for this activity. Play a bit of a Bach concerto, then a little of a Mozart symphony. Ask: **Which of these composers was a Christian?** (Bach.) Play an instrumental section from a contemporary Christian rock song, then a similar section from "secular" rock. Ask: **Which of these musicians is a Christian?** Finally, play part of a song that's recorded by a Christian (like Bruce Cockburn) but that doesn't have an overtly Christian message—and one that's recorded by another Christian and has an obviously Christian message. Ask: **Which of these musicians is a Christian?** Discuss the fact that the influence of faith on an artist doesn't always show on the surface, and the same is true of historical events.

STEP 5

Consider showing and/or discussing portions of three videos that depict the role of Christians in history. (1) *Chariots of Fire*. Eric Liddell, who went on to serve as a missionary to China, honors God as an Olympic runner. Portrayal of Christianity: Mostly positive. (2) *The Mission*. A Catholic priest tries to convert a South American tribe, while a mercenary fights to defend it against an institutional church that's allied with the government. Portrayal of Christianity: Mixed. The priest is sincere; the church comes off looking corrupt and hypocritical. (3) *The Crucible*. The Puritans get scorched for burning alleged witches. Portrayal of Christianity: Mostly negative. Questions for discussion: **How do these movies make you feel about being a Christian? Is one more accurate than the others? Why or why not? Since *The Crucible* is often read and performed as a play in public high schools, what impression of Christianity do you think kids get from it?**

STEP 1

Combine Steps 1 and 2 into a shorter opener, replacing "Twenty Questions" and the quiz. Before the session, ask a group member who collects baseball cards (or other sports cards) to show his or her collection to the group and explain which cards are most valuable. (If no one in your group has sports cards, buy a few packs of cards, pass them out, and let kids decide which cards they think will be most valuable someday.) Then, on the board, make a list of the following people from the Step 2 quiz: Augustine, Charles Martel, Christopher Columbus, Martin Luther, John Wesley, Robert Raikes, James Madison, William Jennings Bryan, and Jimmy Carter. Ask: **If there were such a thing as "Christian history cards," showing great Christians from history, which of these people would belong on those cards—and why?** Answers will vary, and are partly a matter of opinion. Use the quiz answers in the basic session plan as needed. To save time in Step 3, skip the skit.

STEP 4

Instead of studying the stories of Joseph, Assyria, and Cyrus, read Daniel 2:48-49. Have kids speculate on how religion might have affected this government move. Then read Daniel 1:1, 3-4, 6-7, 17-20; 2:1, 19, 47. Ask: **How did devotion to God make these young men better able to influence history? Do you think godly people are better at running countries than unbelievers are? Why or why not? How might God prepare you to have an effect on history?**

STEP 2

You may want to consider adding the following two questions to the quiz.

1. Which black denominations were begun as a result of exclusion from ordination in white denominations?

(a) African Methodist Episcopal

(b) National Baptist

(c) Progressive Baptist

(d) All of the above

[The answer is d—All of the above.]

2. Slavery in America found its false religious justification mainly through what religion?

(a) Islam

(b) Buddhism

(c) Christianity

(d) Jehovah's Witnesses

[The answer is c—Christianity.]

[NOTE: If you use question #3, immediately discuss why some people try to use Scripture to oppress, rather than liberate, others.]

STEP 3

If you used the previous questions for Step 2, ask: **Why do you suppose some Christian textbooks leave out American Christianity's oppressive past—which includes slavery, confinement of Native Americans, and imperialism?**

STEP 2

Younger kids may be totally stumped by the quiz. Simplify it by using just the following true/false statements (all are false):
(1) From A.D. 64 to 311, the Christians persecuted the Romans. (2) The Crusades were wars over the Holy Land, fought between Catholics and Protestants. (3) Christopher Columbus sailed in 1492 strictly to find a new route to the East Indies. (4) The Pilgrims who landed at Plymouth Rock based their colony on the idea that all religions are equal. (5) The U.S. Constitution contains the words, "All … are endowed by their Creator with certain unalienable rights." (6) The man who started Sunday school wanted only to teach the Bible. (7) All Christians supported slavery before the U.S. Civil War. (8) Harvard University was started by people who believed the Bible was full of mistakes. (9) No U.S. President in the last 50 years has publicly admitted to being a "born-again Christian." (10) Religion had nothing to do with the fall of Communism in Eastern Europe. After the quiz, elaborate as needed, using relevant answers to the quiz in the basic session plan.

STEP 3

The skit probably will be over the heads of younger kids. Instead of using it, brainstorm the names of twelve living, famous people—four politicians, four movie or TV stars, and four sports stars or musicians. Write these on the board. Ask: **What religions are these people connected with? What do they believe about God? If you don't know, why don't you?** Point out that reporters, publicists, and others usually ignore "religious stuff" because they think no one's interested or it's too controversial. Some public schools have had the same attitude about mentioning the role of religion in history.

STEP 4

Challenge kids with the truth that God's people, with His help, can influence governments and thereby history. Study the cases of Daniel in Babylon (Dan. 9:1-6, 17-24) and the apostle Paul in Rome (Eph. 6:19-20; Phil. 4:21-22). About Daniel, ask: **What did Daniel want to happen? How did he go about getting it? How did God react?** About Paul, ask: **What did Paul want to happen? What was the key to making it happen? In what way was he an ambassador? What could be the results of making converts in Caesar's household?** Note that in both cases prayer and the right attitude were catalysts for changing history.

STEP 5

Offer a prize to any group member who'll do an oral, written, or videotaped report on a Christian who influenced history. For background material, order several back issues of *Christian History* magazine. (To order, write *Christian History*, Past Issues Sales, P. O. Box 550-A, Church Hill, MD 21690. If you must have the magazines more quickly, try calling the editorial offices of *Christian History* at 708-260-6200.)

PLANNING CHECKLIST

DATE USED:

Approx. Time

STEP 1: *Twenty Questions* _____
- ❏ Extra Action
- ❏ Small Group
- ❏ Fellowship & Worship
- ❏ Extra Fun
- ❏ Short Meeting Time

Things needed:

STEP 2: *An Extracurricular History Quiz* _____
- ❏ Large Group
- ❏ Mostly Girls
- ❏ Media
- ❏ Urban
- ❏ Combined Junior High/High School

Things needed:

STEP 3: *What's Missing?* _____
- ❏ Large Group
- ❏ Heard It All Before
- ❏ Little Bible Background
- ❏ Mostly Girls
- ❏ Mostly Guys
- ❏ Urban
- ❏ Combined Junior High/High School

Things needed:

STEP 4: *He's Got the Whole World …* _____
- ❏ Extra Action
- ❏ Heard It All Before
- ❏ Little Bible Background
- ❏ Short Meeting Time
- ❏ Extra Challenge

Things needed:

STEP 5: *Thanksgiving* _____
- ❏ Small Group
- ❏ Fellowship & Worship
- ❏ Mostly Guys
- ❏ Extra Fun
- ❏ Media
- ❏ Extra Challenge

Things needed:

Truth or Consequences

SOCIAL SCIENCE 101

Right

WRONG

YOUR GOALS FOR THIS SESSION:
Choose one or more

☐ To help kids learn the importance of biblical values in the study of human behavior and interaction.

☐ To help kids understand how their school social sciences courses may be missing the boat by attempting a "values-free" approach to their subjects.

☐ To help kids choose to stand up for God's truth.

☐ Other:_____
_____

Your Bible Base:

Romans 1:18—2:4; 8:5-9; 13:9-14

Logic Problems

Choose three volunteers from the group, preferably those who speak well and can think on their feet. Explain that you will give each of them a simple statement, and they will each have 60 seconds to convince the group that the statement is true. Afterward, the group will vote on who was most persuasive.

The statements are as follows:
- **Two plus two equals five.**
- **Red is really blue.**
- **The sun revolves around the earth, which is flat.**

After the game (and the vote), discuss the activity. Ask: **What was the problem with this contest? Why did the speakers have such a hard time convincing us that the statements were true?** (Because the statements *weren't* true.)

But isn't truth just a matter of personal opinion? If a person really believes that two and two is five, what right do I have to say he's wrong? (He may have the right to believe what he wants, but I don't want him grading my SAT's. There are standards of truth that we all accept, and he is wrong. He may have the right to be wrong, but that doesn't mean we have to claim that he's right.)

The Theory of Relativity

(Needed: Copies of Repro Resource 8)

Ask for two volunteers to participate in a brief skit. Give each a copy of "Class Struggle" (Repro Resource 8). Let the actors read through the skit once; then have them perform.

Afterward, ask: **What sort of attitudes do you find in school about right and wrong? Do your teachers try to present a "values-free" education?** Get a couple of responses. If group members don't fully understand what a "values-free" education means, use the following questions to get more specific.

- **What would happen at school if someone, in the middle of a class discussion on lifestyle choices, said, "I believe homosexuality is a sin"?**
- **What would happen if someone said she believed abortion was wrong?**
- **What would happen if someone said it was morally wrong to have sex before marriage?**
- **What would happen if someone said that the only way to have a relationship with God is through Jesus Christ?**

Would these people be encouraged or discouraged by teachers at your school? Encourage group members to be open and honest about how things are at their schools. Perhaps some of them will say that they *don't* receive a "values-free" education at school. If so, refer to the general philosophy of society that we see regularly on TV talk shows. A relative, values-free attitude is regularly preached over the airwaves.

Explain: **In this session, we'll be looking at what the Bible says about values and right and wrong. Then we'll try to find some practical ways to be true to our faith without being viewed as obnoxious bigots.**

STEP 3

The Romans Road Map

(Needed: Chalkboard and chalk or newsprint and marker, copies of Repro Resource 8, pencils)

Have group members turn to Romans 1. Ask someone to read aloud verses 18-20. Then ask: **Why is God angry?** (Because of the godlessness and wickedness of humanity.)

How do we find "truth"? (God has made it clear to us. He is truth, and He has revealed Himself to us through His creation. Also, we find truth in God's Word.)

In what way do people "suppress the truth"? (They choose to live wickedly, and do not seek the truth about God. Or they deny or twist the truth of God to suit their own purposes.)

How does creation reveal information about God and His nature? (The spectacle of nature itself surely teaches something about God's greatness and power. But perhaps verse 20 is also referring to

OPTIONS

a moral fabric built into human nature. We know instinctively what behavior is best for society.)

Ask someone to read aloud verses 21-23. Then ask: **What did the "truth suppressors" not do that they should have done?** (Glorify God and give thanks.)

What did they do that they shouldn't have? (They worshiped animal and human images instead of God.)

Do people today worship images, or was this just a problem for primitive cultures? (Today people worship human images such as Madonna and Arnold Schwarzeneggar. They also worship cars, sports teams, rock groups, etc.)

Point out that the next few verses specifically talk about sexual immorality, including homosexuality. But the sin list doesn't stop there.

Have someone read aloud verses 29-32. Then ask: **Are people today guilty of these things?** (Absolutely. "They disobey their parents"—does that sound familiar to anyone?)

Note that this society not only does these things, it also approves of doing these things. Ask: **Do you think our society encourages people to be greedy, envious, and murderous? Do we encourage gossip, slander, and arrogance? Do we invent ways of doing evil? Are you ever urged to disobey your parents?** If possible, get an opinion—as well as an example or two to back up that opinion—from each group member on this topic. If no one mentions it, suggest that a casual glance at most TV shows or any newspaper would seem to confirm that our society is very much like the one described in Romans 1.

Write the following point on the board: "Creation reveals what's right." Say something like: **Whether you're Christian, Jewish, Hindu, or atheist, there are certain truths and standards that you just instinctively know. If you reject them, you're on dangerous ground.**

Suggest that when we argue for moral values in school and in society, we are not pushing a specifically *Christian* agenda. We are merely asking our society to accept the standards that God has built in to human nature.

Have someone read aloud Romans 2:1-4. Then ask: **Who is this passage talking to?** (Those who pass judgment on others.)

Why is it wrong for us to pass judgment on others? (Because we too are guilty of violating God's standards.)

Write the following point on the board: "Do not be judgmental." Then ask: **Does this mean we can't express our ideas of right and wrong?** (No. But we must have an attitude of kindness. "Judge the sin, but not the sinner," as some have said. We do not condemn or accuse individuals without recognizing our own sinfulness; yet we can uphold God's standards.)

Have someone read aloud Romans 8:5-9. Then ask: **What two kinds of people are described here?** (Those who live according to the sinful nature and those who live by the Spirit.)

What does the Spirit do for us? (He gives us life and peace. He controls us, so that our behavior can conform to God's standards.)

Write the following point on the board: "God's Spirit gives life."

Have someone read aloud Romans 13:9-14. Then ask: **How does Paul sum up the commandments of God's law?** ("Love your neighbor as yourself.")

Isn't that a little too easy? Does that mean if we love our neighbors, we don't have to keep the rest of the commandments? (Love keeps the commandments for us. The idea is that if we devote ourselves to showing God's love for others, we will naturally keep the commandments without thinking about it.)

Write the following point on the board: "Love sums up the law."

Summarize: **So what can you do about our society? You probably won't change what happens on Geraldo or Oprah. And you probably won't change the way courses are taught in your school. But among your friends, you can have a great influence.**

Encourage group members to write down the following guidelines (at least what's in italics) on the back of Repro Resource 8.

(1) *Don't be intimidated from holding a belief you know is right.* The Bible indicates that people have an inner, God-given sense of what is right and wrong. God created us that way.

(2) *Be humble and not judgmental.* Don't spout off your opinions if no one wants to hear them. Be willing to consider the fact that you may be interpreting a situation, or the Bible, incorrectly.

(3) *Live fully.* Show your friends an example of an exciting life, lived by God's standards, in God's spirit.

(4) *Love others.* Care for the people around you. Even if you disagree with their behavior, it's because you want what's best for them. Show them God's love.

What to Watch For

(Needed: Copies of Repro Resource 9, pencils)

Ask: **So while you're living and loving and being a great Christian example, how do you get through sociology class? How can you keep your mind from being twisted by the school curriculum? How can you tell good teaching from bad?** Suggest that the first step is recognizing the errors in the logic of those who oppose your beliefs.

Distribute copies of "Bad Vibes" (Repro Resource 9). Go through the sheet as a group, giving group members an opportunity to read the comments on each "logic error."

After each logic error is read, have group members raise their hands to indicate whether or not they've heard someone use that logic before. Ask volunteers to share their experiences. Then ask them if and how they responded to the logic at the time, and how they would respond now.

Close the session with a group prayer. Ask each person to offer a sentence prayer relating to one of his or her classes or teachers at school. For instance, someone might pray for courage to debate evolutionary teachings in biology class. Someone else might pray for wisdom in dealing with a social sciences teacher who insists on the importance of unrestricted freedom of sexual choice. Invite group members to share their school concerns with the rest of the group.

After group members have offered their sentence prayers, close by praying aloud for wisdom and strength for your group members as they seek to live for God daily in school.

NOTES

Class Struggle

TEACHER: So, class, we see that Einstein's Theory of Relativity has had vast implications, even in the social sciences. The traditional divisions between matter and energy have disappeared, as have the traditional philosophical constraints of our society.

ALEC: Do we have to know this for the test?

TEACHER: Yes, Alec, you have to know everything for the test. Now what do I mean by "philosophical constraints"? Anyone?

ALEC: Is that, like, straitjackets for guys who think too much?

TEACHER: Poor Alec. A mind is a terrible thing to waste.

ALEC: Yeah, and for fat people, a waist is a terrible thing to mind.

TEACHER: Now, Alec, we mustn't make fun of people who are horizontally challenged. And that just proves my point. It used to be that society had certain expectations, and it would judge anyone who did not fit in with those expectations. But now we know better. We used to make fun of people who were too short or too fat or of a different race or sexual persuasion. But now we know there is no right or wrong about these things. Each person has the right to be what she or he is.

ALEC: Whew! That's a relief!

TEACHER: Why?

ALEC: Well, I thought you were going to give me detention for being late to class today.

TEACHER: I am.

ALEC: But that's just the way I am! How can you discriminate like that? I am punctually challenged!

TEACHER: That's enough, Alec. I will now hand back the quiz you all took last week. I must say I was quite disappointed in most of you. (*Hands paper to Alec*) Especially you, Alec.

ALEC: (*Excited*) All right! I got a 19! I knew I'd score higher than my age if I kept trying. But, Miss Corcoran, I have a problem with this one.

TEACHER: Obviously you had a problem with most of them.

ALEC: But, you see, number one here. You marked it wrong.

TEACHER: Well, it *is* wrong.

ALEC: Maybe in the old days. But, now, there is no right or wrong, is there?

TEACHER: I didn't mean—

ALEC: How can you give me a grade like this when I sincerely believe these answers? Don't I have a right to my own opinion?

TEACHER: But, Alec, the first question is "Who was Albert Einstein?" You said he was a shortstop for the Dodgers.

ALEC: He was! That's what I truly believe! Einstein to Fuller to Kant, what a double-play combination! I think Einstein led the league in fielding percentage one year.

TEACHER: You got it wrong, Alec!

ALEC: I'm just doing what you taught me.

Bad Vibes

Whether you're in class, among friends, or watching TV, beware of the following errors in logic. Often people will use them to discount biblical views of right and wrong. Challenge these errors if you can; ignore them if you have to. But don't get tripped up by them.

Logic Error #1: There's no right or wrong, so all choices are equal and no choice really matters.

We may be uncertain about an *absolute* right or wrong in certain situations—but there still could be a "better" or "worse" choice. Choices *do* matter. They can mean the difference between pleasing God and displeasing Him. In other situations, there *is* an absolute right or wrong.

Logic Error #2: Millions of people can't be wrong.

Yes, they can. This logic frequently pops up when surveys are reported. "Eighty percent say money is more important than health—so it must be true!" Ridiculous. This logic is also often used with behavior questions. If it's reported that 70% of kids have sex before they're 18, you might think you're weird if you're in the minority. Don't believe it.

Logic Error #3: Do your own thing. Everyone must have freedom to choose.

That's great, but freedom has fences. Your choice may limit someone else's choice. If you choose to play your trumpet at 3 a.m., you may override your parents' decision to sleep. These things must be worked out. Even personal freedom of choice is not absolute.

Logic Error #4: Old ways are bad.

Not necessarily. Some old ways are bad. Some new ways are worse.

Logic Error #5. If you're sincere about a belief, that belief is true for you.

OK—I sincerely believe I can fly like a bird.

Logic Error #6: If you criticize what a person does, you hate that person.

No! Criticism can be a form of love. We must be able to determine what is good and bad (or better and worse) behavior without hurting the individuals who choose the bad behavior.

Logic Error #7: You can't change the way you are. If you're born a certain way, that's the way you'll be for your whole life.

You hear this logic a lot in regards to sexual orientation. There is also the idea that childhood trauma dooms people to difficult lives. Don't minimize the impact of childhood problems; but recognize that people can find healing and hope. People *can* change the way they are (or let God change them).

EXTRA ACTION

STEP 1

In place of speeches, try some relativistic recipes. You'll need an oven, mixing bowls, pans, and ingredients for making cookies. Have group members form teams. Say: **We're going to make cookies. Each team will get the ingredients it needs. But each team will get a different amount of each ingredient. After all, we don't believe in rigid rules and recipes anymore, do we? Different strokes for different folks!** Pass out ingredients, giving different amounts to each team. (Example: One team might get two cups of flour and one teaspoon of sugar; another might get two cups of sugar and one teaspoon of flour.) After kids mix up their ingredients, bake the cookies (move on to Step 2 while you wait). Let kids taste the results, some of which will be pretty awful. Ask: **Why do we have recipes and rules? Why do schools teach rules about cooking but not about what's right or wrong?** (Most people agree about cooking, but not about religion—which is the basis for morality.)

STEP 3

Bring a cordless phone that has a "page" button on the base unit. When pushed, this button makes the hand-held receiver beep for easy finding. Plug in the base unit and hide the receiver somewhere in the building. Have group members form teams. Tell group members you've hidden the phone, and that each team should position itself somewhere in the building—in the hope that it's closest to the hiding place. Then you'll push the "page" button. The first team to follow the beep, retrieve the phone, and bring it to you wins. Use this as an illustration of how truth has been revealed to us by God, just as the phone's location was revealed by its beeping. Most people choose to ignore the "beeping" of the truth, even when it's right under their noses.

SMALL GROUP

STEP 1

If you don't have many kids who could meet the challenge in the basic session plan, try the following activity instead. Bring one of each kind of toothpaste dispenser available—the traditional tube, the pump, and the tube that pulls excess toothpaste back inside. Have group members form three teams. Give each team a dispenser. Each team must try for 30 seconds to convince the others that a law should be passed making it mandatory to use only its type of dispenser—and that the others should be banned. Award a prize for the most convincing argument if you like. Then ask: **Should the government really tell people what kind of toothpaste dispenser to buy? Why or why not? Should the government—through public schools—tell kids what's morally right and wrong? Why or why not?**

STEP 3

Reading the four guidelines at the end of the step may seem too preachy, especially when you're reading to a small group. Try writing each guideline on an index card. Give each card to one person or pair of kids. Each person or pair should come up with a way to teach its guideline to the rest of the group. (Methods might include acting out a fable that has the guideline as its moral, performing a rap, or making a poster.)

LARGE GROUP

STEP 1

Delivering an impromptu speech to a large group could be intimidating. For an alternative, try the following activity. Before the session, make a stick-on name tag for each group member. But use names that no one in the group has. Also create a seven-foot height chart on poster board—but mix up the inch-mark numbers so that they're totally random. (For instance, a kid who's really 63 inches tall might be 74 inches on the chart, and one who's really 72 inches might be 41 inches on the chart.) Pass out name tags as kids enter; make sure the kids put the tags on. Then offer prizes for the shortest and tallest group members—as measured on your mixed-up chart. Ask: **How do you feel about your new name? Your new height?** At least some of the kids won't be comfortable with either. Discuss the fact that most people see names and numbers as absolutes. But some people think moral values—ideas of right and wrong—are just a matter of opinion.

STEP 3

For more group involvement, try the following activity. Bring a ladder and a Polaroid camera. Have group members form teams—the larger the better. Have one team at a time lie on the floor and arrange itself in a shape (star, flower, pop bottle, Roman numeral, etc.) without telling others what it is. Members of the other teams, lying down with their chins touching the floor, will try to guess what the shape is. As they do, climb the ladder and take a photo of the shape. Then pass the picture around the group. Repeat the process to give all teams a chance. Point out that just as it was hard to see the shapes from the floor, it's hard to see God in creation when you don't have the right perspective. Tie this into Romans 1:18-23.

STEP 3

Kids may have heard passages like these before and have taken them to mean, "We're right and everybody else is wrong." They can't swallow that assertion in a pluralistic society. Try to address this concern by looking at the following verses. Read Job 38:1-13. Ask: **On what basis does God claim authority to do as He wishes?** (His all-powerful and eternal nature, His role as Creator, etc.) Read John 14:6. Ask: **Who claims that Jesus is the only way to heaven?** (Jesus Himself.) Read 2 Peter 3:9. Ask: **Is the purpose of Christianity to screen "undesirable" people out of heaven? Explain.** (God wants everyone to be saved, and is allowing extra time for more to accept His Son.) Point out the bottom line: **When we say Christ is the only way, it's not because we're right or because we think others are less deserving of heaven than we are. It's because we believe the claims of God the Father and God the Son, as recorded in the Bible. People can disagree with that belief, but in doing so they should compare the Bible's trustworthiness against that of their own philosophies—not just their opinions against ours.**

STEP 4

Kids may be nearly immune to exhortations to "stand up" for their beliefs at school. Ease into the subject by asking what they would do if a false rumor about a good friend were spreading at school—a rumor that the friend was dealing drugs. Would they stand up for the friend? If so, how? What if other kids in the youth group were making snide remarks about their school? Would they stand up for their school? If so, how? What if a family member were falsely accused of murder? Would they stand up for him or her? If so, how?

STEP 2

Asking the "What would happen if . . ." questions may be a problem if kids don't know what the Bible has to say about issues like homosexuality and abortion. If you need to address this, try passages like these: Leviticus 18:22 (homosexual practice); Psalm 139:13-16 (abortion, if it's taken to indicate that aborting a fetus would interfere with God's intent to bring a new person into the world); Hebrews 13:4 (sex outside marriage); John 14:6 (Jesus as the only way to God).

STEP 3

The Romans study might be tough for kids to digest. Have three teams study these passages instead: Proverbs 1:1-9; Proverbs 2:1-15; Proverbs 3:1-8. All three teams should answer these questions: **What is the source of real wisdom? What are the benefits of getting wisdom from this source? Why do you think public schools don't teach the principles in this passage? Should they? If you can't get this kind of wisdom at school, where will you get it?** You may want to explain that "fear of the Lord" (1:7; 2:5) refers to greatly respecting and submitting to Him, not just being afraid.

STEP 1

To begin the session with worship, try the following activity. Meet in a room that's as dark as you possibly can make it. Try to play "follow the leader" in the dark. The leader can say only, "Now do this," rather than giving specific instructions. (To avoid accidents, clarify beforehand that all actions should be performed without moving around the room.) After a minute or so, ask: **How does it feel to guess what your leader is trying to tell you?** (Confusing, irritating, etc.) Explain that this is what it's like when people are in spiritual "darkness"—they can only guess what God is like and what He wants of them. Then turn on the lights. Note that God has revealed through Christ and in the Bible what He's like. Sing a couple of songs about light and seeing (like "Shine, Jesus, Shine," "The Light of the World Is Jesus," and "Have You Seen Jesus My Lord?"). Pray briefly, thanking God for not leaving us in the dark. You may want to refer to this activity during the Romans study in Step 3.

STEP 4

Hold a "pep rally" to build group identity and remind kids that they all face similar challenges at school during the week. Some elements you might want to include: making large "school spirit"-type posters that encourage group members to stand up for their beliefs at school; upbeat background music; refreshments. If possible, form a circle and have each group member step into the middle for a few moments while you announce his or her "stats" (name, school attended, etc.) through a bullhorn. If your budget allows, you might even want to give kids "uniforms" (T-shirts with your group name or logo on them).

MOSTLY GIRLS

STEP 2

Do "Class Struggle" (Repro Resource 8) as a group skit. Change the name of Alec to Alice and have your two volunteer performers act out the skit as it is written. However, the rest of your group members will portray other members of Miss Corcoran's class. Have them ad-lib lines in responding to the comments made by Alice and Miss Corcoran.

STEP 3

After discussing the verses in Romans, have group members form teams of four or five. Instruct each team to choose a value (such as honesty, respect, concern for others, etc.) and come up with a way to explain to the rest of the group the significance and importance of that value. (For instance, a team might perform a skit demonstrating what happens when its chosen value is absent in a relationship.) Each team will have two minutes to make its presentation.

MOSTLY GUYS

STEP 1

The prospect of impromptu speech making may petrify most guys, who tend to be less verbal than girls at this age. If you want an activity that's not so threatening, try this. Before the session, get three large, opaque plastic eggs. To start the session, place the eggs on a table at the front of the room. In two of the eggs place a piece of already-chewed gum. The other egg should be empty. Tell group members that you've filled two eggs with gum and that the other is hollow. Let three volunteers come up and point to the eggs they'd like. (Let the youngest kid pick first.) Kids may not touch the eggs before all are chosen. After they discover that all the eggs are filled with already-chewed gum or hollow, read Colossians 2:8, which warns against being taken "captive through hollow and deceptive [philosophies]" of the world. Ask: **What are some hollow or deceptive philosophies that you've heard at school? Do you think schools teach these things on purpose? If not, how does it happen?** If you like, give all three volunteers some gum to make up for your trick.

STEP 4

Many guys, faced with unbiblical or anti-biblical teaching at school, may react in one of two ways: by itching for a fight, or by just saying, "Aw, they're stupid," and never confronting teachers or students. Acknowledge that people sometimes go to these extremes because they're afraid of talking things over—afraid that they wouldn't be able to defend their faith or convince the other person. Read John 14:26-27, a passage about how we don't have to be afraid because the Holy Spirit lives in us. One of the things He does is to remind us of the things we've learned and need to say.

EXTRA FUN

STEP 1

You'll need two tables, two tablecloths, and a lot of plastic dishes and cups. Put the cloths on the tables. Have group members form two teams. Give each team an equal number of dishes and cups. Teams will have two minutes to see which one can build the higher tower of cups and dishes on its table. Towers must stay in place for at least 15 seconds after the two-minute mark. Then challenge teams to pull the tablecloths out from under the dishes without disturbing the towers. After they try (and probably fail), point out that just as the whole tower rested on the tablecloth, many of the things we need to learn in school are based on ideas of right and wrong. Some people claim you can leave "values" out of school without affecting the rest of the curriculum. But when all moral teachings are pulled out of classes, the effect can be like yanking a tablecloth from beneath a tower of dishes.

STEP 4

Wrap up your meeting with an open-ended scavenger hunt. Instead of giving kids a list of specific items to find, describe items in a general way. (For example, you might say: **Find something that's cold and purple, something green and smelly, something sharp and yellow, and something brown and fuzzy.**) After teams return and you award prizes to the winners, point out to your group members that they had to think for themselves during this hunt instead of just reading a list and finding the items. That's how we should respond to what we hear about moral values in school; we should think for ourselves rather than just going along with what we're told.

STEP 3

Bring a color TV to your meeting place. Attach it to an antenna or VCR—whatever allows you to have a program going during this part of the meeting. As you discuss the Romans passage, manipulate the picture and sound on the TV to reflect what you're talking about. For instance, when you discuss how people "suppress the truth" (vs. 18), turn the sound off. When you describe how the truth can be clearly seen in creation (vs. 20), turn the sharpness or contrast controls to make the picture as clear as you can. On "their foolish hearts were darkened" (vs. 21), turn the brightness control to darken the picture; then brighten it again. During the rest of the passage, use the color and tint controls to distort and remove colors in reflection of the idol worship and other sins listed. [NOTE: You may want to practice this before the session for maximum effect. Try to show a relatively bland program (such as a newscast or talk show) to avoid distracting kids from the study.]

STEP 4

Before the session, use a tape recorder to capture an hour or so of talk radio (preferably a call-in show about a controversial topic, and not a program on a Christian station). Pick a five to 10-minute segment that includes some discussion of right and wrong. Play this for kids after you've gone over Repro Resource 9. As they listen, have them practice spotting logic errors, values expressed, and rejection of absolutes. If it's easier, you could record a segment of a TV talk show (like Donahue, Oprah, or Geraldo) and play it back for your group.

STEP 1

To save time, replace Steps 1 and 2 with a new opener. Bring a few blindfolds and several magazine pictures of fruit and vegetables. Don't let kids see the pictures yet. Ask: **Which of you can tell the difference between grapes and bananas just by touching them?** (Adapt the question to fit the items in your pictures.) Get a few volunteers who think they can tell the difference; blindfold them. Then give them the pictures and challenge them to tell the difference by touch. They won't be able to, of course. After thanking volunteers, say: **Some people say we can't really tell the difference between right and wrong either. They say one person's idea of right is another's idea of wrong. Are they right, or are they wearing some kind of blindfold? How do you tell the difference between right and wrong? Do you think kids should be helped in school to tell the difference? If not, why? If so, how?** After discussion, go directly to Step 3.

STEP 3

Shorten the Bible study by skipping Romans 8:5-9 and 13:9-14. To save more time in Step 4, pass out Repro Resource 9 for kids to consider at home rather than going over it as a group.

STEP 2

Explain that the theory of relativity recognizes light as a "universal invariant." That means that no matter how, when, where, or under what conditions you observe it, the characteristics and speed of light remain the same. Then say: **School systems are, in theory, "value-free" so that no religion can impose its judgments. But this does not alter the course of Christians who reflect Jesus' light. Their light is constant, and comes from inside.** Have volunteers read in succession John 1:4; Matthew 5:14; Psalm 119:105; and Psalm 27:1. Then, as a group, discuss how light—Jesus' light, which does not change and extends to all—can affect each of the situations addressed by the questions in the session.

STEP 3

This activity will aid group members in practicing the points they wrote on the back of Repro Resource 8. Before the meeting, ask a group member who you know can be convincingly argumentative to help you by pretending to have a strong belief in something you know the rest of the group will disagree with. For instance, the person may argue that everyone should remain celibate for life or that men who have children shouldn't have to be responsible for them. When group members finish Repro Resource 8, suggest that they should practice what they wrote. Then change the subject to your "hot issue," debate the topic a little, have your opinionated teen sound off, and let the arguments begin. Afterward, gently evaluate how group members acted and remind them of their duty to "correct one another in Christian love."

STEP 1

Younger kids may be tongue-tied by the challenge of impromptu speech making. Instead, have them do a taste test. Bring samples of regular, fat-free, and sugar-free versions of various foods for comparison. (For example, you might bring regular and fat-free cookies, ice cream, or cheese—and regular and sugar-free soft drinks, candy, or gum.) Ask: **Which versions do you like better? If you'd never tasted the regular version, how might you feel about the "free" version?** Then say: **You can see what fat-free and sugar-free mean. What might "values-free" mean?** (Education that supposedly doesn't favor one view of right and wrong over another.) **Which version do you think you'd like better—with values or without? Why?**

STEP 2

Portions of the skit may be hard for younger kids to follow, so skip it. In Step 3, you may want to substitute a simpler study from Proverbs (see "Little Bible Background" option). In Step 4, take care to apply the principles to classes that junior highers are familiar with—social studies, for example, rather than sociology or social sciences. Challenging younger kids to debate teachers and students may be unrealistic; helping these group members spot errors may be enough for now.

STEP 3

More mature kids may want to discuss these questions: **Which values are absolute, and which aren't? The Bible doesn't set rules for every possible situation, does it?** While you won't have time to settle these questions, you could gain insight from the following passages. Read Micah 6:8. Ask: **Is this instruction simple, complicated, or both? How has God shown us what is good? What parts of the Bible help us know how to "act justly and to love mercy and to walk humbly with...God"?** (The Ten Commandments, the Sermon on the Mount, etc.) Read Matthew 22:37-38. Ask: **How is the command to love God and your neighbor a condensed version of the rest of the Bible? Can you think of any truly loving act that the Bible prohibits?** Read Acts 15:5-6, 12-14, 19-21. Ask: **Why did the apostles reduce the number of rules that the Gentiles had to follow? Does that mean the rules were wrong?** (No, but they weren't absolute; they didn't apply to the Gentiles.) **What nonbiblical rules do Christians today tend to impose on each other?**

STEP 4

Challenge kids to follow through on what you've been discussing. Give each person a pad of sticky stick-on notes. Kids should use these to flag school textbooks and notebooks when they encounter a "logic error" while doing homework or listening in class. These notes can help them to remember to search out "the rest of the story" in such cases. The notes could also be used to mark logic errors in books or magazines they read at home.

DATE USED:

Approx. Time

STEP 1: *Logic Problems* _____
- ❑ Extra Action
- ❑ Small Group
- ❑ Large Group
- ❑ Fellowship & Worship
- ❑ Mostly Guys
- ❑ Extra Fun
- ❑ Short Meeting Time
- ❑ Combined Junior High/High School

Things needed:

STEP 2: *The Theory of Relativity* _____
- ❑ Little Bible Background
- ❑ Mostly Girls
- ❑ Urban
- ❑ Combined Junior High/High School

Things needed:

STEP 3: *The Romans Road Map* _____
- ❑ Extra Action
- ❑ Small Group
- ❑ Large Group
- ❑ Heard It All Before
- ❑ Little Bible Background
- ❑ Mostly Girls
- ❑ Media
- ❑ Short Meeting Time
- ❑ Urban
- ❑ Extra Challenge

Things needed:

STEP 4: *What to Watch For* _____
- ❑ Heard It All Before
- ❑ Fellowship & Worship
- ❑ Mostly Guys
- ❑ Extra Fun
- ❑ Media
- ❑ Extra Challenge

Things needed: